RHS

GARDENING
M**BY**NTH
MONTH

RHS

GARDENING
MONTH
BY
MONTH

IAN SPENCE

LONDON, NEW YORK,
MELBOURNE, MUNICH, DELHI

Project Editor Caroline Reed
Project Art Editor Elaine Hewson
Senior Editor Helen Fewster
Senior Art Editor Joanne Doran
Designer Becky Tennant
Managing Editor Esther Ripley
Managing Art Editor Alison Donovan
Production Editors Joanna Byrne, Luca Frassinetti
Production Controller Mandy Inness
Publisher Jonathan Metcalf
Associate Publisher Liz Wheeler
Art Director Peter Luff

DK India
Editor Nidhilekha Mathur
Designer Nitu Singh
DTP Operator Rajdeep Singh

First Edition
Project Editor Katie Dock
Project Art Editor Elly King
Editor Caroline Reed

First published in Great Britain in 2007 by
Dorling Kindersley Limited, 80 Strand, London WC2R 0RL
Penguin Group (UK)

ISBN 978 1 4053 6305 1

Colour reproduced by MDP, Wiltshire, UK
Printed in China by South China Co. Ltd

To find out more about RHS membership, visit our website
www.rhs.org.uk or call 0845 062 1111

Discover more at
www.dk.com

CONTENTS

SYMBOLS USED
IN THIS BOOK

♟ RHS Award of
    Garden Merit
↕ Height of plant
↔ Spread of plant

Gardeners are born optimists: we look forward to the next year, convinced our gardens will do even better, but to get the best results we have to plan ahead. This book is your guide to what to do and when to do it. Use it as checklist to keep on top of routine jobs throughout the year.

Each month, the tasks you need to carry out are listed to help you plan your time and work out your priorities. Keep an eye on the weather, too – it will help you to judge when your garden is ready for these tasks. Bear in mind that conditions vary widely between different parts of the country and from year to year; if there's a thick layer of snow on the ground in April then you cannot sow seeds outside!

Gardening is my passion, and one I would like to share with you; I hope this book fires your enthusiasm so that it lasts a lifetime. Happy gardening!

IAN SPENCE

WHAT TO DO IN **JANUARY**

WEATHER WATCH

In January the garden may seem dead to the world, but there is more going on than you think. Evergreens provide reassuring silhouettes in a spartan landscape, while a covering of snow can bring true magic, and it may even do your garden some good too.

WINTER CHILL

Temperatures during winter are largely governed by the temperature of the sea, with January and February being the coldest months. The chilliest nights occur when there is no wind, the skies are clear and there is snow on the ground, and the coldest air will be found on low ground. Average daily temperatures in January are 6–8°C (43–46°F) in the south and 2–4°C (36–39°F) in the north.

WINDY WEATHER

This is a month of gale force winds associated with deep depressions crossing near or over the British Isles, with high ground experiencing the worst of all. The number of days with gales and their strength varies considerably between north and south. Northern parts of the country, especially those on exposed western coasts, experience the strongest winds, with on average 7.5 days of gales, whereas the south is much less blustery, with only 0.2 days.

SUNSHINE IN PLACES

Southern regions get the most sunshine, mainly because they are flatter. In the north, eastern parts get more sun for the same reason. Southern regions receive on

average 57.2 hours of bright sunshine in January, whereas in Shetland they will get only about 22 hours this month.

RAINFALL HERE AND THERE

The amount of rain falling on different parts of the country also varies according to its topography (how hilly or flat it is), southern and eastern regions being the driest. In some parts of the north-west Highlands 236mm (9¼in) of rain may fall this month; on the south coast of England, 81mm (3in).

SNOW ON THE HILLS

Snow is rare in coastal areas, more frequent over high ground inland. The amount varies hugely from almost none at all in many areas to heavy falls, which can last throughout the winter. North-east Scotland fares worst, averaging 16 days of snow, with the south coast of England having only on average 0.8 days.

AROUND THE GARDEN

ORDER SEEDS

There is a bewildering array of seeds and young plants available from all the seed companies. It can sometimes be daunting, even for experts, trying to decide which seeds to choose. But it's a pleasant job leafing through catalogues and planning what to grow in the year to come. If you stick to older, tried and tested varieties, you won't go wrong, but it can be great fun trying some of the new ones that are brought out every year.

When seeds start arriving, store the packets in a cool spot. The ideal place is in a plastic container with a sealable lid; just pop it in the bottom of the fridge.

GET TO KNOW YOUR SOIL BETTER

It is disheartening to see plants struggle because your garden soil does not suit them. Testing your soil for its type and pH – its acidity or alkalinity – is a good idea.

Fast-growing annuals, like these colourful nasturtiums, produce masses of flowers from seed within a few weeks.

This will help you decide which plants and seeds to choose. Feel the soil in your hands to get to know its structure. It might contain a high proportion of clay, making it heavy and wet, or sand, making it light and dry – or something between the two, the perfect balance being known as "loam".

Clay holds together well.

The pH of soil can be tested with kits from garden centres. There are many available, costing anything up to several pounds. The cheaper ones with colour-coded charts are adequate for most purposes. Knowing more about your soil will help you choose plants that thrive in your garden, either by scrutinising labels when you buy, or, if you prefer to plan at home, getting yourself a good "plants for places" guide.

Sand feels dry and gritty.

Regularly adding bulky organic matter to soil – such as digging in compost or well-rotted manure, or mulching with leafmould – can do wonders to improve extreme soil types, preventing plants drowning in heavy clay or drying out in free-draining sand. But it's generally better and easier not to change the pH of your soil in beds and borders, and to simply choose plants that like the soil. You can always grow other plants in containers filled with tailor-made soil mixes.

DESTROY WEED SEEDLINGS

On your winter rambles around the garden, take a hoe with you so that you can knock out weed seedlings before they get too big. This will save a huge amount of time and effort when spring arrives. Collect up annual weeds and put them on the compost heap. Any perennial weeds should be dug up with as much of their roots as possible, and then binned. Pieces of root left in the soil or put on the compost heap often start to grow again, actually increasing the weed problem.

SPREAD ORGANIC MATTER

There isn't much to do outside when the soil is rock-hard, but a job that will save you time later is spreading out well-rotted manure or garden compost. It's quite acceptable to walk on the soil if it is frozen hard. Barrowing muck or compost about can be a messy job, but in these conditions the barrow

Spread manure over the ground; rain and earthworms will mix it into the soil.

can be wheeled over the ground with little effort and without getting caked with soil. Don't, however, take the barrow over a frozen lawn; if you can't avoid going over the lawn put down planks to protect it.

Spread the load evenly over the surface and the ground will soon thaw out when the weather improves. It's a job to keep you warm on a cold day. No need to sit huddled indoors by the fire!

COLLECT DECAYING LEAVES

It is best to compost leaves, not to burn them, as they can then contribute to the goodness of the soil. Pay particular attention to clearing the crowns of herbaceous perennials, as these are likely to rot in prolonged damp conditions under fallen leaves. Be very careful when disturbing large piles of leaves in which a hedgehog may be hibernating – in these cases, it might be safer to put aside your rake and instead use either garden grippers or the "big hands" that are advertised in magazines.

KEEP AN EYE ON PONDS

There is little to do with ponds this month, but be sure to keep a watch for freezing temperatures. If the pond is left frozen over for long periods, any fish within it will die from lack of oxygen.

A thick layer of leaves on the lawn can kill off the grass, so remove them on a regular basis.

Every morning, check the pond; if it is frozen over, melt a small area of ice with a pan of hot water. Simply sit the pan or a kettle on the ice for a few seconds and it will melt. Under no circumstances should you try to break the ice with a hammer or stick, as the shock waves could kill the fish and any other wildlife in the pond, and could even cause damage to the pond liner.

Alternatively, float a small plastic or rubber ball on the pond. This is especially useful in ponds with rigid sides, such as those made from cement or preformed fibreglass liners. The ball absorbs the pressure of the sheet of ice (as water expands when frozen) so that strain is not put on the sides of the pond. You can pop the ball out to create an airhole in the ice, but remember to replace it at night, which may involve enlarging the hole if temperatures have stayed low.

If you have trouble bending down or your pond is very large,

there is a handy alternative to using a ball: when you've finished with a plastic milk or juice container that has a handle, part-fill it with water. Tie a cord around the handle, then peg it at the side of the pond; the benefit of this technique is that you will be able to pull it out without leaning over too far.

KEEP OFF ICY GRASS

Don't walk or work on the grass at all when it is frozen or frosted, otherwise later, when it thaws out, your footprints will show up as yellow patches on the lawn where the grass has been damaged.

DISPERSE WORM CASTS

Worms are quite active in lawns at this time of year and are most noticeable by the casts they leave on the lawn's surface. Brush these off regularly; if they are left, they will be trodden into the surface of the lawn, looking unsightly and encouraging weed seeds to grow in these small patches. However, worms do a lot of good in other parts of the garden and should be encouraged. It doesn't take long to clear even a large lawn if you use a long, flexible cane and swish it back and forth over the lawn to scatter the casts. On smaller lawns you can use a stiff broom. Try to do the job when the surface of the lawn is dry and the worm casts will spread more easily.

IMPROVE DRAINAGE

You can improve the drainage of the lawn using a garden fork. It's quite easy to identify badly draining parts of the lawn: they are lower patches where the water tends to collect and takes much longer to drain away. Wait until the surface of the lawn dries out a bit, then push a garden fork 15cm (6in) into the ground and wiggle it about to open up the holes, at about 15cm (6in) intervals over the affected area.

Immediately after aerating the lawn, spread some sharp or horticultural sand (not builder's sand), or a sand and soil mixture, over the area and work this into the holes with a stiff broom. This prevents the holes closing up too quickly and further improves the drainage. It is a tedious job, but well worth doing. If you have a large lawn you can hire a mechanical aerator to make the job a bit easier.

Use a garden fork to aerate grass. You can hire mechanical spikers for large areas.

REPAIR HOLLOWS AND BUMPS

Even out bumpy lawns this month if the weather is mild and dry. Hollow areas where water tends to collect can be raised level with the rest of the lawn quite easily. First make 'H'-shaped cuts in the lawn with a spade or lawn edging iron, and then carefully push a spade under the turf and roll each half back. Add soil to the exposed area, firm it well and carefully roll back the turf. You may have to add some more soil to get the turf very slightly higher than the surrounding lawn to allow for settling. After rolling back the turf, tamp down firmly with the back of a rake and the job's done.

To repair bumps in the lawn do exactly as for repairing hollows, but when the turf is rolled back, scrape some soil from underneath to lower the level of the turf.

To even out bumps and hollows, lift a flap of turf and scoop out or fill in with soil.

GET THE LAWN MOWER SERVICED

Send the mower off now in order to avoid the servicing agents' busiest time and get the mower back quickly – because, believe it or not, the lawn can be given a light trim now and then even through the winter. It only needs a light topping with the blades at their highest setting. Don't do it if the lawn is very wet or frozen as this will ruin the grass. An occasional winter trim keeps the lawn looking healthier, because the less grass you take off every time you mow the lawn, the better it is for the grass plants – this applies in summer as well.

WATER CONTAINER PLANTS

Plants growing at the base of house walls can be sheltered from rain by the overhang of the house eaves. It is surprising how dry plants can get in this position, so check on them regularly.

PROTECT POT-GROWN SHRUBS

It is not the hardiness of the plant that is the issue; during very frosty weather, plants in pots are more vulnerable to damage because the roots in the pots are above ground. If you haven't already protected them, there are several ways to do so. Pots can be wrapped in bubble plastic, or hessian sacking if you can get it. Extra protection can be given by wrapping straw or bracken around the pot and holding this in place with bubble polythene, hessian or old compost sacks. Grouping the pots will give them some mutual protection.

Alternatively, if there is space, move plants into the house or a

Wrapping your pots in hessian sacking or bubble wrap helps to insulate vulnerable plant roots against cold weather.

shed when temperatures outside drop. You can also wrap pots to be on the safe side. Remember that empty ornamental pots, especially glazed ones and old terracotta, can be vulnerable to cracking by frost, and may need protection.

TREES, SHRUBS & CLIMBERS

ERECT A WINDBREAK

Windbreaks protect newly planted trees and shrubs, especially evergreens, from wind damage. They can be in the form of hessian, horticultural fleece, bubble plastic, or strong polythene, tied securely to a framework around the plants. To increase the level of protection, some straw can be placed inside the windbreak framework, but it's important to make sure air can circulate and light can get in, particularly for evergreens.

CHECK TREE TIES AND STAKES

Young trees and bushes which are blown about by strong winds will never last long. It is therefore essential to check ties and stakes regularly. When trees and bushes are planted loosely, a sunken area develops around the base of the main stem, caused by the constant rocking back and forth. This is where water can collect, and it is here that the plant will begin to rot and die off.

Ties should be secure, but not so tight that they restrict the growth of the plant. Check them regularly, and if they are constricting the main stem, loosen them a little to allow for expansion.

Inspect all stakes and ties regularly, especially on the stems of young trees.

MOVE DECIDUOUS TREES AND SHRUBS

No matter how expert we think we are, we all make mistakes in placing plants. There is still time to move deciduous trees and shrubs if they are in the wrong place, or have outgrown their allotted space. Never underestimate the effort needed to move large plants, because you want to take as much of the root system and the soil around it as you can, so enlist the help of a friend if necessary.

Once the tree is planted, gently firm the soil with your heel to reduce the risk of it sinking. Fill with more soil if necessary.

PLANT BARE-ROOT TREES AND SHRUBS

When preparing the ground, keep the roots of the tree or shrub protected from the wind and sun so they don't dry out – use a plastic bag, or cover the roots with a mound of compost. Once the plant is in, firm the soil very gently so that it doesn't become too compacted (*see also p.56*).

If conditions are not on your side and the soil is too hard or wet for planting, heel in the plants in a corner of the garden until the soil is suitable. Dig a trench big enough to hold the root system, and cover the roots with soil, firming gently. The plants will survive like this for quite some time.

If the soil is too frozen even to heel in the plants, wrap the roots in hessian or sacking, and keep them indoors. Unwrap the top growth if packed in straw to let it get some light, and keep the wrapping around the roots moist. Look after them, and plants can stay like this for a few weeks.

PLANT DECIDUOUS HEDGING PLANTS

Provided that weather conditions permit, hedging plants such as beech, hawthorn, and hornbeam can be planted this month in ground that has been well prepared. The cheapest way to buy hedging is as young, bare-rooted plants known as "whips", sold in bundles. If the weather has caused the soil to freeze or become waterlogged, you can simply heel in the plants temporarily (*see previous page*).

To prepare the ground prior to planting, mark out a strip at least two spade-blades wide along the length of the proposed hedge. Then take out a trench to one spade's depth at one end of the area, and put the soil into a wheelbarrow. If the soil at the bottom of the trench is composed of heavy, compacted clay, you can always loosen it up with a garden fork, but if you do this, make sure you don't bring any of the poorer subsoil to the surface.

Incorporate as much organic matter as you can into the soil at the bottom of the trench, and then cover this with soil by digging the next section of the trench, repeating the process until you reach the end of the line, when the last part can be filled with the soil in your barrow. Space the young plants out along the trench, then fill in around the

Well-rotted farmyard manure worked into the bottom of the trench will give plants a good start.

Before choosing your hedge, consider its purpose and what will best suit your space. Popular choices include (clockwise from above) beech, Berberis, and Cotoneaster.

plants, and firm with your boot. In exposed sites, a windbreak of, for example, plastic mesh stapled between posts on the windward side of the hedge will help the plants establish. Pampering the hedging plants in the first few years after planting will encourage them to become healthy specimens as they grow in size.

PRUNE TREES TO SHAPE

Young trees often grow out in all directions into other plants in the border, throwing out shoots along the whole length of the trunk. You should prune out misplaced stems this month, always cutting to a junction or the main stem. If you want to make a standard tree with a length of bare trunk, cut back some of the side growths now too.

Don't do it all at once, but over two or three seasons, shortening some this year and completely removing them next year. The extra leaves left on the main stem over summer help to encourage the vigour of the tree; cutting side branches off all at once would severely affect the tree's growth. Use a pruning saw, or secateurs when branches are thinner than your little finger.

CLEARING A TREE TRUNK

First year   *Second year*

Future years: when pruning off any thicker stubs, leave the slightly swollen ring (branch collar) intact when you remove branches.

PRUNE WISTERIA

In summer, you should have cut back the new long shoots to five or six buds from the main stems. Now these same shoots should be shortened even more, to two or three buds from the main stems. You can do the same to any new sideshoots that have grown since summer. The advantage of doing this now is that with no leaves on the plant, you can see exactly what you are doing.

Shorten the sideshoots from the main wisteria framework to encourage flower buds. You should have a terrific show of colour by early summer (see Wisteria floribunda *'Multijuga', left).*

KEEP CLIMBERS IN CHECK

Plants such as wisteria, ornamental vines, ivies, Virginia creeper, Boston ivy, and climbing hydrangea have a habit of working their way into window frames and doors. Try to keep climbers clear of gutters and drainpipes, as they can cause expensive structural damage if left to their own devices.

Left unchecked, climbers like Parthenocissus *(left),* Hydrangea petiolaris *(right), and ivy (below) can overwhelm their supporting structures and might cause structual damage.*

FLOWERING PLANTS

BRING BULBS INSIDE

Bulbs planted in pots and bowls last autumn should be brought into the house in batches to give a prolonged flowering display. Bring them inside when they have made about an inch of growth. It's best to put them in a cool room or greenhouse for a week or two first; if they get too warm too quickly, they will grow fast, becoming leggy, and produce poor flowers. Water bulbs in bowls without drainage holes carefully or you may overwater them.

At the same time, locate a sheltered spot outdoors, out of sight but still in the light, where you can put pots of bulbs as they finish flowering indoors. Remove the spent flowerheads to prevent the plants' energy going into producing seeds. Feed them with a high-potash fertiliser to build up flower buds for next year.

Continue feeding regularly until the foliage dies back, and then in spring, the bulbs can be planted in the garden. It is not a good idea to force the same bulbs year after year. Forcing saps a plant's energy, and they rarely flower well if forced more than once.

Create fertiliser for bulbs by adding water-soluble feed to a watering can. Be sure to follow the manufacturer's instructions carefully.

ORDER SUMMER-FLOWERING BULBS

Leafing through colourful catalogues at this time of year is a pleasant occupation, allowing you to dream of the summer to come. Ordering early and by mail will give you the best choice of varieties, especially useful if your local garden centre only stocks a limited selection. Lilies are the most popular, but why not try some of the more unusual bulbs, such as *Galtonia candicans* (wood hyacinth) or *Ornithogalum* (star of Bethlehem). Even the frost-tender bulbs such as tigridias are easy to grow – but bear in mind that, like dahlias and gladioli, they will need lifting and storing in a dry frost-free place over winter.

Try something a little different: nowadays there are lots of unusual bulbs on offer, such as ornithogalums (top) and tigridias (right).

INSPECT DAHLIA TUBERS

Take a close look at stored dahlia tubers from time to time to see if there is any disease present. Any that are showing signs of rotting off should be removed from the rest, or the disease may spread through the lot. Any individual tubers infected can be cut from the main crown of the plant, while the rest are retained. Early stages of rotting can be controlled by cutting out the infected area and dusting with flowers of sulphur.

ORDER HERBACEOUS PERENNIALS

Now is the time to look through bits of paper to find all those notes you made of "must-have" plants seen at shows and gardens last year. Order them from nursery catalogues now for delivery and planting in the spring. There is a bewildering array of plants to choose from these days, and you can have plants in flower, if you choose them carefully, almost all the year. For interest all season, and to act as a foil for the flowering plants, it's also a good idea to select from some of the beautiful foliage plants on offer, especially the increasingly popular grasses, sedges, and ferns.

Dust dahlia tubers with sulphur powder to discourage rot, then store in boxes of peat substitute with the crowns above the surface.

Ornamental grasses (left), sedges (bottom left), and ferns (below) have the advantage of both acting as a foil for flowering plants and being low-maintenance.

SOW SWEET PEAS

These like a good root run, so sow them in long sweet pea tubes, available from garden centres. Alternatively, make your own with newspaper rolled into tubes and held together with sticky tape – or keep the cardboard centres from toilet or kitchen rolls. Place the tubes side by side in a seed tray and fill with peat-free compost. Some seed varieties need soaking overnight to soften the seed coat.

Another method is to "chit" the seed – to remove a sliver of the seed coat carefully with a garden or craft knife at the opposite end from the "eye", where the root will start growing. This allows water to penetrate the seeds more easily, hastening germination. Sweet peas don't need very high temperatures to germinate so there is no need for a propagator – a cool, light room or even a sheltered cold frame is sufficient.

Sow sweet peas now to be rewarded by a flowering display in summer.

PREPARING
SWEET PEA SEEDS

If necessary, soak the seeds overnight to soften the seed coat, or chit (nick) the tough coating to help the seeds germinate.

Push a couple of seeds into the compost in each tube to a depth of about 2.5cm (1in). Water well, and keep in full light.

KITCHEN GARDEN

COMPLETE WINTER DIGGING

The sooner cultivation of empty beds and new vegetable plots is completed, the better. This will help the winter weather break down large clods of earth, improving the soil structure and making it easier to work in spring. If you cannot dig now because the ground is frozen hard, you can at least barrow out manure or compost and spread it on top of the soil. When the soil is very wet, keep off it, or it will compact down and become a sea of mud that dries to a hard crust.

Each winter, spread organic matter as a surface layer over the beds rather than digging it in. The level will fall over the season.

You will then have great difficulty working it in later months trying to make seed beds.

One way to avoid walking on the soil is to use the deep bed method of growing vegetables: beds that are only about 1.2m (4ft) wide can be tended by reaching over from paths each side, so you never need to tread on the soil. Initially double-dig the beds, incorporating plenty of organic matter. Double-digging is essentially the same as single-digging, but soil is taken out to two spade depths rather than one. Once this is done, you need never dig these beds again.

Every winter, you simply add organic matter as a surface layer, and the healthy worm population that should exist in the beds will take it down into the soil for you. Crops can be grown much closer together because you don't need to leave extra space between rows to get at the plants. The soil is not compacted in any way, and you'll get much higher yields than on a conventional arrangement of rows.

Cover the ground with polythene where your earliest sowings and plantings will go, to dry and warm the soil.

COVER GROUND WITH POLYTHENE

When you have dug over an area, cover the ground either with cloches, or with a large sheet of polythene, anchored round the edges or tucked firmly into the soil. This will keep off the worst of the winter weather so that the soil can easily be raked down into seedbeds next month. It also helps to warm up the soil for any young plants set outdoors early, or alternatively for early outdoor sowing. This way you'll get the earliest vegetables when they are at their most expensive in the shops.

BEND LEAVES OVER CAULIFLOWERS

This will protect the developing curds, which actually are the plants' undeveloped flowerheads. When exposed to a prolonged period of light the curds tend to turn green and, after a while, the flower buds develop, making them inedible. By bending a few leaves over the curd this process is slowed down, making the crops last a bit longer. It's very easy to do: just snap the leaves near the base of the midrib and tuck them in around the curd. You can tie the leaves up to keep the curds covered in windy weather.

START EARLY POTATOES

Freshly dug potatoes are in a class of their own when it comes to flavour, better than anything in the supermarket. It's time to look out for seed potatoes as they need to be chitted (started into growth) before planting in March. As well as advancing the date on which the potatoes will be harvested,

A cardboard egg tray or shallow box are ideal for sprouting seed potatoes.

chitting them will also increase the overall yield.

To start them off, lay the tubers in a tray with the "rose" end (the end with most buds on it) uppermost. Put them in a light, cool, but frost-free place – a spare room, porch or utility room – and after two or three weeks, shoots will begin to sprout. To get the best crop, thin the shoots to two or three per tuber. Plant out from March.

FORCE RHUBARB

Doing this will encourage growth of tender young stems in the spring. Clear away all dead foliage from the crown. If the winter has been mild, you may see fresh growth already starting at ground level; be careful not to damage it. Cover the plant with an old dustbin or large pot. Alternatively you can buy terracotta rhubarb forcers. These are upturned clay pots with a lid to check on the forced rhubarb, and are usually decorative. Place one of these over the crown of the plant, and if you can get it, cover the forcer with a pile of fresh horse manure. The heat generated by the manure as it rots will force the rhubarb on even quicker.

APPLY ORGANIC FERTILISER

Although you may not notice it, even in late January things are beginning to stir; sap is beginning to rise and trees are awakening after their winter rest. An organic fertiliser such as blood, fish, and bone or seaweed meal is ideal, because organic fertilisers release their nutrients slowly over a long period; the plants don't get the sudden boost to growth they would get with inorganic, or chemical, fertilisers. Too much soft growth early in the season is more susceptible to damage from frosts, pests, and diseases. Pull away any mulch around the base of trees and bushes if necessary before feeding; then water the ground, and renew the mulch.

Terracotta forcing pots, that have a lid for checking the progress of the rhubarb, make attractive garden features.

JANUARY PROJECT

POTTING UP LILIES FOR EARLY COLOUR

Lilies are the epitome of summer with their sweetly scented flowers. Grow some in a container near the door and they will greet you with their perfume as you go by. However be aware that their pollen can stain clothes.

Extend the flowering season by planting lily bulbs in pots from January through until spring. Put a few bulbs in each pot at intervals of about four weeks and enjoy a long succession of flowers. Lilies are perfectly hardy, but starting them off in pots in the greenhouse or on a windowsill will get them off to a good start. There are many eye-catching species available that are renowned for their scent, such as *Lilium auratum*, *L. candidum*, *L. hansonii*, *L. regale*, and oriental hybrids, like 'Star Gazer' (*right*) and 'Arabian Red'.

1 **Buy fresh bulbs** from a reputable grower. Choose a deep container, as lilies are planted about 20cm (8in) deep. Cover the drainage holes with broken pieces of pot, or coarse gravel, and then add a layer of multi-purpose compost.

2 **Add a layer of horticultural grit**, 3cm (1½in) deep, over the compost and lay the lily bulbs on their sides on top. Planting the bulbs in this way allows water to drain out of their scales, which may otherwise collect and cause rot.

3 **Cover the bulbs** and top up the container to around 5cm (2in) below the rim with a 50:50 mix of compost and horticultural grit. Place the pot on "feet" to help drainage, and place in a sheltered spot. Move into a sunny position as soon as shoots appear.

4 **Water the container** every few days and apply a high potash feed every two weeks in summer. Keep watering and feeding your lilies until the foliage dies down, then move the pot to a sheltered site over winter. In spring, renew the top 5cm (2in) of compost.

BULB OPTIONS

There are many flowering bulbs, corms and tubers suitable for pots, including jewel-like dwarf dahlias (*below*) and fiery-flowered *Crocosmia*. Begonias grown from tubers also

come in many colours. Also try elegant *Gladiolus communis* subsp. *byzantinus* with its vivid, deep magenta flowers.

CHRISTMAS BOX   [1]

Sarcococca hookeriana var. *digyna* ♀
A thicket-forming, evergreen shrub with glossy, lance-shaped leaves. In winter, it bears clusters of fragrant, white flowers with pink anthers, followed by round black or dark blue fruits.
‡ 1.5m (5ft) ↔ 2m (6ft)

CULTIVATION Grow in fertile, moist but well-drained soil in shade, or in sun if soil remains moist. Needs little pruning. Dig out suckers at the margins of the clump if it encroaches on other plants.

HEATHER   [2]

Erica carnea 'Springwood White' ♀
A robust, spreading, slightly trailing evergreen shrub. From winter to mid-spring, it is covered with small, dense spires of white flowers.
‡ 15cm (6in) ↔ 45cm (18in)

CULTIVATION Best in an open, sunny site in well-drained acid soil; it will tolerate slightly alkaline soils. After flowering, trim off the old flowers with shears and top-dress with leafmould, garden compost, or similar.

WINTER ACONITE 3

Eranthis hyemalis ♀ A hardy perennial with small, knobbly tubers. In late winter and early spring, bright yellow flowers appear above a ruff of dissected, bright green leaves.
‡5–8cm (2–3in) ↔5cm (2in)

CULTIVATION Grow in full sun, in any fertile soil that is not too dry in summer. Plant tubers 5cm (2in) deep in autumn, or buy plants "in-the-green" and plant when the soil is not too wet or frozen.

2

3

WITCH HAZEL ⓵

Hamamelis × intermedia **'Arnold Promise'** ♀ Slow-growing, deciduous shrub of vase-shaped outline. Bare branches are spangled with fragrant, spidery, yellow flowers in early to midwinter. The leaves turn yellow before falling in autumn.
‡to 4m (12ft) ↔ to 4m (12ft)

CULTIVATION Grow in fertile, moisture-retentive soil, and a sheltered spot, in sun or part-shade. Needs little pruning, but remove damaged shoots after flowering.

HONEYSUCKLE ⓶

Lonicera × purpusii Moderately vigorous, semi-evergreen or deciduous shrub. During winter and early spring, it bears small clusters of fragrant white flowers with conspicuous yellow anthers. It has purple shoots and dark green leaves in the summer.
‡2m (6ft) ↔ 2.5m (8ft)

CULTIVATION Grow in any fertile, well-drained soil in sun or dappled shade. After flowering, cut back the flowered shoots to strong buds, but only to confine to bounds.

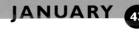

SKIMMIA 3

Skimmia japonica Tough, dome-shaped, evergreen shrub. In winter, it produces dense clusters of pink buds that open to reveal scented white flowers. It has slightly aromatic, glossy dark green leaves all year. Female plants bear red berries, if male and female plants are grown together. ‡ to 5m (15ft) ↔ 1.5m (5ft)

CULTIVATION Grow in dappled or deep shade, in any fertile, humus-rich soil. It needs little, if any pruning other than to shape if necessary after flowering.

2

3

SNOWDROP [1]

Galanthus plicatus* subsp. *byzantinus
A hardy perennial bulb. In late winter
or early spring, it bears nodding, honey-
scented, white flowers with green
markings on the inner petals.
‡20cm (8in) ↔ 8cm (3in)

CULTIVATION Grow in dappled shade
in any fertile garden soil that does not
dry out in summer. Lift and divide the
bulbs when congested, after flowering
but before the leaves have faded. May
self-seed.

ALGERIAN IRIS [2]

***Iris unguicularis* 'Mary Barnard'** ♀
A robust, rhizomatous perennial.
In midwinter it produces scented,
bright violet, yellow-marked flowers.
The flowers are excellent for cutting.
Has tough, grass-like leaves throughout
the year.
‡30cm (12in) ↔ 5cm (2in)

CULTIVATION Grow in full sun in poor
to moderately fertile, very freely draining,
neutral to alkaline soil in a sheltered site
against a south or west facing wall. Once
planted, leave undisturbed; they flower
with increasing freedom as they settle in.

ROSEBUD CHERRY 3

Prunus x *subhirtella* **'Autumnalis Rosea'** ♀ A moderately vigorous, spreading deciduous tree. From late autumn to spring, it bears small, semi-double, pale pink flowers. The leaves are bronzed when young and yellow in autumn.
‡8m (25ft) ↔ 8m (25ft)

CULTIVATION Grow in fertile, moist but well-drained soil in sun or light dappled shade. It needs minimal pruning; in late summer, remove damaged or badly placed shoots.

2

3

PAPER BIRCH 　　　1

Betula papyrifera A deciduous, fairly
vigorous tree of conical outline. The
peeling white bark is beautiful when
the tree is leafless in winter. Dark green
leaves turn yellow and orange in autumn,
and long golden catkins appear in spring.
‡20m (70ft) ↔ 10m (30ft)

CULTIVATION Grow in fertile, humus-
rich soil in sun or dappled shade. In
winter, prune out the lowest branches
when very small to create a clear trunk.

SILK TASSEL BUSH 　　　2

Garrya elliptica A dense, bushy
evergreen shrub. From midwinter
through to early spring, it bears swags
of silky, hanging, grey-green catkins. It
has glossy, wavy-margined, dark greyish-
green leaves all year.
‡4m (12ft) ↔ 4m (12ft)

CULTIVATION Grow in any fertile,
well-drained soil in sun or part-shade.
Shelter from cold wind. After flowering,
shorten any shoots that spoil the shape;
if wall-trained, cut back shoots growing
away from or into the wall.

2

3

TIBETAN CHERRY

Prunus serrula ♀ A rounded, deciduous tree. In late spring, it bears small, single, bowl-shaped white flowers. The polished mahogany bark is stunning all year round. The leaves turn yellow in autumn.
↕10m (30ft) ↔ 10m (30ft)

CULTIVATION Grow in fertile, moist but well-drained soil in sun or light dappled shade. It needs minimal pruning in late summer. When young, remove sideshoots from the trunk to display the bark at its best.

CORNUS

Dogwoods include several outstanding deciduous shrubs. These are grown principally for their brightly coloured leafless stems, which bring interest to the winter garden. They bear clusters of white flowers in spring, and white or blue-black fruit in autumn.

CULTIVATION Grow in any moderately fertile soil. They tolerate shade, but stems colour best in sun. For the best effect, prune the stems right back to the base each year in early spring.

TOP ROW LEFT TO RIGHT
• *C. alba* 'Aurea' ♀
  ↕3m (10ft) ↔ 3m (10ft)
• *C. alba* 'Elegantissima' ♀
  ↕3m (10ft) ↔ 3m (10ft)
• *C. sericea* 'Kelseyi'
  ↕75cm (30in) ↔ 1.5m (5ft)

BOTTOM ROW LEFT TO RIGHT
• *C. alba* 'Sibirica' ♀
  ↕3m (10ft) ↔ 3m (10ft)
• *C. sanguinea* 'Winter Beauty'
  ↕3m (10ft) ↔ 2.5m (8ft)
• *C. sericea* 'Flaviramea' ♀
  ↕2m (6ft) ↔ 4m (12ft)

WHAT TO DO IN FEBRUARY

WEATHER WATCH

February is a month of anticipation, as spring is on the way. On the mildest days you can get on with winter-pruning jobs and cultivate the soil, but if you're huddled up indoors, why not fill the time with a spot of garden planning.

RISK OF FROST

As far as temperatures are concerned, January and February are similar, with February being, on average, colder. Temperature over land is largely governed by the temperature of the sea, which is at its lowest in February. Average daily temperatures in the south will be around 6–8°C (43–46°F), and in northern regions 4–6°C (37–43°F). Hard frosts are still common, so continue to protect vulnerable plants outdoors.

WINDY DAYS

February can still be windy, but less so than January. The north of the country will have on average 3–4 days of gales this month, the south only about 0.1 day. These figures vary according to height above sea level and the local topography. Coastal areas are always windier than inland.

MORE SUNSHINE

Generally there is more sunshine in February compared to January, with southern parts of the country getting around 7.6 days, and northern parts around 5.2 days of bright sun. The days are getting appreciably longer, too. Sunny days make you want to get on with jobs such as seed-sowing, but don't hurry as there can still be a lot of bad weather to come.

WINTER WET

Rainfall varies from one part of the country to another, south-eastern parts generally getting the least rain, with on average 35–38mm (1–1½in). In Scotland this month, the north-east coast is driest, but the south-west is one of the wettest parts of the country, with on average 110mm (4⅓in) of rain, due mainly to the predominance of high ground.

PERSISTENT SNOW

Thick snow can persist in high areas for most of the winter, but on lower ground amounts vary. Western coastal areas have very little snow and mild temperatures – there are gardens on the west coasts of Scotland and Ireland growing plants usually found in warmer regions. In the north, on high ground above 100m (300ft) there will be on average 2–3 days of snow, increasing to around 15 days over 300m (984ft). In southern parts 1–2 days is the average snowfall for the month.

AROUND THE GARDEN

CHECK GARDEN EQUIPMENT

Examine your tools and machines to ensure they are in working order. Once the busy gardening season really gets under way, it is maddening to go to the shed, and only then remember that your favourite spade has a broken handle – just when you need to get on with digging or planting a newly bought plant. Wiring of all electrical appliances should be checked for cuts too, and if you are not sure what to do, contact a qualified electrician, or take it to your nearest stockist for advice.

HAVE A CLEAR-OUT

If you use chemicals in the garden, even "organic" kinds, it is a good idea to go through them and see which ones have been lying around for a long time and can be discarded. There may be bags that have split open with the contents spilt on the floor or shelves, or bottles with only a few drops left in them, or even some that have been in the shed unused for years.

Care for and preserve the wooden parts of your tools, first by sanding them down, and then by wiping them over with linseed oil.

Don't just pour them down the drain or scatter old fertiliser over the garden as you may cause a lot of harm. Take this sort of material to your local authority waste site, and let them deal with it. Look for contact numbers in your local phone book.

LEAVE FOOD FOR GARDEN WILDLIFE

Make sure birds have food and water. It's a very hungry month for wildlife, and putting food out may distract birds and small mammals from taking buds and bulbs. If you put up bird boxes, do not worry if birds don't start using them straight away: they may need a little time to get used to new boxes before they will select them to nest in.

APPLY ORGANIC FERTILISER

This is a good time of year to do this; organic fertilisers release their nutrients more slowly than inorganic ones, so they will be available to the plants just as they

Set aside time to put up a bird box, which should be sited as high as possible to prevent cats from reaching it.

start into growth in the spring. A sprinkling of organic fertiliser, like seaweed meal, blood, fish, and bone, or pelleted chicken manure, around the plants will do them the world of good after the long winter. Spread the fertiliser according to the manufacturer's instructions, and then lightly stir it into the surface of the soil, either with a hoe or a garden fork.

TREES, SHRUBS & CLIMBERS

PLANT BARE-ROOT TREES AND SHRUBS

This can be done any time during the dormant season from November to March, but recent research indicates that February is the ideal time. Provided the soil is not frozen, or so wet that it sticks to your boots, plants put in this month get off to a really good start.

By planting now it is not long before the soil begins to warm up.

PLANTING A BARE-ROOT TREE

1 Dig a generous hole that won't cramp the root system. Incorporate plenty of organic matter into the hole.

2 Put in a stake on the windward side so the plant is blown away from the stake – this will prevent rubbing.

3 Plant to the tree's original depth (the darker part of the stem near the roots). Fill in the hole and firm in gently with your boot.

New roots grow before you know it, helping to establish the plant. Remember to look after new plants and water thoroughly during dry spells, as they are at their most vulnerable during their first year.

Plant new climbers exactly as you would trees and shrubs (although they are more likely to be container-grown rather than bare-rooted), digging holes at least 22cm (9in) away from walls and fences so that the plant is not in a dry "rain shadow", and leaning the plants into the support.

TRIM WINTER-FLOWERING HEATHERS

Carry this out as they finish flowering, otherwise they become straggly and the centre of the plant will be bare. Use a pair of garden shears to trim back to the base of the flower stalks: this will encourage sideshoots to grow, keeping the plant bushy and compact. Mulching with a peat substitute and feeding in a few weeks' time will do a lot to promote growth.

TEND TO CONIFERS

If you didn't tie in conifer branches before winter arrived, it's possible that wind or snow could have bent them down, spoiling their shape. Pruning off these branches can leave an unsightly gap, so tie them up instead. Plastic-coated wire is fine provided it is cushioned against the trunk either with a piece of hessian or with a rag cut into strips and folded, otherwise the wire will cut into the trunk eventually killing the tree.

If bent down, conifer branches splay out but rarely break. Tie them back with soft twine, a strip of fabric, or cushioned wire.

PRUNE OVERGROWN EVERGREENS

Provided they are completely hardy, overgrown evergreens such as *Prunus laurocerasus* can be pruned now. More tender shrubs like *Choisya ternata* (Mexican orange blossom) should be left until later in the year when the weather will be a bit warmer. Any shoots that have become overcrowded or have grown out awkwardly can be pruned back to maintain the plant's shape.

Cutting back to ground level may be an option if the plant is one that tolerates drastic pruning – for example, *Prunus laurocerasus*, *Aucuba japonica* (spotted laurel), or *Viburnum tinus*. This drastic method of pruning encourages strong growth from the base of the shrub. Feed after pruning, preferably with an organic fertiliser, and then mulch with organic matter.

PRUNE LATE-FLOWERING SHRUBS

These include *Buddleja davidii* (the butterfly bush), *Caryopteris × clandonensis*, *Ceanothus* 'Burkwoodii' (the deciduous ceanothus), hardy fuchsias, santolina, ceratostigma, lavatera, and leycesteria (the nutmeg bush).

These shrubs flower best on growth made since the spring. It's a terrific job if you've had a bad day, as you can be quite brutal with them! Cut them back almost to the ground, leaving one or two buds or shoots on each stem. You may feel you're cutting off far too much, but it is the right thing to do to get the best show of flowers.

Where you want to increase the size of the shrubs, leave a few stems on and prune these lightly. When you have finished pruning, give them a feed of organic fertiliser and mulch with garden compost or farmyard manure to get them off to a flying start.

◀ *Buddleja davidii* 'Fascinating'

When pruning Buddleja davidii, *use loppers or a pruning saw to cut the thick stems back to a stubby framework.*

When pruning Caryopteris, *cut back all of the whippy stems, and a new crop will grow and flower.*

◀ *Hamamelis × intermedia* 'Jelena'

It's worth noting that larger winter-flowering shrubs like witch hazel (*Hamamelis*) don't as a rule need regular pruning. However, once flowering has completely finished, you can remove any stems that are rubbing or spoiling the shape of the plant.

PRUNE LATE-FLOWERING CLEMATIS

Towards the end of the month, you can prune *Clematis orientalis*, *C. texensis*, *C. viticella*, and its many varieties, such as 'Madame Julia Correvon' and 'Gravetye Beauty', and also the late large-flowered hybrids such as 'Ville de Lyon' and 'Jackmannii'. These are often referred to as "group 3" clematis.

In sheltered parts, they may already be producing shoots. They can be rather brittle, so be careful when pruning and pulling away the old growth. Apart from this, they are the easiest of all clematis to prune. Cut the growth down to 23–45cm (9–18in) from the ground, cutting each stem back to just above a healthy bud. They are ideal for growing through other shrubs, because as they start afresh each year, they never become so overgrown that they swamp their host. After pruning, feed with an organic fertiliser and then mulch with organic matter, or put a large stone at the base of the plant. Clematis like their heads in the sun but their roots shaded and cool.

To prune group 3 clematis, wait for the buds to break, then cut all growth close to the ground.

PRUNE JASMINE

Winter-flowering jasmine can be pruned once the flowers have gone over completely. First prune out any dead or damaged wood. Then tie in any stems that you need to extend the framework or coverage of the plant, and then shorten all the side growths from this main framework to 5cm (2in) from the main stems. This will encourage plenty of new shoots for flowering next winter. Feed and mulch as for clematis.

Summer-flowering jasmines can also be pruned, but you must tackle this type by taking out an entire main stem or two to the ground. If you prune back all the side growths as with winter jasmine, they produce a mass of tangled leafy growth that is no good to anyone.

This lanky plant, Jasminum nudiflorum, *needs some attention to prevent it becoming very untidy.*

PRUNE OVERGROWN HEDGES

Overgrown or misshapen hedges can be pruned this month – this will benefit them by improving both their health and shape. The majority of deciduous hedges can be pruned back hard, as can broadleaved evergreens such as *Prunus laurocerasus* and laurel, but don't ever cut conifers back into bare wood. The exception to this rule, however, is yew.

Yew is often considered to be a slow-growing hedge, but it is surprising how quickly it actually grows. Even if trimmed regularly, it has a tendency to gradually creep outwards if it is not trimmed hard enough. Unlike other conifers, such as Leyland cypress, yew will take very hard pruning: cut it back as much as you like and it will grow away again from the stumps. Other conifers should be lightly but regularly trimmed from the very beginning to keep them compact; don't ever allow them to become overgrown.

TOP-DRESS POT-GROWN SHRUBS

Shrubs grown in large pots over the course of several years will benefit from yearly top-dressing with fresh compost. Scrape away about 2.5cm (1in) of the old compost from the surface. Then add fresh potting compost that contains some slow-release fertiliser. This will feed the plants over several months, doing away with the chore of feeding them every week or month through the spring and summer.

To top-dress a plant, scrape off the top layer of soil and replace it with fresh multipurpose compost.

FLOWERING PLANTS

FINISH WEEDING AND DIGGING

To save yourself a bit of time at a later stage, you could incorporate organic matter into borders and new planting areas at the same time as you complete all of your weeding and digging. It's probably also worth keeping an eye out for any old, dead growth from plants such as sedums and acanthus that was left on for effect over winter – this should be cut down now. The sooner all of these tasks are carried out, the better, as it's likely that new shoots will already be emerging from some plants by the end of the month, and they are easily damaged.

Towards the end of the month herbaceous perennials will be starting into growth; they will benefit from being fed with an organic-based fertiliser, as this will encourage them to get off to a really good start.

START DAHLIA TUBERS

To produce shoots that make good cuttings, you should now start up dahlia tubers that were stored during the winter. The tubers can be potted up singly, or several can be put into large trays. Place the tubers in good light, and spray them every now and then with clear water – this will encourage the buds to grow. If you didn't store any dahlias over winter, you can buy some from the garden centre. These should be treated in exactly the same way.

To start dahlia tubers, fill a shallow tray with compost, and set the tubers on top.

DAHLIAS TO TRY

'Glorie van Heemstede'

'Hamari Gold'

'Zorro'

'Kathryn's Cupid'

'Ivanetti'

'Moonfire'

Unlike most other bulbs, snowdrops and aconites are planted while in leaf.

PLANT SNOWDROPS AND WINTER ACONITES

Do this after flowering, but while the foliage is still green. Both of these bulbs should be bought "in the green" as it is known. Look through the gardening press now and you will see plenty advertised by specialist nurseries, who will supply them in the green by mail order. Many garden centres also sell them in pots. It's as well to buy snowdrops in particular from a reputable supplier, then you can be sure that they haven't been uprooted from the wild, an illegal practice which is causing great conservation worries.

Work in some compost or leafmould to enrich the soil before planting; a little bonemeal won't go amiss either. Put the plants in a little deeper than they were and water them if the soil is dry. Overcrowded clumps in the garden can be lifted with a fork after flowering, and separated out. Replant them singly in informal drifts at the same depth as before.

Plant snowdrops (left) and winter aconites (right) now for flowers that will noticeably brighten your garden come next winter.

KITCHEN GARDEN

LIME BRASSICA BEDS

About one-third of the vegetable plot needs to be limed every year, generally where the brassicas (Brussels sprouts, cabbages, and cauliflowers) will be, as these all like alkaline soil. But before applying any lime always first check the existing pH of the soil – its acidity or alkalinity – with a soil-testing kit, as this will determine the amount of lime you put on. It may be that if you naturally have a very alkaline soil, you do not need to add lime at all.

The pH of the soil is a scale of 1–14 by which the alkalinity or acidity of the soil is determined. Around seven is neutral; values less than 7 are acid, and higher than 7, alkaline. Soil-testing kits are easy to use; most come with a numbered chart to which you match the colour of your soil sample, after mixing it with the solutions provided.

Once you know your soil's pH, the instructions on the packet will help you add the correct quantity of lime. Wear gloves, goggles, and a face mask, and choose a still day. It's safest to use the ordinary sort of garden lime, calcium carbonate – or the organic alternative, dolomitic limestone – rather than quicklime or slaked lime, as although more effective these are highly caustic.

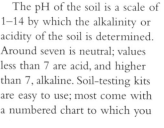

Lime should be added at least two months before planting anything.

SOW PEAS

An ideal way to sow peas is in a piece of plastic guttering, choosing an early variety such as 'Douce Provence'. Drill drainage holes in the bottom of the guttering, then fill with a peat-free seed compost. Sow the seeds evenly in two rows 2.5–5cm (1–2in) apart and 2.5cm (1in) deep, and water. Keep them on a windowsill or in a greenhouse; it does not need to be heated, although heat will speed up germination. When the seedlings have a few leaves they can be planted out under a cloche by sliding them out of the guttering into a shallow trench in the soil.

PLANT SHALLOTS

Prepare the ground thoroughly, incorporating plenty of organic matter. Add an organic fertiliser, following the instructions on the packet, and rake the soil to a fine tilth. Plant the shallots 15–18cm (6–7in) apart, in rows the same distance apart. Don't just push them into the soil, or the new roots will push the bulbs up and out again. Birds love to pull them out too if they see them. Plant shallots with a trowel, with the bulb tips just beneath the surface.

Space out all of the peas before pushing them in, so you don't lose track of where you've got to.

Once the seedlings have a few pairs of leaves, the whole lot can simply be "shunted" into a trench.

POTTING UP MINT

1 Clumps of mint will now be looking tatty and overgrown, and slugs may be eating the shoots. Dig up a section and separate out the healthiest-looking parts.

2 Shake or rinse off most of the soil and cut a few small sections of thick, fleshy root, 2.5–5cm (1–2 in) long. Replant other sections in the garden if needed.

3 Pot up cuttings in multipurpose compost, stand on a windowsill, and water regularly. Soon a new crop of fresh shoots will grow.

A few roots of mint potted up now will provide sprigs you can use in a few months' time with the first vegetables of the season.

POT UP MINT

Mint is an excellent herb to use along with the first of the early potatoes dug fresh from the garden. Confining mint to pots is generally the best way to grow mint outside, as it can be very invasive, easily taking over parts of the garden. Grow it in a large pot and stand this on the terrace, or plunge the pot into the ground, leaving the top 5–10cm (2–4in) of the pot proud of the soil surface. This will usually prevent the mint from creeping over the rim into the soil, but it is wise to keep an eye on it anyway.

MULCH FRUIT TREES

It is well worth doing this with well-rotted manure or garden compost after all the pruning and feeding has been done. Not only will a mulch help to keep down weeds, it will also hold in moisture. This cuts down the amount of watering you will have to do in the warm summer months, and will give you better quality fruit to enjoy.

If by some strange circumstance the soil happens to be dry, soak the ground first before applying the mulch. Mulch is as good at keeping water out as retaining it in the soil. You can lay a seep- or tricklehose beneath the mulch to make watering in the summer simple.

PRUNE AUTUMN-FRUITING RASPBERRIES

There is a distinction to be made between the pruning times and methods for summer- and autumn-fruiting raspberries. If you get it wrong then you lose a crop for the year.

Autumn-fruiting raspberries, which are the ones to be pruned this month, produce their fruit from August or September onwards on long stems (canes) that grew during that summer. In my opinion, the best variety is called 'September'. Summer-fruiting raspberries will fruit on the canes that grew the previous year. So the new canes that they produce this summer will fruit the following summer.

Prune autumn-fruiting raspberries, quite simply, by cutting all of the canes down to the ground.

PLANTING RASPBERRY CANES

To give the plants a really good start, plant them in a trench to which plenty of organic matter has been added.

Erect a sytem of support for the canes — for example, a post at each end of the row with three wires stretched between them.

In spring, when new canes have grown, you can cut the original one back to ground level.

PLANT BARE-ROOTED CANE FRUITS

Towards the end of February is the latest time you should be planting bare-rooted cane fruits – raspberries, blackberries, and hybrid berry canes – which are usually sold in bundles. Make sure the soil is thoroughly prepared by digging a trench all along the proposed row and working in plenty of organic matter, if this was not carried out during the winter months.

All bare-rooted cane fruits, except the autumn-fruiting raspberries, will need support for their fruiting canes. This is usually provided by a system of posts at either end of the row with a minimum of three horizontal wires strained between the posts. Freestanding rows should be at least 1.5m (5ft) apart.

If you are using a wall or fence for blackberries and hybrid berries (raspberries prefer to be in the open), then you may be able to attach the wires to vine eyes screwed into the wall. Plant raspberries about 45cm (18in) apart in the row. Blackberries and hybrid berries need to be at least 1.5m (5ft) apart, and some vigorous cultivars may need even more space. If you are unsure, ask the nursery for advice.

Prune the newly-planted canes to about 22cm (9in) from the ground. You will probably have to summon up a bit of courage to do this, but it is essential to encourage the production of good, strong fruiting canes from the base of the plant. Later in the summer you can cut it right out. Tie the canes to the wires as they grow through the season, but don't take a crop this year. The odd fruit is fine, but be sure to remove flowers if there are a lot of them. At this time you are trying to get the plants established. They will then give a good crop next year.

FEBRUARY PROJECT

GROW A LEMON TREE

Growing your own citrus fruits is great fun. Commercially grown citrus plants are widely available, but children particularly love watching a lemon tree grow from a pip (*see opposite*). Although it will take years before a citrus seedling matures into a tree and bears fruit, it still makes an attractive ornamental plant. As the tree reaches the fruiting stage, there will be the added bonus of highly fragrant flowers. The plants seem to have a few flowers and fruits at different stages of development most of the year.

Citrus trees don't need much heat in winter but they do need to be protected from frost, either in a cool room or greenhouse. In the warmer months, you can stand them outside in a sunny corner. Give them plenty of water during spring and summer.

1 **Cut open a lemon** and remove the pips and dry them. Plant several pips in a pot, 1cm (½in) deep, in seed compost. Water them well and put the pot in a warm spot. Keep them well watered.

2 **Pot on the lemon seedlings** once they are well established. Carefully lift them from the soil, without damaging the roots, and plant them individually in their own pots of soil-based compost.

3 **Place the pots in a sunny spot,** and keep well watered. Over winter, grow in a cool room indoors; when the threat of frost has gone, stand pots outside for lengthening spells to acclimatize gradually.

OTHER CITRUS

Lemons are the most popular fruits to grow but you can also try growing tangerines, grapefruits, or limes. They all require the same growing conditions.

CORNELIAN CHERRY 　1

Cornus mas Spreading, fairly vigorous deciduous shrub or small tree. In late winter, it bears small but profuse clusters of yellow flowers on bare branches. The dark green leaves turn red-purple in autumn. It sometimes produces small, bright red fruits.
↕5m (15ft) ↔ 5m (15ft)

CULTIVATION Any fertile, well-drained soil, including chalky ones. Best in an open sunny site, but will tolerate light shade. Keep pruning to a minimum.

CAMELLIA 　2

***Camellia* x *williamsii* 'Anticipation'** ♡
A strong-growing, evergreen shrub of narrowly upright growth. Beautiful, peony-like crimson flowers appear from midwinter to mid-spring. The lustrous, dark green foliage is delightful all year.
↕4m (12ft) ↔ 2m (6ft)

CULTIVATION Thrives in sun or dappled shade, but needs shade from early morning sun, which may damage flowers in frosty weather. Grow in humus-rich, lime-free (acid) soil, or in ericaceous compost in pots. Trim lightly to shape after flowering if necessary.

EARLY CROCUS 3

Crocus tommasinianus ♥ A robust,
cormous perennial. In late winter or early
spring, slender, goblet-shaped flowers
appear. They come in white, lilac, and
red–purple, often with silvery overtones.
‡10cm (4in) ↔ 2.5cm (1in)

CULTIVATION Best in full sun but will
tolerate dappled shade. Grow in fertile,
well-drained soil. Plant corms in the
autumn, 8–10cm (3–4in) deep.

2

3

EUONYMUS [1]

Euonymus fortunei 'Silver Queen'
A hardy, brightly variegated evergreen
shrub. The shiny green leaves with white,
often pink-flushed margins make good
ground cover all year round. Tiny,
greenish white flowers in summer,
followed by pink fruits with orange seeds.
↕2.5m (8ft) ↔1.5m (5ft)

CULTIVATION Foliage colour is best in
full sun, but it tolerates light shade. Grow
in any well-drained soil. Trim in mid- to
late spring; remove any all-green shoots.

LAURUSTINUS [2]

Viburnum tinus A bushy, moderately
vigorous, evergreen shrub. In winter
and spring, it bears flattened clusters
of perfumed white flowers. It also
has attractive, glossy, dark green leaves
and black berries.
↕to 3m (10ft) ↔to 3m (10ft)

CULTIVATION Grow in sun or part-
shade in any fertile, moist but well-
drained soil. Shorten overlong shoots
that spoil the plant's outline.

1

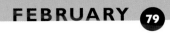

LENTEN ROSE `3`

Helleborus orientalis An upright
evergreen perennial. From midwinter
to spring, it bears white or creamy green
flowers that flush pink with age. Leathery,
divided, deep green basal leaves persist
throughout the year.
‡45cm (18in) ↔ 45cm (18in)

CULTIVATION Happiest in dappled
shade, but tolerates sun if the soil is
reliably moist. Grow in any good garden
soil. Trim away old leaves before flowers
emerge to display them at their best.

HEATHER [1]

Erica × *darleyensis* 'Jenny Porter' ♥
A dense, bushy shrub with mid-green
leaves; the young foliage has pale cream
tips in spring. From late winter until
spring it bears pinkish white flowers.
A good ground cover plant.
↕30cm (12in) ↔60cm (24in)

CULTIVATION Best in an open, sunny
site in well-drained acid soil. After
flowering, trim back with shears to the
base of the flower spikes and top-dress
with lime-free compost or leafmould.

CLEMATIS [2]

Clematis cirrhosa var. *balearica*
An evergreen, early-flowering clematis.
It bears cup-shaped, fragrant, pale cream
flowers with reddish-brown speckles,
either singly or in clusters, from late
winter to early spring. The foliage is an
attractive bronze colour beneath. Silky
seed heads in summer.
↕3m (10ft) ↔1.5m (5ft)

CULTIVATION Grow in sun or dappled
shade in fertile, humus-rich, well-drained
soil, with the roots in shade. Protect from
cold wind. After flowering, remove dead
or damaged shoots; shorten others to
confine to bounds.

JAPONICA

3

***Chaenomeles × superba* 'Nicoline'** ♀
A rounded, spreading deciduous
shrub with broadly oval, mid-green
glossy foliage. An abundance of large,
sometimes semi-double, scarlet flowers
are borne in spring and summer. Green
fruit ripens to yellow in autumn.
‡ 1.5m (5ft) ↔ 2m (6ft)

CULTIVATION Grow in moderately
fertile, well-drained soil in sun or part-
shade. After flowering, shorten flowered
shoots to strong buds. When mature, take
out one in five of the oldest shoots.

2

3

HARDY CYCLAMEN 1

***Cyclamen coum* Pewter Group** ♀
Low clump-forming winter-flowering
cyclamen with attractive silver and
dark green marbled leaves. Charming
reddish pink flowers. Self-seeds freely,
forming extensive colonies with time.
‡8cm (3in) ↔ 10cm (4in)

CULTIVATION Grow in moderately
fertile well-drained soil, ideally beneath
a canopy of trees or shrubs to protect
them from excessive summer rain when
dormant. Give a deep, dry mulch of
leafmould as the leaves wither.

DWARF IRIS 2

***Iris* 'Harmony'** A small, sturdy perennial
bulb suitable for rock gardens, containers,
or beneath deciduous shrubs. Yellow-
marked, royal-blue flowers appear in late
winter amid a sheaf of narrow leaves.
‡10–15cm (4–6in) ↔ 5cm (2in)

CULTIVATION Best in full sun. Plant
bulbs at twice their own depth in late
summer or early autumn in well-drained
soil. Add coarse grit to heavy clay soils to
improve drainage.

WILD NARCISSUS 3

Narcissus cyclamineus ♀ A vigorous, perennial bulb. In early spring, it bears nodding, golden yellow flowers with backswept petals.
‡15–20cm (6–8in) ↔ 2.5cm (1in)

CULTIVATION Grow in sun or dappled shade in any moderately fertile, well-drained soil. Plant bulbs in autumn at twice their own depth. If grown in turf, allow the foliage to fade naturally before mowing.

WHAT TO DO IN
MARCH

WEATHER WATCH

The clocks going forward gives gardeners extra time for getting everything done – and there's quite a list. But the riot of spring colours will give plenty of encouragement. You can mulch and prune, take cuttings, reseed lawns, and sow half-hardy annuals.

CHANGEABLE WEATHER

Although March can be a cold month, on the whole temperatures are rising. However, sharp frosts may descend on the land on clear nights, turning the ground hard, so don't put out tender plants yet. Cloud cover and wind will also have a direct effect on temperatures throughout each day.

COLD WINDS

March winds can be bitterly cold, but they do help to dry out the soil after winter rains and snow. High ground above 100m (300ft) and exposed coastal areas, especially the west coast, can still be subject to gales for 0.6 to 4.3 days. In the south gales will occur on an average of 0.2–1.5 days during this month. All coastal areas, whichever way they face, are windier than inland, and the winds carry salt spray, which can damage plants.

MORE SUNSHINE

The longer days of spring bring more chance of increased hours of bright sunshine each day. The northern half of the country will still have less, on average, than the south. Cloud cover will, however, cut down the amount of direct sunshine everywhere on most days.

RAINFALL

The amount of rain falling around the country depends on how hilly or flat it is. Areas such as the Lake District and the Western Highlands have significant rainfall at this time of year, with a March average of 228mm (9in). But in the south-east of England the average is 41mm (1½in). Low-lying areas may be prone to flooding as snow on the hills begins to thaw.

LATE SPRING SNOW

Heavy snowfalls are rare this month, but in north-eastern areas, especially, snow can still be thick on the ground, making spring very much later than in other regions. At Braemar in north-east Scotland, one of the coldest places in the country, even in March there will be 10 or more days of snow. In the milder south of England 0.9 to 1.4 days of snowfall is an average figure. It is rare that snow will lie on the ground at sea level.

AROUND THE GARDEN

MULCH BARE SOIL

Weed and tidy the soil before mulching with organic matter – well-rotted farmyard manure, garden compost, cocoa shells, chipped bark, or spent mushroom compost (don't use the last around acid-loving plants like rhododendrons, because it contains lime). Soil in borders left bare will very quickly lose water in dry spells. Covering with a thick layer of organic matter will cut down the rate at which water evaporates from the soil, reducing the need to water.

This is especially important for young trees, shrubs and perennials that have recently been planted. After spending hard-earned cash on plants, never let them go short of water in their first year. A mulch will also suppress weeds, and it looks good too. Never put a mulch on top of dry soil: if the

Always spread a generous layer, at least 5cm (2in) deep, for a mulch to do its best.

soil is dry, water it first. A layer of compost is just as good at keeping water out as sealing it in.

PREPARE PONDS FOR SPRING

Take netting off the pond or, if the pond was not netted in the autumn, remove as many leaves

It's time to take pumps out of store: check them and put them back in the pond.

from the pond as you can, as well as any other winter debris. If too many leaves are left in the pond the water will become stagnant and stifle aquatic life. At the same time, remove any old foliage from pond plants. Remove pond heaters put in for winter to prevent the pond from freezing.

Submersible pumps and lighting systems can now be taken out of store and returned to the pond. Circulating water helps keep the water oxygenated for fish and other creatures – with the added bonus that the sound of water is very soothing. If anything doesn't work, ask an electrician to take a look at it – don't tinker.

If you have fish in the pond, you should begin feeding them now. Little and often is the watchword at this time of year. Too much food in the pond left over by the fish will encourage the growth of algae.

PLANT CONTAINERS WITH HARDY PLANTS

Many plants can be grown in containers: small trees, shrubs and climbers, herbaceous perennials, annuals, alpines and ground cover plants. Let your imagination run riot. The only real rule is to look after the plants well, by watering, feeding, and deadheading regularly. Using slow-release fertilisers and the water-retentive crystals now available can save some work through the year.

It is worth noting that roses, particularly the "flowering carpet" varieties, miniature roses, and elegant standards, all look excellent on the patio, in containers filled with a soil-based compost. These composts (such as John Innes No.3) are far better than other composts for shrubs in containers; they hold a supply of nutrients more easily than ones without soil, and they also retain moisture much more readily, reducing the amount of watering to be done.

Remember to move containerised patio roses into the shade to prevent scorching if the weather becomes fiercely sunny.

After planting, make sure you prune the roses hard to encourage plenty of new growth. After a couple of months have elapsed, you can feed regularly with a high-potash feed to encourage a profusion of flowers, and you will be rewarded with a smashing display for weeks on end. Remember, though, that in dry weather watering may have to be done once if not twice a day.

START MOWING REGULARLY

By this time in most parts of the country, grass will be growing steadily, and needs to be cut regularly to keep it in good condition. A lawn will be much healthier and stay greener the less grass you remove every time it is cut. For the first few cuts, set the blades at their highest setting. Even if you tend to leave clippings on the lawn in summer, keep the box on the mower in spring, so that air, rain, and fertiliser can penetrate the turf.

REPAIR DAMAGE TO LAWN EDGES

Over the summer, lawn edges can easily be damaged, and often, especially with light sandy soils, edges can crumble away in places. To repair a broken edge, cut out the entire damaged portion of turf and turn it around. Fill in any hollows with soil and sow grass seed onto this. Water, and peg polythene over the top to encourage the grass seed to grow, and then you will have a perfect repair.

You can continue to reseed other bare patches in the middle of the lawn like this all through the summer, by scarifying the bare patch to roughen the surface and spreading on a mix of potting compost and grass seed mixed together in equal proportions.

REPAIRING DAMAGE TO EDGES

1 Cut out a square of turf surrounding the damage to the edge, undercut it with a spade, lift it, and rotate it by 180°.

2 The "good" side of the turf will form a perfect edge, with no dip. Fill the hole with soil and reseed it to cover the gap.

TREES, SHRUBS & CLIMBERS

GET BARE-ROOT PLANTS INTO THE SOIL

If you didn't get around to planting these last month, or you still have to finish off the job, this really is the last month before autumn to get these plants in. With the leaves opening up they find it much more difficult to establish, because they are losing water rapidly from the foliage. Plants grown in containers can be planted year-round, although spring and autumn, the traditional times, are best.

This is also your final chance to plant any bare-root hedging plants you would like in your garden. From now until autumn, you will probably find that only container-grown plants will be available, which can make buying hedges in bulk expensive.

MOVE EVERGREEN SHRUBS

This is a good time of year to relocate your shrubs. Evergreens moved in winter are unable to replace water lost from their leaves through the action of frost and strong cold winds. Plants generally do not take up water from the soil until the temperature rises above 4–5°C (around 40°F). Now the soil is beginning to warm up and the shrubs will shortly begin to grow; they will therefore lose less water, helping them re-establish. When moving shrubs, take as large a rootball as you can manage; if necessary, get a friend to help. Provide protection at first from cold winds with a screen of hessian or similar material. Keep the shrub well watered and it should grow away well.

MOVING A SHRUB

1 Dig a trench around the shrub, following a circle around the outermost extent of the shrub's branches.

2 Work inwards, using a fork to tease soil out from between roots, reducing the weight of the rootball. Try not to damage the roots.

3 Use a spade to undercut the rootball, working from all sides until the shrub is completely free.

4 Half-roll up a sheet of sacking or polythene. Ease the rolled half under the rootball by tipping the shrub.

5 Tip the shrub the other way to unroll the sheeting, then gather it up and secure to enclose the rootball.

PRUNE ROSES

You can prune both bush and shrub roses now. Climbers are usually pruned in the autumn, so that they can be tidied up and tied in before winter winds blow them about. Never prune ramblers in the spring unless you need to drastically renovate them, as you will lose this year's flowers. Prune them after flowering.

The main reason for pruning roses is to build a healthy framework of shoots that will produce a good display of flowers. Thinning overcrowded growth allows in light and air, reducing the chance of pest and disease problems, and it also encourages strong, healthy growth. Cutting bush rose stems to their base will encourage the plant to produce new growth there, keeping it young. Cuts must be clean, not ragged or bruised, so equip yourself with a good pair of

PRUNING BUSH ROSES

Bush roses are free-flowering roses of bushy habit, with upright stems. Large, usually double flowers are borne either singly or in clusters of three buds from summer to autumn on one- and two-year-old wood. They can be used in formal beds, mixed borders, or simply for flower cuttings.

- *Remove any dead and diseased stems, and any crossing in the centre of the bush to open it up.*
- *Cut out any weak shoots.*
- *Prune last year's shoots to within 5–8cm (2–3in) of previous year's growth (see left).*

strong, sharp secateurs. You may also need a pruning saw for thicker shoots.

First of all, remove any dead or unhealthy wood; ignoring this may encourage diseases to invade. Then cut out any shoots that are crossing and rubbing against each other. The flowering wood can now be pruned, and here the method varies depending on the rose type (*see below*). Always prune to outward-facing buds.

The main rule to remember is that the harder you prune, the more vigorous the subsequent growth will be.

Clear up rose prunings carefully, or they will ambush you later. It's best to dispose of or burn them, rather than shredding them for composting, as they can harbour disease. Then mulch around the roses, ideally with well-rotted farmyard manure, or a bagged product such as shredded bark.

PRUNING SHRUB ROSES

Shrub roses produce many stems with a bushy or semi-trailing habit. The single, semi-double or fully double scented flowers are borne through summer, usually with one but occasionally with several flushes of flowers. Little pruning is required.

- *Prune any dead, damaged or diseased stems, cutting to stem junctions or healthy buds.*
- *Once growth becomes crowded, thin central shoots and cut one or two main stems to the base.*
- *Trim off any dead heads or hips left from last year (see left).*

PRUNE WINTER STEMS

Dogwoods and shrubby willows grown for their ornamental coloured stems should be pruned now. The best stem colour from *Cornus* and *Salix* is produced by one-year-old shoots; this is the reason for pruning them in spring. Ornamental *Rubus* with their white stems should be pruned now too. Be careful when doing so, as the stems have sharp thorns. Prune all these shrubs hard, to about one or two buds of last year's growth, to leave a stubby framework.

If you cut your eucalyptus back hard every year, it will produce attractive rounded leaves and will remain a shrub.

PRUNE SHRUBBY EUCALYPTUS

Not all of us have room to grow eucalyptus as a tree, but it responds well to hard pruning, making a lovely foliage shrub. Just prune all last year's growth to about 15cm (6in) from the ground, and you will be rewarded with the attractive round juvenile leaves on a small bushy plant.

In spring, prune back dogwoods and willows grown for winter stems (above), such as Rubus *(top right),* Cornus *(near right), and* Salix *(far right).*

Any climbers that have got out of hand can be pruned drastically this month in order to renovate them.

RENOVATE CLIMBERS

This is a good time to tackle overgrown climbers: before they start fully into growth, yet while they have breaking buds so that you will be able to see where stems are dead. Climbers that can be cut hard back include honeysuckles, ivies, rambling roses, and winter jasmine.

PLANT CLIMBERS

If you didn't plant new climbers last month, you still have time to do so now. Make sure supports such as wires and trellis are fixed up before you buy and plant them. Wires may stand out at first but are soon hidden by the plants. Vine eyes are invaluable when attaching wires to posts or pillars. Giving a vine eye a few twists once the wire is attached at both ends ensures that the wire stays completely taut.

Wire stretched between vine eyes forms one of the simplest and most popular supports for climbers.

VIGOROUS CLIMBERS TO CUT BACK HARD

Hedera helix 'Dragon Claw'

Jasminum nudiflorum

Lonicera periclymenum (honeysuckle)

Rosa 'American Pillar'

FLOWERING PLANTS

PLANT AND DIVIDE PERENNIALS

Hardy perennials will grow quickly if planted now. Feed and mulch them following planting, and be sure to keep them well watered until they establish.

Put aside some time to lift and divide overgrown clumps of summer-flowering herbaceous perennials this month. Most can be lifted and divided in spring just as growth gets under way, and if the divisions are reasonably sized,

DIVIDING PERENNIALS

1 Use a fork to loosen the clump all the way around the edges so it can be lifted clear of the soil.

2 A mature clump can be hard to pull apart, but you can use a spade or a garden knife to cut it roughly into sections.

they should flower later in the year. Plants which need dividing are usually quite easy to identify.

As perennials age the clumps push outwards, with fresh young growth emerging to the edge of the clump, and the centre dying out. This is the stage at which they should be divided. Lift each clump with a fork, insert two forks back to back, and prise them apart; smaller pieces can then be pulled apart by hand.

Add organic matter and fertiliser in order to revitalize the soil, and plant the young divisions in groups of three, five or more, depending on how much space you have available. Water them in well if the soil is dry.

3 Tease out small, chunky pieces to replant. The best bits are often toward the outside of the clump.

4 Fork and water the soil where the plants are to grow. Scoop out small holes and firm the plants in. Water them regularly.

SPLIT PRIMULAS AFTER FLOWERING

Towards the end of March, split up polyanthus–type primulas as the flowers go over. Begin by digging up each clump with a fork. With very large clumps you will have to push two forks back to back into the centre of the clump and push the fork handles apart. Then divide the sections by hand. Trim off most of the old foliage, leaving about 5cm (2in).

Apart from making the plants tidier, this reduces loss of water from the leaves: the plants establish quicker and new leaves soon grow. Either plant the divisions back *in situ*, after revitalizing the soil with garden compost or manure, or plant them in rows in a corner of the vegetable garden to grow in summer and plant out again in the borders in the autumn.

Primulas such as Gold-laced Group *(top right) and* 'Miss Indigo' *(right) will bring a terrific splash of colour to your garden in spring if divided now.*

SUPPORT HERBACEOUS PERENNIALS

These will now be making plenty of growth, and at the first sign of rain or a strong breeze the shoots will be flattened. There are lots of supports available to prevent this.

The easiest to use and cheapest are twiggy sticks (known as pea sticks) pushed in around each clump; plants grow up between them. Prunings from other shrubs are excellent, provided they are straight and strong enough, such as buddleja stems with the old flowers removed. They look unsightly to begin with, but the plants soon hide them. Other supports available include canes, plastic-coated stakes that link together, and round mesh supports through which the plants grow, some of which can be raised as the plant grows.

Get staking done early to ensure the plants look natural as they grow. Don't leave it until they flop

or are blown about; trying to stake stems growing in all directions never looks good.

CUT DOWN GROWTH LEFT AFTER WINTER

Even if seedheads and stems still look good, you need to get rid of them to make way for new growth. After a good tidy up, if you didn't feed plants last month, dress the soil with a fertiliser so it is ready for a layer of mulch.

Get stakes and supports in early so the plants grow up naturally around them.

SOW HARDY ANNUALS

Now that spring is here, it is safe to begin sowing hardy annuals outside in most parts of the country. In northern parts you may have to wait until the end of the month or into early April. Hardy annuals look best grown in informal drifts. If the soil has not been prepared, lightly fork it over, but don't add any manure or garden compost. If soil is too rich, plants produce lots of soft growth and few flowers. All you need to do after forking over the soil is to apply a light dressing of a general fertiliser, then you can rake the soil to a fine tilth.

Now comes the fun part: marking out the informal drifts and sowing. The only rule to remember when planning an annual planting is that the taller

Sow Limnanthes douglasii *seeds now to get vibrant poached egg flowers in summer and autumn.*

plants, like larkspur (*Consolida*) and cosmos, go to the back and the shortest, such as nemophila (baby-blue-eyes), lobularia, and the poached egg flower (*Limnanthes douglasii*) stay at the front. You can, if you want to, spend time making elaborate colour-coordinated schemes, or theme borders around a particular colour. But from these plants all we really want is a good splash of colour, so don't worry too much about colours clashing.

By sowing in drills rather than broadcasting the seed over each drift area, it will be more easy to tell the young seedlings apart from weeds. Once they grow together, you won't be able to tell that they are in rows. You can help avoid a regimented look by varying the direction in which the drills cross neighbouring drifts. When the seedlings are large enough to handle, they can be thinned out.

SOWING ANNUALS

1 *Get some dry silver sand, put it in an empty wine bottle and make irregular shapes by pouring out the sand.*

2 *Sow the seeds thinly in shallow drills made with a stick. Check the back of the packet for distances between drills.*

3 *Lightly cover, water, and label each area. Keep the seed packets for advice on thinning distances when seedlings appear.*

KITCHEN GARDEN

PREPARE SEEDBEDS

Even if it's been left exposed, soil should be beginning to dry out now, and will be in a better state for the making of good seedbeds for sowing. Getting the timing of this job right can be tricky. The soil doesn't want to be so wet that it sticks to your boots, nor so dry that it takes a lot of effort to break it up, but hopefully nature has given a helping hand and broken down the worst of the clods.

Once you have broken down any lumps in the soil, rake it over to even out any hollows and bumps.

If the soil is rather too moist for treading on but you feel you must get on, then use planks to stand on. These will distribute your weight and prevent localised areas becoming too compacted.

Break larger lumps of soil down by bashing them with a fork. Then use a rake to smooth out smaller lumps and create a fine tilth, pushing and pulling the rake back and forth over the surface of the soil to a depth of about 2.5cm (1in). Tread the soil to firm it, and apply an organic fertiliser, such as one based on seaweed, about two weeks before sowing. Rake this in and the seedbed is ready for seed.

START SOWING OUTSIDE REGULARLY

This month, seed-sowing outside can get under way in earnest. In northern parts, it's generally best to wait until late March or early April before sowing outside.

SOWING OUTSIDE

Narrow drills are suitable for fine seeds. Use a cane to create a shallow trench; a string guide will help you make sure the trenches are straight.

Wide drills are good for beans and peas grown in rows each side of supports. When the soil is dry and crumbly, use a spade to make shallow trenches.

Station sowing is another option for large seeds such as broad beans. Traditional dibbers like these can be made from broken spade or fork handles.

Sowings of lettuce, endives, radish, salad onions, peas, broad beans, spinach, cabbage, turnips, and beetroot can be made now. Sow short rows at a time, at weekly or 10-day intervals; this way a succession of vegetables will be ready to harvest throughout the summer and autumn.

Many seeds are sold in vacuum-packed foil sachets within the main packet. When the foil pack is opened the vacuum is broken and air gets in, so it's important to store the seeds between sowings in a cool, dry place – a fridge is ideal. Seeds not packed in foil sachets are also better kept in the fridge. Cool conditions ensure the seeds remain viable (capable of germinating) for longer periods.

To sow all of the fine-seeded vegetables, take out shallow drills with a cane. Water the drills before sowing if the soil is dry. Sow the seeds thinly along the drill and cover lightly with dry soil. Once seedlings are large enough to handle it is important to thin them.

With peas and broad beans the technique is a little different. Take out a trench about 2.5cm (1in) deep with a spade and sow the seeds of peas about 2.5cm (1in) apart in the bottom of the trench and cover over. With broad beans, space the seeds about 15cm (6in) apart in rows and cover over with soil. Peas and broad beans will have to be protected with netting or horticultural fleece to prevent mice and wood pigeons digging them up.

SOW PARSNIPS OUTSIDE

Sowing parsnips requires yet another, slightly different technique, because parsnips are notoriously erratic at germinating. Take out a narrow drill as previously described, but instead of sowing the seeds thinly along the drill, sow them in clusters of three or four seeds at 15cm (6in) intervals along the drill. This way, if some of the seeds don't germinate, there won't be any gaps in the row. Because germination can be slow and erratic, it's a good idea to sow a quick-maturing crop like radishes along the drill between the parsnip seeds; this way the row can be easily identified.

PLANT EARLY POTATOES

The traditional way of planting on allotment-style beds is to take out planting trenches about a spade's depth and 60cm (2ft) apart. Put some organic matter in the trench and scatter an organic fertiliser either along the bottom of the trench, or on the soil removed in making the trench. Plant the tubers in the trench about 30cm (12in) apart, and cover with the soil taken out.

PLANTING POTATOES

Prepare the ground before you plant potatoes by laying plenty of organic material at the bottom of your trench.

When planting early potatoes, plant the chitted seed potatoes with the "rose" end (the one with the most shoots) uppermost.

PLANT ONION SETS

Prepare the ground as for seedbeds – although the soil doesn't have to be as fine for onion sets – and apply an organic fertiliser. Plant the sets about 10–15cm (4–6in) apart in rows the same distance apart. Plant each set with a trowel: don't just push them into the soil, because as the roots form they will push the set up and out again. It is also worth trimming off the dry skin at the tip of the onion set, cutting straight across with a sharp knife, as birds use this to get a hold of the sets and pull them out of the soil.

If growing onion sets on deep beds, plant them about 8cm (3in) apart. The onions that grow may be smaller but you will achieve a higher overall yield.

Raising onions from sets rather than from seed usually produces a smaller crop, but in a much shorter time.

SOW HERBS

Hardy herbs can be sown outside now. These include chervil, chives, dill, fennel, marjoram, coriander, and parsley. Sow the seeds the same way as for vegetables – in drills – and plant them out when they are large enough to handle. Young herb plants that are more difficult to raise from seed can be bought from garden centres or specialist herb nurseries. These include mint, tarragon, and shrubby herbs such as thymes and rosemary.

Coriander (left) and chives (below left) can be planted this month for harvesting in summer.

Choose French tarragon rather than Russian, which has a coarser taste and is a very invasive plant. So is mint in nearly all its forms: plant it in a pot and partially sink the pot in the ground to stop it taking over the whole garden.

A dedicated herb garden is undoubtedly one of the most attractive ways to grow these plants, but they also look wonderful growing in borders along with other plants, so if your garden is too small for a separate herb feature, grow them in with other plants, or in pots on the patio by the house.

DIVIDE CHIVES

Chives serve as attractive edging for beds. When dividing them, lift each clump with a fork and divide quite ruthlessly. You can replant small clumps in soil that has been revitalized with organic matter. Water well following replanting.

MARCH PROJECT

SOW A FLOWER MEADOW

Meadows are one of the wonders of nature. As well as being beautiful to look at, they are also easy to maintain and provide a perfect habitat for wildlife. The flowers and grasses thrive on poor soils in a sunny site, and only need to be cut once a year, in autumn, after the plants have set seed.

Meadows look particularly effective on a large scale, but you don't need an extensive garden to create your own earthly paradise. Just sow a meadow seed mix – including hardy annuals, such as poppies, corn chamomile, ox-eye daisies and cornflowers – in a sunny corner to create a swathe of instant colour, which is useful if you are starting a garden from scratch. Your mini meadow will also attract beneficial birds and insects and aid conservation.

1 *Mix meadow seed* with horticultural sand as it helps to spread seed evenly. Seed is sown at 3 grams per sq metre: weigh first, then add sand. Also add some slug pellets to protect emerging seedlings.

2 *To prepare the seedbed* remove weeds and stones then rake over the soil to break down lumps and level the area. Use canes to mark the area into square metres; it makes sowing easier.

3 *After sowing* use the back of a rake to firm the soil gently, ensuring good contact between seed and soil to help germination. This also makes the seed less visible to hungry birds.

4 *To prevent birds* from eating seed, set up a series of strings with CDs threaded on to them across the sown area – or you could use netting. Remove once your seedlings have got going.

ANEMONE [1]

Anemone blanda **'Violet Star'** A fairly
vigorous, spreading, tuberous perennial.
In spring, it produces clear amethyst
flowers with a white reverse to the petals.
The dark green leaves are pretty, but
fade away during summer dormancy.
‡15cm (6in) ↔ 15cm (6in)

CULTIVATION Plant tubers 5–8cm
(2–3in) deep in autumn, in humus-rich,
well-drained soil, in sun or dappled shade.

KINGCUP [2]

Caltha palustris ♀ A hardy, creeping,
rhizomatous perennial. In spring, it bears
glossy, yellow, cup-shaped flowers, often
with a second flush of bloom later in
the year. The heart-shaped leaves are
attractive for many months.
‡40cm (16in) ↔ 45cm (18in)

CULTIVATION Best in full sun but
tolerates light shade. Grow in boggy,
permanently moist soil at the water's
edge, or in planting baskets, in water
to 23cm (9in) deep.

1

GLORY OF THE SNOW 3

Chionodoxa forbesii **'Pink Giant'**
A moderately vigorous, bulbous
perennial. In early spring, it bears
spikes of starry, white-centred, pink
flowers. Dies back after flowering.
↕10–20cm (4–8in) ↔ 3cm (1¼in)

CULTIVATION Plant in autumn, 8cm
(3in) deep, in any well-drained soil. Best
in sun or dappled shade. Lift and separate
the bulbs after four to five years if they
become congested.

DAPHNE [1]

Daphne mezereum An upright, deciduous shrub. From late winter until early spring, it produces clusters of perfumed pink to purplish-pink flowers, on bare branches. Fleshy red fruits in summer. All parts of the plant are highly toxic.
‡1.2m (4ft) ↔ 1m (3ft)

CULTIVATION Grow in sun or part-shade. Prefers a slightly alkaline, humus-rich, moist but well-drained soil. Mulch to keep the roots cool. After flowering, prune to shape to take out dead wood.

SKUNK CABBAGE [2]

Lysichiton americanus ♀ An extremely vigorous, spreading herbaceous perennial. In early spring, before the leaves appear, it bears club-like spikes of tiny green flowers surrounded by large, glossy yellow spathes. The large, paddle-shaped, leathery green leaves elongate after flowering.
‡1m (3ft) ↔ 1.2m (4ft)

CULTIVATION Grow in full sun or light dappled shade in moist, fertile, humus-rich soil. Allow plenty of room for the leaves to grow.

DUTCH CROCUS 3

***Crocus vernus* 'Pickwick'** Robust, cormous perennial. From early to late spring, it produces striking white flowers, striped pale and dark lilac, with dark purple bases.
‡12cm (5in) ↔ 5cm (2in)

CULTIVATION Grow in sun or light dappled shade, in fertile, well-drained soil. Plant corms in autumn, 8–10cm (3–4in) deep.

CORKSCREW HAZEL [1]

***Corylus avellana* 'Contorta'**
A deciduous shrub with contorted
branches. The twisted shoots look
attractive in winter, especially when
snow-covered. Yellow catkins hang
from bare branches in late winter
or early spring. The heart-shaped,
wrinkled leaves are also twisted.
‡5m (15ft) ↔ 5m (15ft)

CULTIVATION Thrives in any good
garden soil in sun or part-shade.
Remove any suckers which grow
from the base and carefully prune
out any misplaced shoots in winter.

CROWN IMPERIAL [2]

Fritillaria imperialis A robust, strongly
upright, bulbous perennial. In late spring
or early summer, at the tips of stout
stems, it bears large, nodding, orange,
yellow or red flowers crowned by
leafy bracts.
‡to 1.5m (5ft) ↔ 25–30cm (10–12in)

CULTIVATION Grow in full sun in
fertile, well-drained soil. Plant bulbs
in autumn, at four times their own
depth, setting on a layer of sharp sand
to improve drainage. The bulbs will
rot in wet soils.

GRAPE HYACINTH 3

Muscari armeniacum ♀ A vigorous, bulbous perennial. In spring, it produces spikes of tubular, bright blue flowers with white mouths.
↕20cm (8in) ↔ 5cm (2in)

CULTIVATION Grow in full sun in any well-drained, moderately fertile soil. Plant bulbs, 10cm (4in) deep, in autumn. Lift to divide congested clumps as the leaves fade in summer.

2

3

FORSYTHIA ⬚1

Forsythia × intermedia **'Lynwood'** ♀
A strongly upright, deciduous shrub.
In spring, it bears bright, rich yellow
flowers in great profusion all along
the bare branches. Undistinguished in
summer, but a good host for clematis.
↕1.5m (5ft) ↔ 1.5m (5ft)

CULTIVATION Thrives in any fertile soil
in sun or light dappled shade. Shorten
the flowered shoots to strong buds after
flowering; when established, cut out one
in four of the oldest stems to encourage
new growth from the base.

SCILLA ⬚2

Scilla siberica **'Spring Beauty'**
A slender, perennial bulb. In spring, it
bears loose spikes of small, nodding, deep
blue flowers amid narrow, strap-shaped,
shining green leaves.
↕20cm (8in) ↔ 5cm (2in)

CULTIVATION Grow in full sun or light,
dappled shade, in any fertile, humus–rich
soil. Plant the bulbs in autumn at twice
their own depth.

1

DOUBLE NARCISSUS 3

Narcissus **'Cheerfulness'** ♀ Robust, bulbous perennial. In mid-spring, each stem produces several sweetly scented, double white flowers with clustered, creamy-white segments at the centre.
‡40cm (16in) ↔ 8cm (3in)

CULTIVATION Grow in sun or light, dappled shade. Plant the bulbs in autumn at twice their own depth, in any fertile, well-drained soil. If flowering declines, and bulbs are congested, allow the foliage to die down and lift and divide the clumps.

2

3

MIMOSA [1]

Acacia dealbata ♧ A native of Australia
and Tasmania, this is a fast-growing,
evergreen, spreading tree that can also
be grown as a shrub. It has attractive,
fern-like, blue-green foliage and, from
late winter to spring, it produces long
clusters of globular, fragrant, bright
yellow flowerheads.
‡15m (50ft) ↔ 10m (30ft)

CULTIVATION Grow in good, fertile,
neutral to acid soil in a sheltered, sunny
position. After flowering trim any shoots
that spoil the shape of the plant.

BLUE COWSLIP [2]

Pulmonaria angustifolia **'Azurea'**
A vigorous, spreading, herbaceous
perennial. From early to late spring, it
bears funnel-shaped, bright blue flowers,
tinted red in bud. The smooth, unspotted,
glistening dark green leaves make good
ground cover.
‡25cm (10in) ↔ 45cm (18in)

CULTIVATION Grow in deep or dappled
shade, in damp, humus-rich soil. Cut
back after flowering for a fresh crop
of new leaves. Divide every three to
four years to maintain vigour.

JAPONICA 3

***Chaenomeles* × *superba* 'Pink Lady'** ♥
A spiny, spreading shrub with glossy,
mid-green leaves. Dark rose-pink, cup-
shaped flowers are borne in clusters from
late winter to spring, followed by green
fruits that ripen to yellow in autumn.
↕1.5m (5ft) ↔2m (6ft)

CULTIVATION Grow in any fertile,
well-drained soil in sun or part-shade.
After flowering, shorten flowered shoots
to strong buds. When mature, take out
one in five of the oldest shoots.

SARGENT'S CHERRY   1

Prunus sargentii ♀ A deciduous tree with a wide-spreading crown. In early to mid-spring, it bears hanging clusters of large, single, bowl-shaped flowers of soft pale pink; the leaves are bronze-red as they emerge with the flowers. Small, glossy, crimson fruits attract birds into the garden, and the leaves turn to brilliant shades of orange and red in autumn.
‡to 20m (60ft) ↔ 15m (50ft)

CULTIVATION Grow in any moist, but well-drained soil. It needs minimal pruning; remove badly placed or crossing branches in winter.

SPECIES TULIP   2

Tulipa tarda ♀ A vigorous perennial bulb. In early to mid-spring, each stem produces four to six open, star-shaped, greenish-white flowers that are yellow inside. Lance-shaped, shiny, bright green leaves.
‡to 15cm (6in) ↔ 5cm (2in)

CULTIVATION Best in full sun, but it will tolerate light, part-day shade. Grow in any poor to moderately fertile, well-drained soil. Add coarse grit to heavy clay soils. Plant the bulbs at twice their own depth in late autumn.

1

CANDELABRA PRIMULA ③

Primula 'Inverewe' ♀ A robust, semi-evergreen herbaceous perennial. During summer it produces several stems bearing tiered clusters of up to fifteen brilliant red flowers.

‡75cm (30in) ↔ 60cm (24in)

CULTIVATION Grow in part-shade in slightly acid soil enriched with well-rotted organic matter. They will tolerate a sunny position so long as the soil does not dry out. Divide plants between autumn and early spring.

KILMARNOCK WILLOW 1

Salix caprea **'Kilmarnock'** A top-grafted, stiffly weeping, deciduous tree. In mid- and late spring, it produces grey male catkins, studded with yellow anthers, on bare shoots. Forms a dense umbrella of stout, yellow-brown stems and narrow dark green leaves that are grey-green beneath.

↕ 1.5–2m (5–6ft) ↔ 2m (6ft)

CULTIVATION Grow in full sun or light shade, in any moist but well-drained soil. Prune annually between late autumn and early spring to thin out congested shoots.

HYACINTH 2

Hyacinthus orientalis **'City of Haarlem'** ♀ A vigorous, upright bulb. In late spring, sturdy stems arise bearing dense spikes of highly scented, soft primrose-yellow flowers.

↕ 20–30cm (8–12in) ↔ 8cm (3in)

CULTIVATION Best in full sun. Plant bulbs in autumn, 10cm (4in) deep, in fertile, well-drained soil. Use prepared bulbs for winter flowers indoors. Plant in bowls of bulb fibre with the tip of the bulb exposed. Keep in a cool, dark place for six weeks. When shoots are about 2.5cm (1in) long, bring into light and warmth.

2

PRIMULA

3

Primula **'Miss Indigo'** Small but
showy semi-evergreen perennial. From
late winter to late spring, it produces
clusters of double, indigo–purple flowers
with creamy white tips. Has rosettes of
wrinkled, bright green leaves for most
of the year.

↕20cm (8in) ↔ 35cm (14in)

CULTIVATION Grow in dappled shade
in damp, fertile, humus-rich soil. Divide
after flowering to maintain vigour.

3

WHAT TO DO IN **APRIL**

WEATHER WATCH

Now we are well and truly into spring the garden begins to look green and vibrant. You can begin to prune early-flowering shrubs now and start dividing perennials. Regular weeding and deadheading will keep your garden in trim.

COLD SNAPS

On the whole, days are warming up, but do beware of very cold nights with sharp frosts. These can damage fruit-tree blossom. Clear, warm, balmy weather makes it very tempting to put young plants out now, but slightly tender plants still need daytime protection with cloches. Some garden centres will have bedding plants for sale; don't buy yet unless you have a frost-free greenhouse.

SOME STRONG WINDS

Winds are generally much calmer now, but some parts, especially coastal areas in the north-west, will still have 1–2 days, on average, of gale-force winds. In southern

parts winds can still be strong at times, so give newly planted plants some protection.

EVEN SUNSHINE

The amount of sunshine over the country as a whole is fairly even: Argyll, in Scotland, gets around 170 hours on average this month, and Plymouth, on the south coast of England, 180 hours. Cloud cover on a day-to-day basis will have a dramatic effect on the amount of direct sunshine brightening up each area.

SHOWERS

April showers may well bring forth May flowers, but we all hope the showers ease off soon. High ground in the north-west of the country can still experience high rainfall. Fort William in the north-west Highlands gets an average of 100mm (4in) of rainfall in April, while in the Home Counties the average is much lower: 42–47mm (1½in). There is, therefore, more need to conserve water in the south-east, by collecting rain and only watering when necessary.

RARE SNOWFALL

Heavy snowfalls are rare now, but there can be exceptions. One April in the mid-1980s, 15cm (6in) of snow fell in Ayrshire on the south-west coast of Scotland. This area is usually quite mild and rarely gets any snow.

AROUND THE GARDEN

PROTECT PLANTS

The warmth and spring rains now will bring about huge increases in the populations of slugs and snails, which can cause a great deal of damage to plants. If you're not organic, spread slug pellets in amongst the plants affected. There is no need to put down a lot of pellets; it doesn't take many to kill off slugs. There are several organic ways to combat slugs, including a biological control: a tiny nematode that attacks them that can be watered onto the soil. Traps are also effective. One of the oldest and best known is the beer trap: a jar sunk into the ground with the lip just proud of the surface, filled with beer, which will attract slugs.

Hedgehogs, frogs, toads and thrushes all prey on these pests, so encourage them to stay. Lay a flat stone in a border, and you might soon notice a thrush using it as a handy "anvil" on which to smash snail shells. Pests are also on the move with the warmer weather. Get on top of problems as soon as you spot them, and nine times out of ten you can prevent them from getting a hold.

A copper band around the rim of a pot will help to protect the plant by repelling slugs and snails.

APPLY SYNTHETIC FERTILISERS

If you didn't give plants an organic fertiliser earlier in the spring, a chemical fertiliser will give them an instant boost now, when they really need it. Pull back any mulch, lightly fluff up the soil with a rake and apply according to the maker's instructions. Then replace the mulch.

Like us, all plants need nutrients to survive, but there is no need to feed absolutely everything every year. Trees and shrubs, for example, will on the whole grow quite happily for many years provided that the initial preparation before planting has been done thoroughly.

All you might be required to do is to apply some fertiliser in the first two or three years after planting. Following that, unless there is any obvious deficiency, they will usually cope well on their own. But always remember to water them well during dry spells in the early stages of getting established.

When you sprinkle the fertiliser around a plant, make sure that none of it comes into contact with the stem or leaves.

The areas of the garden that are most in need of being fertilised every year are the vegetable and fruit garden, annual borders, and plants in containers, where the plants are taking more out of the soil. The more we deplete the soil, the more we have a duty to put nutrients back in to keep the soil in a healthy state. With all fertilisers, whether organic or artificial, make sure you wash your hands well after using them.

TIDY BORDERS

Set aside a morning or afternoon to go round the garden doing those small jobs that make all the difference to its appearance. Lightly fork over the soil, pulling out any weeds you see. Any plants taking up too much space and growing into other plants can be lightly pruned into shape to tidy them up. Don't be too hard with the pruning, or you may cut off all this year's flowers. Put in plant supports as you go, then you don't have to keep treading over the borders to do different jobs.

KEEP ON MOWING AND WEEDING

If grass is left to grow long and is then cut short it will turn yellow, look unsightly, and be weakened, so regular mowing is advisable. Blades should be at a high setting when you start mowing in spring. By the end of April, you can start lowering them each time you mow.

Be sure to level lumps and bumps in lawns – they cause the mower to scalp the grass, weakening it and encouraging weeds and moss. Remove coarse grasses by criss-crossing the clump with an old knife, then pulling tufts of grass out. After this, regular mowing will discourage coarser grasses.

Although you can treat moss with a mosskiller now, bear in mind that this treats the symptoms, not the cause. The main causes of moss in lawns are poor drainage, weak grass and compacted soil. The best way to remedy these faults is to aerate the lawn each year using a fork or a machine to spike the lawn, and to rake out "thatch": this is the dead grass and moss that accumulates. By doing this regularly, the grass will be much healthier and it will be harder for moss and weeds to establish in it.

For lawns with very few weeds, use a spot-treatment weedkiller to minimise damage to grass. Common weeds include (clockwise from top left) plantain, self-heal, mother of thousands, and dandelions.

FEED ESTABLISHED LAWNS

Always use fertilisers according to the manufacturer's instructions. There is absolutely no point in putting on a little extra to speed things up. Plants will only take up a certain amount, and the excess leaches into the water table and into streams and rivers, contributing to pollution.

There are several methods of applying lawn fertiliser. One is to mark out the lawn into square metres or yards with string and canes, then measure out and scatter the fertiliser by hand (wearing gloves) in measured doses, as when sowing seed. This can be laborious if you have a large lawn – if this is the case, you could use a fertiliser spreader instead. There are many types available, and they can be bought or hired.

CLEAN OUT PONDS

This isn't a job that has to be done every year, but only when the plants get overcrowded – usually after five or six years, although larger ponds may need cleaning less frequently. If you have fish in the pond, they will have to be put

CLEANING OUT A POND

1 Lift all plants in their baskets, or scoop them out with your hands, and put them in trays of water before removing any fish. Fish can be removed using a net and placed in a container with pondwater.

into a temporary container – filled with pond water, not tap water. If the pond is lined with a butyl liner, be careful not to puncture it.

Once any fish are out, the pond can be emptied and the plants divided up and replanted. Larger clumps of waterlilies and other plants can be divided up in exactly the same way as for dividing herbaceous perennials. After the pond is refilled it is possible the water might go green for a while, but it will soon sort itself out when the plants re-establish.

2 Bail or pump out the water, then gently scoop out mud from the bottom, using plastic implements so that you do not damage the liner.

3 Hose and wash down the liner using a soft brush or broom, and then clean out the murky water left as residue.

4 Refill the pond, then tidy up and divide the plants, and replace them. Lastly, put fish back along with the water they have been sitting in.

DIVIDING WATERLILIES

1 Gently rinse as much soil as you can from the clump of roots.

2 Use a sharp knife to divide the fleshy rhizome into sections, each with a shoot. Discard any old, lifeless pieces. Replant the new sections in fresh aquatic compost.

INTRODUCE AQUATIC PLANTS

Now the water in ponds is warming up, it's the ideal time to plant new aquatic plants, as they then have the whole season to get themselves established. When you get the plants home, if there is any delay before planting, make sure they do not dry up.

Special containers are available for aquatic plants from the vast majority of garden centres. The modern containers are made of fine mesh and don't need lining with sacking, as in the past. Fill them with garden soil or special aquatic compost – don't use ordinary potting compost, as this has fertilisers added to it, and it will encourage the growth of algae in the pond.

Place the plant in the container and then fill around it with compost to about 2.5cm (1in) from the rim of the container. Then put a layer of coarse grit on the surface of the soil. This prevents the soil from floating out.

If you plant up waterlilies now, they should be flowering by the time summer arrives.

Don't forget to add some oxygenating plants. Water in a pond turning green with algae is a constant problem, and the smaller the pond the more of a problem it is. Most algae grow in water that is low in oxygen, so adding plants that increase the oxygen in the water suppresses them. Most algae problems occur in small, shallow ponds where the volume of water is relatively small and the water heats up quickly in warm weather. You could, as a last resort, renovate the pond and dig it deeper, as this will help to keep the temperature of the water down. Installing a fountain or building a waterfall feature would also help, as they increase oxygen levels in the water.

TREES, SHRUBS & CLIMBERS

PLANT EVERGREEN HEDGES

This is a good time to plant evergreens, not only conifers but the many broad-leaved plants that make excellent hedging. Most can be clipped to shape or grown informally, only being trimmed when they become overgrown. By planting evergreens at this time of year there is less chance of them being damaged by cold winter winds, but they may still need some protection.

It's not just winter winds that cause problems, though. Even in spring and summer, high winds can be just as damaging. The speed of the wind going over the surface of the leaf draws water from it more quickly than the plant can replace it from the soil, especially in summer if the ground is dry, and this causes withering.

If your plants are regularly scorched in this way, consider erecting more screens and windbreaks to shelter your garden – or research some more wind- and drought-tolerant shrubs to replace casualties.

Once hedging is planted, water it in well, and add a thick mulch of manure, compost, or shredded bark around the plants.

EVERGREEN HEDGING PLANTS TO TRY

Ilex aquifolium 'Handsworth New Silver'

Buxus sempervirens 'Suffruticosa'

Garrya elliptica

Escallonia rubra 'Woodside'

PLANTING A CONTAINER-GROWN TREE

1 Soak the rootball in a bucket of water for an hour or two. Then mark the digging area as shown, remove any turf and weeds, and dig the hole, to 1½ times the depth of the rootball.

2 Loosen some soil from the sides of the hole by scarifying them with a fork, then mix the soil you have removed with some rotted organic matter.

3 Hammer a stake into the hole just off-centre, on the windward side. Add a little of the soil and organic matter mix.

4 Lay the tree down, and slide it out of its pot. Tease out the roots and remove any weeds without breaking up the rootball.

5 Hold the tree next to the stake, and add the soil and organic matter mix. Firm the soil by treading it, then lightly fork the top layer and water well.

6 Secure the tree to the stake using a tie. Cut back any damaged stems and long sideshoots, then apply a thick mulch around the tree.

PLANT TREES AND SHRUBS

Spring and autumn are the best times to plant container-grown trees and shrubs. However, they are actually sold ready to plant at any time of year, even at times that bare-root stock would no longer be available.

If the soil in the pot is very dry, begin by watering the plant thoroughly in its pot about an hour or two beforehand, then ease the rootball out of the pot. Dig a generously-sized hole – about three or four times the diameter of the rootball – and mix the soil you've removed with some rotted organic matter. Hammer in a stake, and set the tree firmly in the hole, so that the top of the compost is level with the ground around it. Then add the soil and organic matter mix, water well, and mulch around the plant to lock in that precious moisture.

PRUNE FORSYTHIAS AND CHAENOMELES

These two shrubs put on a terrific show of colour in the spring, on wood made the previous summer. Now is the time to prune them for flowers next spring. The method of pruning for both shrubs is the same. When the flowers are over, cut back the flowered shoots to two or three buds from their base. On more established shrubs cut out about a third of the older growth to the base of the plant. This will encourage new shoots to grow from the base.

These shrubs can also be trained against walls or fences, where they look very attractive. Pruning in this situation is slightly different. After you have tied in any stems you need to fill gaps, prune all flowered shoots to one or two buds from their point of growing. You can do the same in summer to keep chaenomeles, and also pyracanthas, flat where space is limited. Leading shoots can be pruned to keep the shrubs within their allocated space.

To prune forsythias, cut the flowered stems back to strong new leafy sideshoots, pointing upwards and outwards.

To avoid sparse flowering on chaenomeles (above left), prune the sideshoots back to one or two buds to encourage flowers (above right).

CUT BACK SILVER-LEAVED SHRUBS

This should be carried out once the plants approach the size to which you want them to grow. If lavender plants are left unpruned, the centre of the shrwub grows sparse and the plant looks unattractive; they don't like being pruned into older wood. So it is wise to prune them every spring to keep them bushy and compact. Other silver-leaved shrubs that should be pruned in this way are *Helichrysum serotinum* (curry plant) and *Santolina* (cotton lavender).

Prune the tips of lavender (above) and Helichrysum serotinum *(top right) shoots in order to encourage bushiness.*

Go over the whole plant, trimming off 2.5–5cm (1–2in) of growth. Use shears for speed if you have a lot of lavender, for example a low hedge. It may seem a bit harsh, but by doing this the plants stay compact and the centre does not open up.

If you didn't last month, you should now also trim winter-flowering heathers with shears. The spent flowering stems will probably be looking quite tatty, so remove them to show off the more attractive new growth.

The best coloured foliage on Sambucus *(above left) and* Cotinus *(above right) is produced by new stems, so it's a good idea to prune them now.*

PRUNE SHRUBS FOR COLOURFUL FOLIAGE

There are some shrubs that are grown primarily for their distinctively colourful foliage, such as *Sambucus* (elder) and *Cotinus* (the smoke bush). If you want to increase the size of the plants it is worthwhile leaving two or three shoots unpruned and these can grow on, making the plant larger without compromising on the colourful foliage. As always, after pruning the shrubs need to be fed with a general fertiliser and watered in if the weather is dry.

TIE IN CLIMBERS

Climbing and rambling roses should now be tied in, training the shoots as near to horizontal as possible. By doing this the flow of sap is restricted; this causes more sideshoots to develop along the whole length of the main stems, which in turn produces more flowers. If left to grow vertically, all the flowers are produced at the tips of the stems where they are difficult to see.

This is also an ideal time to tie in shoots of twiners such as clematis, as they will be growing fast now. Once they get a hold of their support they can usually be left to get on with it, especially if they are growing through other shrubs, but they may need some guidance if encroaching too much on other plants.

To train a climbing rose, tie in shoots horizontally. This will encourage the development of more flowering sideshoots.

To grow roses on a post, wind the stems around the post in a spiral fashion and tie them in. This will restrict the flow of sap.

FLOWERING PLANTS

KEEP PLANTING AND DIVIDING PERENNIALS

Getting plants in the ground now gives them time to establish while the weather is still mild and wet, so that they will put on good growth during the season. Water the new plants regularly, as spring winds can dry them out quickly. Whenever possible, revitalize the soil with well-rotted farmyard manure or garden compost before replanting perennials, and remember to water in well following planting if the weather is dry.

To encourage flowering later this year, divide summer- and autumn-flowering perennials and bulbs such as nerines this month.

DIVIDING BULBS

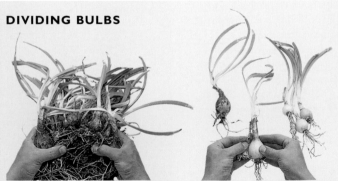

1 Lift the clumps and shake off as much soil as possible. Separate out and clean each bulb, retaining as much root as you can.

2 Replant singly at the same depth, 5cm (2in) apart. Peel off brown, flaky debris, leaving a layer of white, papery skin intact.

Remove daffodil flowers by pinching through the stem, just under the seed pod.

DEADHEAD DAFFODILS

Now the flowers are going over, snap the flowerheads off behind the swollen parts; you can leave the stalk intact. If the spent flowers are left on, the plant's energy will be diverted into the production of seeds. By removing the old flowers, the plant's energy is instead diverted into the formation of next year's flower bud within the bulb. For this to happen, the foliage must be left on the plant.

For many years the practice was to allow the foliage of the bulbs to die back completely, to give the plants the longest time to build up that flower bud for next year.

However, recent research has shown that the foliage can be cut down six weeks after the flowers are over. You can choose whichever method you like. The old foliage of daffodils can look rather messy, but don't tie it up with raffia or elastic bands. The best way to hide it is to grow daffodils in amongst other plants like hostas which have large, bold leaves.

PLANT SUMMER BULBS

To produce a succession of flowers, plant summer-flowering bulbs such as dahlias, cannas, and gladioli this month. They enjoy a sunny position in well-drained soil. All of these bulbs, if planted at intervals over a period of a few weeks, will give a succession of flowers throughout summer and into autumn.

Tender bulbs like gladioli can go out now wherever you live. For the best effect in ornamental borders,

Planted now, Eucomis comosa *will bear white flowers on long stalks in late summer.*

plant gladiolus bulbs (or more correctly, corms) in groups of five or more. They should be 10–15cm (4–6in) apart and 7–10cm (3–4in) deep. Note that the deeper the corms are planted the less staking they will need in the future. They will do best in a sunny spot in well-drained soil, so if you garden on heavy clay, put a layer of coarse grit in the bottom of the hole and plant the corms on this to improve drainage.

Plant tigridias 5–8cm (2–3in) deep and 10–15cm (4–6in) apart. Galtonias should be 10–15cm (4–6in) deep and 22–30cm (9–12in) apart, and eucomis 15cm (6in) deep and 15–22cm (6–9in) apart.

Other bulbs you could consider planting now include lilies and the de Caen anemones. Lilies can be planted outside in well-prepared soil in groups in any mixed border.

Gladioli can be grown in a number of ways: in rows for cutting, in tubs, and in groups in borders.

Plant the bulbs to three times their own depth and 7–10cm (3–4in) apart. Don't forget that lilies don't like to sit in damp soil, so aid drainage in clay soil by planting bulbs on a layer of coarse grit. De Caen anemones should be planted about 2.5cm (1in) deep and 10–15cm (4–6in) apart.

All bulbs should be planted by the end of the month in time to flower during the summer.

THIN SHOOTS ON PERENNIALS

To get top quality flowers from border plants it is sometimes necessary to thin out overcrowded shoots. Plants most likely to need thinning include delphiniums and lupins, especially if you are growing these for showing at your local flower show. Phlox will also put on a bolder show if thinned. Remove about one in three or four of the shoots, depending on how crowded they are.

CONTINUE SOWING HARDY ANNUALS

If you live in a colder part of the country, it is probably best to wait until this month before sowing outside, as this will give the soil more of a chance to warm up. Heavy clay soils in particular take longer to warm up than light sandy soils.

Some perennials flower better if you reduce the number of shoots at the base by thinning them out.

SOW AND PLANT SWEET PEAS OUTSIDE

It is advisable to only do so this month in warmer southern areas. The easiest way to grow sweet peas is to sow them where they are to flower. There are many ways of growing sweet peas, and they have a variety of uses in the garden. The scented varieties are the best to grow: a sweet pea without scent is like a rose without thorns. Erect a support, either by fashioning wigwams from canes or bean poles, or by letting them scramble up through shrubs.

Improve germination by soaking seeds overnight to soften the seed coats. Then plant two seeds at 30cm (12in) intervals and 1cm (½in) deep. When the seeds have germinated, the weaker of the two can be removed, or moved to fill in any gaps. The young plants may need to be attached to the support with sweet pea rings initially, just to get them started. Soon the tendrils will twine themselves around the support.

SWEET PEAS ON A WIGWAM

1 Make a wigwam of 2m (6ft) canes, tied together at the top. Sow two sweet pea seeds at the base of each cane.

2 Mixed colours and scented varieties are best for a cottagey effect. Pick the flowers regularly and more will be formed.

SOW UNUSUAL ANNUAL CLIMBERS

Climbing plants have many uses: adding height to a border, or hiding ugly buildings or other unsightly places like the compost heap. To use permanent perennial climbing plants like roses and clematis can be expensive, and many do take some time to get established and cover a given area. For a cheap and quick way to cover an eyesore, or to add height to a planting, annual climbers are ideal. Another way to use annual climbers is to let them scramble through evergreen shrubs or trees, extending their period of interest.

Sweet peas and nasturtiums (*Tropaeolum majus*) in a range of shades from brilliant reds to yellows can be sown directly into the soil now, but other more

Sown now, Eccremocarpus scaber (left), Ipomoea tricolor (top, near right), and Rhodochiton atrosanguineus (top, far right) will flower between late spring and early autumn.

unusual climbers can be raised in pots and planted out in June. Many are tender perennials grown in our climate as annuals.

Lovely plants to try include *Ipomoea* (morning glory), with large blue or pink flowers; *Cobaea scandens*, with violet and purple flowers; *Canarina canariensis*, the Canary bellflower, with almost courgette-like orangey flowers; *Eccremocarpus scaber* (Chilean glory vine), with funnel-shaped red and yellow flowers; purple rhodochitons; black-eyed Susan, or *Thunbergia alata*; *Tropaeolum peregrinum*, and in small spaces, *Asarina procumbens*,

which makes an effective trailing plant in a raised rock garden.

Sow the seeds thinly and cover them lightly with vermiculite as some of them need light to germinate. They will all need a temperature of around 18°C (65°F). These plants can also be bought in as mini-plants or plugs for potting on. This is an easy way to grow them, as it cuts down on the cost of providing heating to germinate the seeds. They will need at least frost-free conditions to grow on until the threat of frost is passed, generally around the beginning of June.

SOW ANNUAL GRASSES

The delicate foliage and attractive seedheads of these grasses contrast with broad-leaved plants in the borders. It's an inexpensive way to try out the new way of growing perennials among grasses for a "naturalistic" border look, and the seedheads can be dried and used in flower arrangements.

Annual grasses can be sown outside from now onwards. You can sow *in situ* in drifts as with annual flowers (in drills, so you can tell them from weed grasses when they germinate), or in drills on a spare piece of ground, to transplant in among plants in the border when big enough. Sow the seeds in shallow drills scratched out with a stick and water the drills if the soil is dry. Cover the seeds lightly and label them. Thin out the young seedlings, and transplant if necessary when they are large enough to handle.

Look out for seeds of Hordeum jubatum *(squirrel tail grass, above left),* Lagurus ovatus *(hare's tail grass, above right), and* Briza maxima *(quaking grass, right), which will all be at their best during the summer.*

KITCHEN GARDEN

THIN OUT SEEDLINGS

If seedlings are not thinned out the plants will become straggly and won't crop well at all. The distances to thin each type of vegetable will vary and it is best to check the back of the seed packet for details of individual plants. The thinnings of most vegetables, except root vegetables such as carrots, beetroots, and turnips, can be transplanted. The advantage of this is that these thinnings, having been disturbed, will mature that little bit later than the seedlings left in the row, therefore extending the succession of cropping. Water seedlings before and after thinning in dry weather. Seedlings being transplanted should also be watered gently but well after planting.

Be careful not to damage the remaining plants as you thin along the row.

SOW LEEKS

It is now safe to sow leeks outside, in a nursery bed (a spare piece of ground used to raise plants before transplanting them to their final cropping positions). Sow them in short rows by taking out narrow drills in the usual manner. Water the drills if the weather is dry, and sow the seeds thinly along the drill. Cover with dry soil and label the row. When they are 10cm (4in) high they can be transplanted. Make holes for planting using a large dibber – if you don't want to buy one, you could fashion one from an old spade handle. Drop one plant into each hole, then water in, and some soil will be carried into the hole, anchoring the plant.

SOW FLORENCE FENNEL

Do so in drills 60cm (24in) apart, and then thin the seedlings to 38cm (15in) when they are large enough to handle. These are quite decorative plants with feathery foliage, and grow to a height of around 1.25–2m (4–6ft). The swollen stem bases have a striking aniseed flavour.

Place a few seeds into your palm, then tap your hand gently so the vegetable seeds are distributed evenly throughout the drill.

KEEP SOWING SUCCESSIONAL CROPS

Keep up with sowing vegetables such as lettuce, radish, beetroot, peas, broad beans, salad onions, and turnips. By sowing little and often you will avoid having a glut of produce all at one time. Sow in shallow drills made with a stick, watering the drills before sowing if the soil is dry. Sow the seeds thinly and cover with soil and label them. Thin out when the seedlings are large enough to handle.

The stem bases of florence fennel can be cooked as a vegetable, while the leaves can be used in garnishes and salads.

Bush tomatoes make interesting hanging basket displays.

SOW TOMATOES

There is no point sowing tomatoes to grow outdoors much more than six to eight weeks before you can plant them out. Sow the tomato seeds in small pots containing seed compost. Overfill the container, give it a sharp tap on the bench to settle the compost, strike off the surplus and then firm gently to level off. Water the container before sowing. Sow the seeds thinly and cover with vermiculite until the seeds just disappear.

Cordon tomatoes will need to be supported with a cane.

There are numerous tomato varieties from which to choose – from the small cherry tomatoes to the large, beefy slicing types. Which ones you choose to grow is simply a matter of taste. However, note that different varieties grow in different ways. Cordon tomatoes are tall plants with a single central stem which needs support. There are also bush varieties, many of which are relatively hardy, do not need training and look very decorative, especially in containers on the patio.

CONTINUE SOWING AND PLANTING HERBS

By this time of year most herbs can be sown outside, and any sown inside earlier can be planted out from the end of the month, after hardening off in a cold frame. Many varieties of young herb plants are available from garden centres and by mail order from specialist herb nurseries. But it's a real treat to make a trip to a herb nursery, to see, and of course to smell, all the different herbs on offer.

SOW SWEETCORN AND COURGETTES

Make sure you sow these towards the end of this month. If they are sown any earlier, they will get drawn and starved before it is safe to plant them out, at the beginning of June. Sow these two seeds per 8cm (3in) pot, pushing them into the compost on their edge. They don't need quite as high a temperature as tomatoes to germinate: 16°C (61°F) is sufficient. Once the seeds have germinated, remove the weaker one and grow on the other one. Pot up into larger pots if necessary before planting out in June.

To start courgettes into growth, push two courgette seeds into the soil, then cover with some more compost.

SUPPORT PEAS

Peas have rather straggly growth, and if they are not supported some of the crop will become spoiled lying on the soil. There are several ways to support peas. You can either buy plastic green support mesh from the garden centre, or you can use twiggy sticks. Use prunings from other shrubs in the garden provided they are strong and fairly straight. An ideal shrub for this is buddleja (the butterfly bush).

It produces large purple or white flowers on long shoots made through the summer. If you don't grow buddleja, any other shrubs with reasonably straight stems will do. Keep them to one side after pruning from the shrub in spring. The tips with the old flowerheads may have to be removed to make them more presentable.

Twiggy prunings are ideal to give a backbone of support to rows of peas.

PLANT MAINCROP POTATOES

This is the latest month to plant maincrops if you want a decent crop. Take out trenches 60cm (24in) apart to the depth of the spade, heaping the soil to one side. If no organic matter was dug in earlier in the year, put some well-rotted manure or garden compost in the trench. Place the tubers on this, about 38cm (15in) apart. Sprinkle fertiliser in the gaps along the row, then cover the tubers with soil, leaving it slightly mounded up.

After digging a trench, place the potatoes within it, making sure that the sprouts are facing upwards, then cover them with soil.

EARTH UP EARLY POTATOES

Drawing a little soil up over the emerging potato shoots not only protects them from any late frosts, it encourages the development of roots further up the stems, which in turn increases the yield. Carry out this task sooner rather than later as it is easier to do as the shoots emerge. Any new potatoes that are exposed to sunlight will go green, making them poisonous.

FEED BERRIES AND CURRANTS

Blackcurrants, blackberries and hybrid berries should all be fed with a high-nitrogen feed. These plants make a lot of growth during this season, and an extra dose of a high nitrogen feed will give them a welcome boost. Don't use too much – follow the directions on the package. Too much nitrogen will result in very soft growth, which is more susceptible to attack from pests and diseases.

PLANT CONTAINER-GROWN FRUIT TREES

By this month it is too late to plant bare-root fruit trees and bushes, but there are many different kinds available in containers that will have been trained in attractive ways. The major advantage of container-grown plants is that they can be planted at any time of the year, because the root system has not been disturbed. You can even buy them in flower and you may get some fruit from them in the first year after planting, but don't be too greedy and take a lot of fruit in the first year. It's far more rewarding to let the plants get established now, and they'll fruit all the better in subsequent years. Lay seephose when you plant new fruit and mulch on top of it to water efficiently and conserve soil moisture.

Apples, pears, plums, cherries, red and white currants, and gooseberries can all be trained in a number of ways: espaliers (tiers of horizontal branches), cordons (single-stemmed trees grown at an angle to save space), and fans (branches are trained like the spokes of a fan). These are all attractive and productive ways of growing fruit, and with modern dwarfing rootstocks they can be fitted into the smallest of spaces.

Plant the tree to same depth it was in the container. Establish the depth by placing a cane across the hole and lining it up with the top of the dark section on the trunk.

Espaliers are particularly suited to apple and pear trees (top right). Vulnerable fruits grown against walls or fences can be trained as fans, such as this cherry tree (right).

APRIL PROJECT

POT UP STRAWBERRIES

Home-grown strawberries are far better than those bought in a supermarket – the taste of your first strawberry picked fresh from the plant will come as a revelation. Even the scent emanating from a patch of ripe strawberries is delicious. Apart from the question of freshness, you can also select varieties for flavour, which is not necessarily the first consideration in commercial growing.

You do not have to make space for strawberries in your garden beds – you can grow them in pots on the patio or indoors, which has several advantages. On the patio the strawberries will be kept clear of muddy soil and slug control will be easier. Indoors, the plants are protected from the elements and by planting in succession you can have fruits earlier in the season than is possible outdoors.

1 *It is best to buy young plants* from a specialist nursery to ensure that they are free from any virus. Water the young plants well before transplanting them into larger pots.

2 *Partially fill* 12.5cm (5in) or 20cm (8in) pots with multi-purpose potting compost. Pot up the plants, one each in the smaller pots or three round the edges in the larger size.

3 *Place the crown* of the strawberry plants (where the stems and roots join) level with the surface of the compost. Water them in and firm down the soil with your fingers.

4 *Removing all the flowers* the first year may help to build up the plants, giving you a better crop the following year, so it is advisable to resist the temptation to grow fruit as soon as possible.

LILY-OF-THE-VALLEY [1]

Convallaria majalis ♀ A creeping, upright perennial with fleshy roots. In late spring, arching stems of small, nodding, waxy white flowers appear. They are sweetly scented. The attractive leaves make excellent ground cover.
‡23cm (9in) ↔ 30cm (12in)

CULTIVATION Tolerates deep or part-shade. Grow in damp, leafy, fertile soil. A top-dressing of leafmould in autumn is beneficial. Pot some up in autumn and grow under glass for a scented display indoors.

PIERIS [2]

Pieris japonica 'Flamingo' A dense, bushy, evergreen shrub. In late winter and spring, it bears hanging clusters of urn-shaped, dark flamingo-pink flowers that open from dark red buds. The glossy green leaves are attractive all year round.
‡to 4m (12ft) ↔ 3m (10ft)

CULTIVATION Grow in leafy, moist but well-drained, acid (lime-free) soil in sun or dappled shade. Shelter from cold dry winds. Keep pruning to a minimum.

BLEEDING HEART   3

Dicentra spectabilis ♥ An elegant,
clump-forming, herbaceous perennial.
In late spring and early summer, tall
arching stems bear hanging, heart-shaped
flowers with rose-pink outer petals and
white inner ones. Finely cut, fern-like,
grey-green leaves.
‡ 1.2m (4ft) ↔ 45cm (18in)

CULTIVATION Best in part-shade in
damp, fertile, preferably neutral to slightly
alkaline soil. Divide every three or four
years to maintain vigour.

2

3

STAR MAGNOLIA [1]

Magnolia stellata ♀ Compact, slow-growing, deciduous shrub. In early and mid-spring, the silky buds open to star-shaped, white flowers. Has a neat habit and attractive leaves for the summer.
↕3m (9ft) ↔ 4m (12ft)

CULTIVATION Grow in moist but well-drained, fertile, humus-rich soil in sun or dappled shade. It tolerates slightly acid and slightly alkaline soils. Shelter from cold winds and late frosts, which may damage the flowers. Little or no pruning is required.

AUBRIETA [2]

Aubrieta **'J.S. Baker'** A creeping, mat-forming perennial; perfect tumbling over rocks or low walls. In spring, it produces single, white-eyed, purple flowers in profusion. The greyish-green leaves form dense ground cover.
↕5cm (2in) ↔ 60cm (24in)

CULTIVATION Grow in well-drained, preferably neutral to alkaline soil, enriched with organic matter. Cut back hard after flowering to maintain neat, compact plants.

EUPHORBIA

3

Euphorbia polychroma ♀ A bushy, clump-forming, herbaceous perennial. Forms a dense mound of dark green, sometimes purple-tinted, leaves. From mid-spring to midsummer, it bears long-lasting, bright yellow-green flowers at the stem tips. Very bright, even in part-shade.
‡40cm (16in) ↔ 60cm (24in)

CULTIVATION Best in full sun, but tolerant of light, dappled shade. Grow in a light, well-drained soil enriched with organic matter.

2

3

FLOWERING CURRANT [1]

Ribes sanguineum **'Brocklebankii'**
An upright, deciduous shrub with
rounded, aromatic yellow leaves, bright
when young and fading in summer. In
spring, it bears hanging clusters of tiny,
tubular pale pink flowers. The flowers
are followed by small, blue-black fruits.
↕ 1.2m (4ft) ↔ 1.2m (4ft)

CULTIVATION Grow in full sun or light,
dappled shade in any fertile soil. After
flowering, prune flowered shoots back
to strong buds or shoots lower down
the shrub, to keep compact and bushy.

WARMINSTER BROOM [2]

Cytisus × *praecox* **'Warminster'** ♀
A drought-tolerant, arching evergreen
shrub. In mid- and late spring, each stem
is wreathed in pea-like, creamy-yellow
flowers. The wand-like branches bear
small dark green leaves.
↕ 1.2m (4ft) ↔ 1.5m (5ft)

CULTIVATION Grow in moderately fertile,
well-drained soil in full sun. Tolerates
poor acid soils and deep soils over chalk.
After flowering, cut back the flowered
shoots to buds lower down on young,
green wood. Do not cut into old wood.

BERGENIA 3

Bergenia **'Sunningdale'** Clump-forming herbaceous perennial. Rich lilac-magenta flowers on red stems appear in early and mid-spring. The bold, glossy dark green leaves turn copper-red in winter.

↕ to 40cm (16in) ↔ to 60cm (24in)

CULTIVATION Best in sun in well-drained soil enriched with plenty of organic matter, but tolerant of part-shade and poor soils. Lift and divide every three to five years to maintain vigour.

BERBERIS [1]

Berberis darwinii ♀ A spiny, evergreen
shrub of dense, arching growth. In mid-
to late spring, it bears hanging clusters
of deep orange flowers. Small, blue-black
fruits appear in autumn and glossy, spiny,
dark green leaves last all year.
‡1.5m (5ft) ↔ 1.5m (5ft)

CULTIVATION Easily grown in sun or
partial shade, in any fertile, well-drained
soil. After flowering, trim hedges or
prune single specimens lightly to shape.

PASQUE FLOWER [2]

Pulsatilla vulgaris ♀ A clump-forming
herbaceous perennial. Nodding, bell-
shaped, silky-hairy flowers in shades of
purple, or occasionally white, appear in
spring. The finely divided, hairy leaves
grow taller after flowering. Silky, silvery
seedheads follow the flowers.
‡10–20cm (4–8in) ↔ 20cm (8in)

CULTIVATION Grow in fertile, gritty,
sharply drained soil in sun. It thrives on
shallow chalky soils. Protect from excessive
winter wet. Pulsatillas dislike being
disturbed, so choose the site with care.

CORYLOPSIS 3

Corylopsis glabrescens A deciduous shrub of open, spreading habit. In mid-spring, it produces hanging tassels of fragrant, pale yellow flowers. It has oval leaves that are pale to dark green on top and blue-green beneath.

↕ to 5m (15ft) ↔ to 5m (15ft)

CULTIVATION Grow in dappled or part-shade. It prefers well-drained, humus-rich, acid soil, but will tolerate deep soils over chalk. Prune out badly placed shoots after flowering.

ALPINE CLEMATIS   1

Clematis 'Frances Rivis' ♀
A vigorous, deciduous, twining climber.
In spring or early summer, it bears
hanging, blue flowers with slightly
twisted petals. Has attractive foliage all
summer and fluffy seedheads in autumn.
‡2–3m (6–10ft) ↔ 1.5m (5ft)

CULTIVATION Tolerates sun or dappled
shade, but the roots should be shaded.
Grow in fertile, well-drained soil enriched
with plenty of organic matter. After
flowering, remove damaged shoots and
shorten others to confine to bounds.

PRIMROSE JASMINE   2

Jasminum mesnyi ♀ A scrambling,
half-hardy evergreen shrub. In spring
and summer, it bears sweetly-scented,
bright yellow flowers. The divided,
glossy, deep green leaves persist all year.
‡2.5m (8ft) ↔ 3m (10ft)

CULTIVATION Grow in full sun, in
fertile, well-drained soil or potting
compost. Tie in shoots to a support
as growth proceeds. After flowering,
thin out the oldest flowered shoots and
shorten the remainder to strong buds.

1

AQUILEGIA 3

Aquilegia canadensis ♀ This attractive, airy perennial has fern-like, vivid green foliage. From mid-spring to midsummer it bears clusters of up to 20 nodding, coral-red and yellow flowers with showy "spurs" that hang from slender stems. ↕60–90cm (24–36in) ↔30cm (12in).

CULTIVATION Grow in any fertile, moist but well-drained soil in full sun or part shade. Seed can be sown in containers as soon as it is ripe, or in spring.

BISHOP'S MITRE [1]

Epimedium × warleyense A vigorous, clump-forming, evergreen perennial. From mid- to late spring, it bears sprays of nodding, yellow and orange-red flowers. The leaves are tinted red in spring and autumn and form good ground cover.
‡50cm (20in) ↔ 75cm (30in)

CULTIVATION Best in part-shade, but tolerates some sun if soil is moist. Grow in fertile, moist but well-drained soil. Shelter from cold winds. Cut back old foliage in late winter to get the best flowering display.

VIBURNUM [2]

Viburnum × juddii ♀ A bushy, deciduous shrub. In mid- to late spring, it bears rounded clusters of fragrant, pink-tinted, white flowers that open from pink buds. In autumn, the dark green leaves turn dark red.
‡1.2m (4ft) ↔ 1.2m (4ft)

CULTIVATION Best in full sun, but it will tolerate part-shade. Grow in any reasonably fertile, well-drained soil. After flowering, shorten any shoots that spoil the outline.

1

PAGODA FLOWER 3

Erythronium **'Pagoda'** ♥ Upright,
clump-forming, bulbous perennial.
In spring, it bears heads of nodding,
brown-marked, sulphur-yellow flowers.
The bronze-mottled leaves die down
in summer.
↕15–35cm (6–14in) ↔ 10cm (4in)

CULTIVATION Grow in part-shade in
fertile, reliably moist, humus-rich soil.
Plant bulbs 10cm (4in) deep in autumn.
Do not let bulbs dry out before planting,
or when dormant.

RHODODENDRON [1]

Rhododendron yakushimanum A very
hardy, dome-shaped evergreen shrub.
In mid-spring, it bears trusses of funnel-
shaped flowers that open from deep pink
buds and fade gradually to white. The
glossy, dark green leaves are clothed in
dense tawny down when young.
‡ to 2m (6ft) ↔ to 2m (6ft)

CULTIVATION Grow in acid (lime-free),
moist but well-drained, leafy, humus-rich
soil in dappled shade or full sun. Shelter
from cold winds. Trim any shoots that
spoil the shape; deadhead after flowering.

SNAKE'S HEAD FRITILLARY [2]

Fritillaria meleagris A small bulbous
perennial that naturalizes well in grass.
In spring, it bears hanging, bell-shaped
flowers in delicate, chequered shades of
pink, purple, or white.
‡ 30cm (12in) ↔ 5–8cm (2–3in)

CULTIVATION Grow in fertile,
humus-rich, moisture-retentive soil.
Plant the bulbs in autumn at two to
three times their own depth and the
same distance apart. If grown in grass,
delay the first mowing until the leaves
have faded naturally.

AMELANCHIER 3

Amelanchier lamarckii ♀ A small deciduous tree for spring and autumn interest. In spring a profusion of star-shaped white flowers are borne in clusters along the branches. The young leaves are bronzed as they unfold, turning to green in summer and then to blazing shades of orange and red in the autumn. ‡10m (30ft) ↔ 12m (40ft)

CULTIVATION Grow in lime-free (acid) soil in full sun or dappled shade. In winter, prune out any crossing branches and those that spoil the shape.

PRUNUS

Vigorous, free-flowering deciduous trees. In spring, they bear a profusion of fragrant blossom in shades of pink and white, and most have fine autumn colour. All of the recommended cultivars are beautiful specimen trees.

CULTIVATION Grow in any moist, but well-drained soil. They need minimal pruning; remove badly placed or crossing branches in winter, or in midsummer if silver leaf disease is a problem in your area.

TOP ROW LEFT TO RIGHT
- *P. avium* 'Plena' ♥
  ‡12m (40ft) ↔ 12m (40ft)
- *P.* 'Kiku-shidare-zakura' ♥
  ‡3m (10ft) ↔ 3m (10ft)
- *P.* 'Ukon' ♥
  ‡8m (25ft) ↔ 10m (30ft)

BOTTOM ROW LEFT TO RIGHT
- *P.* 'Kanzan' ♥
  ‡10m (30ft) ↔ 10m (30ft)
- *P.* 'Shirotae' ♥
  ‡6m (20ft) ↔ 8m (25ft)
- *P.* 'Spire' ♥
  ‡10m (30ft) ↔ 6m (20ft)

MALUS

Deciduous, mostly vigorous, small trees that are ideal as specimens for smaller gardens. In spring, they bear masses of blossom, from white to pink and purplish reds. In autumn, they produce crab apples in colours ranging from yellow to red (*see p.460*). The leaves also turn attractive shades of yellow and orange.

CULTIVATION Grow in any fertile, well-drained soil in sun; they tolerate light shade, but purple-leaved variants are best in sun. Prune in winter to remove misplaced shoots or dead or damaged wood.

TOP ROW LEFT TO RIGHT
- *M.* 'Katherine'
  ↕6m (20ft) ↔ 6m (20ft)
- *M. x moerlandsii* 'Liset'
  ↕6m (20ft) ↔ 6m (20ft)
- *M. transitoria* ♀
  ↕8m (25ft) ↔ 10m (30ft)

BOTTOM ROW LEFT TO RIGHT
- *M. toringo*
  ↕2.5m (8ft) ↔ 3m (10ft)
- *M.* 'Royalty'
  ↕8m (25ft) ↔ 8m (25ft)
- *M.* 'Evereste' ♀
  ↕7m (22ft) ↔ 6m (20ft)

WEATHER WATCH

Make the most of May's balmy weather to prepare for summer. Your garden should be looking its best this month, with bright spring bedding in flower and trees in full leaf, and the flower-show season will offer even more inspiration for the months ahead.

LATE FROSTS

The days are really warming up now, but be aware that the nights can be cold and it is still possible to get sudden sharp frosts at any time this month. These late frosts are the scourge of fruit growers. Most varieties of fruit trees will be in flower now and it only takes one sharp frost to destroy a potential crop for a whole year. Tender plants should be watched carefully and given protection whenever frost is forecast.

WINDY DAYS

It's not a month for frequent gales, but there may be windy days. Exposed north-western coastal areas still get 0.5–0.7 days of gale-force winds, but this is rare in sheltered south-eastern parts.

SUNSHINE AND CLOUD

The amount of direct sunshine will depend on the cloud cover, but generally southern parts of the country get the lion's share of sunshine during this month, although some north-eastern parts compare favourably with the south-east. The western half of the of the British Isles is more prone to cloud because weather fronts are driven over the Atlantic ocean, and because of the topography of this part of the country.

RAINFALL LEVELS

Although, in general, rainfall decreases in all parts by now, some areas are inevitably wetter than others. The north-west Highland region of Scotland averages 107mm (4in) of rain this month and the south-west Borders region and the Lake District in England are not far behind with 95mm (3½in). It's not until you reach East Anglia that there is a considerable drop in rainfall: this region will only get around 44mm (1½in) during May.

RARE SNOWFALL

The only places you are likely to find snow this month are in the hills above 100m (300ft), as at Cape Wrath in the northern Highlands of Scotland. Here, in the mountains, snow can persist for most of the year. However, it is extremely rare for snow to fall on other parts of the country during May, but there can still be hail storms from time to time, which can be quite destructive.

AROUND THE GARDEN

BEWARE OF NIGHT FROSTS

Night frosts are not uncommon this month, especially after clear, bright days. Keep a sheet of horticultural fleece or even some old newspapers handy to cover plants vulnerable to frost if night temperatures are forecast to fall.

KEEP AN EYE OUT FOR PESTS AND DISEASES

Pests and diseases are increasingly common in the warmer weather. Chemical controls may be needed in severe cases, but long-term use of synthetic chemicals is a less than ideal situation. Chemicals kill off not only pests, but also the beneficial insects that prey on them,

such as ladybird and hoverfly larvae. If you do spray, do so on a still day, late in the evening when there are fewer beneficial insects around.

Keep plants in the garden healthy and they will be less susceptible to attack. Prepare the ground well, and mulch new plants after watering to retain moisture. Mulch will slow the rate of evaporation from the surface of the ground.

Keep new plants well-watered in dry spells, so that they don't suffer stress – unhealthy plants are more susceptible to disease.

Keep the garden tidy, and remove weeds whenever possible, as they often act as hosts to pests and diseases. The most organic way to control pests is by using your fingers to squash them, but you have to be vigilant to keep on top of them. The memory of two days spent squashing cabbage white butterfly caterpillars on brassicas in a large garden remains with me.

Don't introduce vine weevil into containers along with new plants, where they can wreak havoc. Knock new plants out of their pots and look for the small white grubs, which eat at the roots. The adult weevils are rarely seen as they only come out at night; notched foliage is a giveaway sign. However, it is the grubs that do the most damage.

There are several products on the market to control vine weevil. The most effective organic control is a biological nematode available via mail order. There are also insecticides especially for pot plants to control vine weevil grubs.

Vine weevil grubs eat the roots of plants and can easily kill them.

KEEP MOWING AND FEEDING LAWNS

Now the grass is growing well, mow your lawn once a week. Each time you mow, lower the mower blades slightly, cutting a little closer each time; don't lower them too much, though, or the lawn will be "scalped". This makes the grass turn yellow, and causes bare patches to develop, introducing weeds and moss – and it looks unsightly too.

If you haven't already done so, you can now feed established lawns.

Some modern fertilisers have anti-scorch properties, so if your one does, don't worry about being a little heavy-handed when applying, but read the instructions first. Remember, though, that it is also wasteful to apply too much. Continue to renovate damaged edges and bare patches on lawns all through the summer, as needed.

HOE BARE GROUND

Hoeing will keep down weeds as they germinate. Weeds are much easier to kill off at this stage, rather than leaving them until they grow much larger. Removing weeds when they are young also gives them less opportunity to set seeds which spread around the garden. Mulching with organic matter will help to prevent the growth of further weeds. Water the soil first if it is dry before applying the mulch. Alternatively, put some plants in the gap to add colour to the border.

KEEP WATERING AND FEEDING PLANTS

As the weather warms up, watering containers can become a daily or twice-daily task. Hanging baskets in particular are prone to drying out quickly, as they are exposed to the sun and wind. Mixing up a feed solution every time you need to feed your plants can be very time-consuming; the easiest way to feed lots of plants in containers is to make up a feed solution in bulk, which can be stored and used at each feed.

Use a hoe to cut the roots off weeds just below the surface. Hoe on a dry day, and leave weeds to dry out before composting.

If plants dry out, the compost shrinks away from the edges of the pot, and water drains down the gap. Soak the pot in water for an hour to alleviate this.

Fill a large tank such as a plastic water butt with water, and mix in some plant food. Always do this according to the manufacturer's instructions. This can be fed to the plants at every watering. A high-potash feed is recommended to stimulate flower production and encourage a prolonged display. The major disadvantage of opting for a high-nitrogen fertiliser is that your plants will produce a lot of leafy growth at the expense of flowers, so avoid these fertilisers whenever possible.

Remember also to water recently planted trees and shrubs on a weekly basis. A few days of sunny weather accompanied by a bit of wind will dry out the soil surprisingly quickly. It is important to water new woody plants well until they get established, as their roots need to develop sufficiently to be able to seek out moisture deep down in the soil.

Any organic matter (such as rotted manure or garden compost, dug into the soil or applied as a mulch) has good water-holding potential which will help new, growing roots. Water before you mulch so that the water is locked into the soil rather than out. Even grass clippings spread in a layer about 5–8cm (2–3in) thick around the plant, but not touching the stems, will help to retain moisture. Try to water in the evenings when there is less chance of the water evaporating from the soil, as it will do in the heat of the day.

EXTRACTING POND WEEDS

Duckweed can multiply before lilypads unfurl. One method of removing it is to use a simple block of wood as shown.

If left unchecked, blanket weed can choke other aquatic plants. Wind it round a stick like spaghetti, then lift it out.

REMOVE POND WEEDS

Blanket weed and duckweed must be removed regularly so they don't take over. Duckweed is a floating plant which is almost impossible to get rid of if it gets established. Remove it using a net like the ones sold for children at the seaside, or an old kitchen sieve strapped to a broom handle.

Blanket weed is a type of algae resembling wet, bright green candy floss. It can be removed by twisting it around a cane – quite a pleasant job for a Sunday morning. Once removed, leave it on the bank with an end trailing into the water for the rest of the day so that aquatic creatures can escape back into the water. After that, it makes a highly nutritious ingredient for the compost heap.

To discourage pond weeds, grow plants with floating leaves like waterlilies which cover the water's surface. Once they are in full leaf in the summer, the problem should lessen. Oxygenating plants also help to reduce the growth of algae.

FEED AND THIN OUT AQUATIC PLANTS

Feed aquatic plants using special aquatic plant fertiliser, not garden fertiliser. Rather than sprinkling pellets on the pond's surface, push them into the plant compost. Remember also to thin out excessive growth on aquatic plants, and generally tidy up the pond before summer. Overgrown aquatic plants that have been in place for several years can be lifted out and divided now. Doing this work may turn the water a bit murky, but it will soon become clear again.

FEED FISH REGULARLY

Fish are more active in warm weather, so make sure they have plenty to eat. Give them just enough food to eat in a short time or the leftovers will rot in the water, encouraging algae to grow. Feeding once a day will be sufficient. On the whole, fish tend to fend for themselves so don't worry if you miss a day or two.

If you allow your pond to become overgrown, sunlight cannot penetrate the water, and any plants that are starved of light will begin to decay.

TREES, SHRUBS & CLIMBERS

Keep on top of pruning your pyracanthas: this will encourage the growth of neat bunches of bright berries in autumn.

PRUNE PYRACANTHAS

Where pyracanthas are trained against a wall, prune out shoots growing directly into or away from it. Shorten the others to about 8cm (3in). This encourages the formation of short spurs which bear the flower buds, and then the beautiful berries in autumn.

TRIM FORMAL EVERGREEN HEDGING

Even if hedging has not grown to the desired size, it is wise to trim it to shape every now and then. Box hedging (*Buxus sempervirens*) does not take to being cut back hard, so the sooner it starts being trimmed to keep it in shape the better. This is best done with hand shears rather than with a mechanical hedge trimmer, which can bruise rather than cut the leaves, making them turn brown and unsightly. It may take more time using shears, but the overall appearance of the hedge will be much better.

You can make cuttings from any shoots about 7.5cm (3in) long. Trim each cutting below a leaf joint, put into pots containing cuttings compost, cover with a polythene bag, and stand the pot in a shady part of the garden; in a few weeks the cuttings will root. You can then place them into their own pots, or space them out on a spare piece of ground until autumn or next spring, when they can be put in their final positions.

PRUNE EARLY-FLOWERING SHRUBS

Shrubs such as *Kerria japonica* and *Spiraea* 'Arguta' will finish flowering around now on wood that was produced the previous year. For kerria, prune back all the shoots that have produced flowers to young sideshoots lower down. This shrub has a tendency to spread out using underground suckers; these can be removed if the plant starts to encroach on other plants.

In the same way, prune back the flowered shoots of *Spiraea* 'Arguta' to buds or shoots lower down on the shrub. In addition to this, on older plants you should cut out about one in three of the older stems completely to the ground. This will encourage young growth from the base of the plant, keeping it vigorous and healthy.

TIE IN CLIMBERS

It is important to keep tying in the shoots of vigorous climbers such as clematis, roses, and vines on a regular basis, otherwise they are likely to smother other plants that are growing in the border.

Encourage vigorous new growth from the base of Spiraea *'Arguta' by cutting the oldest stems down to ground level.*

When tying in climbers, make 'figures of eight' with twine so that stems do not rub directly on supports.

Trying to untangle climbers from other plants can be a tedious job, and is one to be avoided if at all possible. Fixing wide-mesh wire netting to walls and fences is the easiest way to provide support for vigorous climbers. Trellis is more decorative, so choose lighter climbers for this so that the plants' growth does not hide it.

PRUNE *CLEMATIS MONTANA*

Pruning should be carried out once this plant has flowered. The amount of pruning to be done will depend on where it is growing. It will thrive in a range of locations, sometimes climbing fences and walls, and other times wending its way through trees and shrubs. In these situations, little pruning will be needed unless it is outgrowing its space.

However, in more confined spaces, some pruning will be necessary to prevent it taking over the whole garden. Pruning is easy, although the untangling can be tricky. Begin by pruning out any dead or diseased wood, then prune the remaining stems back as far as you need to. This encourages young growth to appear which will flower next spring.

Clematis montana is a vigorous climber; let it scramble up through trees and large shrubs or up a large area of fence or wall.

FLOWERING PLANTS

STAKE AND SUPPORT PERENNIALS

You should pay particular attention to tall-stemmed perennials like delphiniums. These need several bamboo canes placed around each plant, and some string tied around the canes. Alternatively, tie each stem to an individual cane.

Twiggy sticks make informal supports for cottage-style annual flowers.

Tall plants like delphiniums need tall stakes. Top them with corks or some other protector to avoid eye injury when working in borders.

THIN ANNUALS

If you do not thin hardy annuals sown earlier, the plants become leggy and will not flower well. Thin out to leave one seedling at least every 15cm (6in). The taller the plants, the more space they require. Check seed packets for precise details on spacing.

The easiest way to thin out the seedlings is to choose the one you want to keep, hold it in position with a finger on the soil each side of the stem, and pull or pinch out the others around it. Measure the gap to the next one and repeat the process until the job is complete.

Most hardy annuals don't transplant well when they grow taller, so if you thin out promptly as soon as the seedlings can be handled, they can be transplanted to fill any gaps in the rows, or put in other parts of the garden. Some of the very tall annuals – for example, cleome – need some support with twiggy sticks to prevent them flopping over. After this is done, all you have to do is enjoy the show.

TIDY CLUMP-FORMING PERENNIALS

This is the time to cut back and divide clump-forming spring-flowering perennials like doronicums and pulmonarias. Doronicums just need the old

flower spikes cut off to neaten up the plant. But pulmonarias should have all the old foliage cut to the ground, as it will often be covered in mildew by now and will look dreadfully shabby. This will transform the appearance of the plants. At the same time, lift, divide, and replant overgrown clumps. After pruning and dividing, feed with an organic fertiliser, watering in if the soil is dry.

Cut down the foliage on pulmonarias now and new foliage will soon grow, complementing the flowers the plant will bear next spring.

DEADHEAD SPRING-FLOWERING BULBS

Snap off tulip heads and let the stalks remain; it's best to leave the foliage intact for a minimum of six weeks after the last flower. If you really must move them before this (for example, if they have been grown in amongst wallflowers and forget-me-nots for a spring display), you can always move them temporarily, heeling them in in a corner of a border or in the vegetable garden.

Tulips can be uprooted carefully and replanted out of the way to die down.

Begin by lifting the bulbs carefully with a fork. Dig a shallow trench, and heel in the bulbs inside it with the foliage above ground. Cover the bulbs with soil, and lift when the foliage has died down. Don't forget to label the row, or if you have a memory like mine you'll forget where they are.

Feeding spring-flowering bulbs now, whether they are heeled in or still in place, encourages the new flower bud in the bulb to develop for next spring. Sprinkle a general organic fertiliser around the bulbs according to the instructions, and water in if the weather is dry.

TRAIN SWEET PEAS

Sweet peas planted out earlier will be growing vigorously towards the end of May, and will benefit from steering in the right direction. If the plants are grown for display in your garden, tie them to the support. You'll probably find this will be all the help they need, as the tendrils will then twine themselves around whatever they touch.

Cut back aubrieta now to produce a mass of vibrant flowers on a neat, compact plant next spring.

CUT BACK ALYSSUM, ARABIS AND AUBRIETA

These spreading and trailing plants have a tendency to become bare and tatty when the flowers have gone over, especially towards the centre of the plant. This month, it's essential to trim them back hard, almost to the ground, as this will encourage the appearance of fresh new growth. If you don't carry out this task every year, then as the plant ages it will be increasingly reluctant to grow from the base when cut hard back. After pruning, feed with an organic fertiliser.

CLEAR OUT SPRING BEDDING

Prepare the ground for summer bedding by clearing spring-flowering bedding plants. Now that spring-flowering plants like wallflowers, forget-me-nots, and winter-flowering pansies are coming to the end of their flowering time they need to be cleared away, and the ground should be prepared for summer bedding to go in. The old spring-flowering plants can be consigned to the compost heap to ensure a supply of valuable organic matter next year.

Bedding does not have time to root deeply, and can be raked or pulled out quite easily.

After the old plants have been removed, lightly fork over the soil, taking out any weeds. At this point it is beneficial to add a small amount of organic fertiliser, as it breaks down slowly in the soil and will therefore be available to the plants when they are planted out. But be careful that you don't apply too much, or you will get a lot of soft growth at the expense of flowers: a light sprinkling is sufficient. Also, don't dig in organic matter at this time for the same reason – wait until autumn to do this.

Most of the tender summer bedding plants we grow come from the warmer parts of the world such as South Africa, where the soil is baked and very poor as far as the availability of nutrients is concerned. This is why they don't require large amounts of fertiliser to grow well.

SOW PERENNIALS OUTSIDE

Growing plants from seed is both cheap and satisfying, especially when seeds are collected from plants in the garden rather than from a packet. Most perennials can be grown this way: achilleas, alstroemerias, and hardy geraniums are especially easy examples. Take out shallow drills in the soil after raking it to a fine tilth. Water the drills if the soil is dry, allowing it to soak away before sowing the seeds thinly, then cover lightly with dry soil. Label each row. After a few weeks, when the seedlings are large enough to handle, they can be transplanted to a nursery area to grow on and bulk up. You can also sow the seed in pots to plant out in autumn.

Growing perennials from seed is a rewarding task; try Geranium maculatum, which flowers from late spring to midsummer.

SOW BIENNIALS OUTSIDE

Spring-flowering biennials include wallflowers, *Bellis perennis*, forget-me-nots, sweet Williams, and winter-flowering pansies that have just been cleared to make way for the summer bedding. Sowing now will mean plants will flower by next spring. Find a corner in the vegetable plot or one in a border to sow the seeds.

Bear in mind that you shouldn't grow wallflowers in the same piece of ground year after year. They belong to the same family as cabbages and cauliflowers (brassicas) and are subject to the same diseases, such as clubroot (swelling of the roots) which is incurable and persists in the soil for many years.

The preparation for sowing is the same as for other seeds. Rake the soil to a fine tilth and level it off.

Sow forget-me-nots just as the old flowers begin to fade; you will be rewarded by new flowers come next spring.

Take out shallow drills with a stick or cane about 15cm (6in) apart, and water them before sowing if the soil is dry. Sow the seeds thinly along the row and cover over lightly with dry soil, then firm gently with your hand. Label each row so you don't forget what is what. In a few weeks the seedlings will need to be thinned or transplanted to grow on with more space between them, before being planted in their final positions in autumn.

Thin out seedlings (here, sweet William) if they are competing for space. If transplanting them, retain the soil around the roots.

KITCHEN GARDEN

SOW CHARD AND LEAF BEET

Swiss chard has large leaves and pure white stems, both of which can be eaten, the leaves being used in a similar way to spinach. There are also ruby and "rainbow" chards, with deep red and multicoloured

Leafy vegetable crops, such as this ruby chard, not only produce an edible crop but provide a decorative summer display.

midribs respectively, which look good among ornamentals. Leaf beet, or perpetual spinach, is also an ideal substitute for spinach as it is, like chard, less susceptible to bolting (running to seed) than spinach is. Often spinach will start bolting just a few weeks after seeds germinate. Sow the seeds in drills according to the directions on the seed packets, watering the drills first if the soil is dry. Thin out the seedlings when they are large enough to handle and keep them well watered during the summer.

SOW BEANS

Runner beans and French beans can be sown this month, despite being tender plants. By sowing outside now the seeds will germinate when the threat of frost has largely passed in most parts of the country. Seeds of runner beans can be sown two to the base of each bean pole or bamboo cane.

These climbing French beans have weaved their way through an open obelisk made from woven willow and twine.

The weaker seedling can be removed when the seeds have all germinated. Sowing two seeds per "station" also acts as an insurance policy in case one seed should fail to germinate.

Seedlings of all of these plants can be damaged by slugs during germination. In order to avoid this problem, after sowing the seeds cover them with plastic lemonade or water bottles that have had the bottom cut out, pushing them into the ground. To get the bottle round a cane, cut the bottle along its length. The added benefit is that these improvised cloches will act like mini-greenhouses, hastening germination and giving some protection should a late frost occur.

PLANT LEEKS

If you sowed any leeks earlier, they can now be planted out. The method of planting will depend on the way the young plants were raised, but with all planting, apply a general organic fertiliser a few days beforehand.

If the seeds were sown in seed trays and the plants left to grow in the trays until 10–12cm (4–5in) high, they can be planted in individual holes. Use a dibber to make a series of holes 15cm (6in) deep.

PLANTING OUT LEEKS

For leeks sown several seeds to a module, try to plant out the entire cluster without disturbing the rootball.

Drop single leek plants into a deep hole made with a cane or dibber. Do not firm them in, but water gently.

Put one plant in each hole until you have completed the row, then water in. The plants should be about 30cm (24in) apart each way. Do not firm: watering them in will automatically wash some soil down the hole to cover the roots.

If seeds were multiple-sown in modular trays for deep beds, the small clumps of five or six plants can be planted in their clusters, 15–22cm (6–9in) apart each way. This way you get more weight of crop within your growing area than if they were grown in conventional straight rows.

PLANT MARROWS AND COURGETTES

These plants are tender and prone to damage from frosts. Plant into soil that has been enriched with organic matter, as marrows and courgettes require a lot of water during the growing season. They take up quite a bit of room, so space them 90cm (36in) each way.

Keep the plants well watered through the summer. If you do

not have room in the vegetable garden to grow these plants, why not grow one or two in ornamental borders? The large leaves are bold and attractive and will provide a good contrast to other foliage plants in the garden, and the edible parts are a bonus. Trailing varieties can be grown up strong canes, bean poles or other forms of support to make an attractive feature, which also saves space at ground level.

PLANTING OUT SWEETCORN

Plant sweetcorn in blocks, 30cm (24in) apart each way, rather than in rows. Sweetcorn is pollinated by wind: by growing the plants in blocks there is more chance of pollination being successful than if plants are growing in conventional rows. The male flowers appear as tassels at the tip of the plant and the pollen falls onto the female parts lower down the plants.

SWEETCORN POLLINATION

Use a marked plank to plant sweetcorn in blocks, the same distance each way.

Planted in blocks, wind will blow the pollen between plants.

PLANT BRASSICAS

Brussels sprouts and other winter brassicas can now be planted in their cropping positions. It's worth noting that they will take up a fair amount of space over a relatively long period of time. However, it's always possible to grow other short-term crops such as lettuce, radishes, and turnips between the brassicas in order to use the space efficiently. This method of double cropping is known as intercropping, and it makes the best use of the land available.

All the brassicas to be planted out should be well watered beforehand as they wilt very quickly, especially in warm weather. One point to bear in mind is that cauliflowers will not produce a proper curd if they receive even the slightest check to their growth. So watering before planting out and afterwards is very important. The ideal stage at which to transplant the seedlings is when they have made two or three true leaves. The plants should be set out at a minimum of 60cm (24in) each way.

If you're not planting through a membrane, then after planting the brassicas put a collar round the base of each one to prevent the cabbage root fly from laying its eggs at the base of the stem. These brassica collars can be bought from garden centres. Alternatively, 15cm (6in) squares of old carpet work just as well.

PROTECTING BRASSICAS

Planting through porous membrane (here, a paper mulching sheet) will protect the plants from cabbage root fly.

NET BRASSICAS

Birds love to eat young brassicas as soon as they are planted out. In fact wood pigeons often seem to sit and watch me planting, ready to pounce as soon as my back is turned. There are many bird scarer products on the market, with varying degrees of effectiveness. Whichever you use, the birds sooner or later come to realise that it poses no actual danger. The only foolproof way of stopping birds eating the plants is to grow them under cover.

Support netting or fine-weave mesh sheeting on stakes with strong twine or wire strung between them, so it is held above the plants like a tent. Always make sure netting is well anchored at ground level so that small garden birds do not get tangled in it. It's not a very pleasant job trying to untangle a bird from netting.

Alternatively, individual collars can be bought or made and fitted around the stem of each plant.

Use cane supports to hold brassica netting off the surface of plants, or the birds will peck through it.

PINCH OUT BROAD BEAN TIPS

Pinching out the tops of broad beans when they flower discourages blackfly, which love the young, succulent tips of the plants. By removing them when several trusses of flowers have developed, there should be less need to spray to control these aphids. Provide support for broad beans with string stretched between canes at either end of the row. The plants tend to flop over when the pods develop.

By removing the tender tip when you pinch out broad beans, you take away the part blackfly like best.

PROTECT CARROTS

Carrots are at risk from carrot fly: the female flies around just above soil level seeking out juicy carrots by their smell, and lays her eggs at the base of the foliage. The larvae of the fly burrow into the carrot root making holes in it, causing rot to set in. This makes the carrots unappealing to eat and certainly useless for storing over winter.

This pest also attacks parsnips and parsley. You can protect all of them by covering with horticultural fleece, leaving it over the crop for the next generation of carrot fly in August. Alternatively, erect a barrier made from horticultural fleece, fine mesh, or polythene supported on a wooden framework, which prevents the carrot fly from getting to the crops.

To minimise the threat of carrot fly, sow seeds thinly to reduce the need for seedling thinning. Don't leave thinnings lying around, as the smell of bruised leaves will attract carrot fly in the area. You could also grow alternate rows of onions

Fence in carrots with fine mesh around canes to keep carrot fly at bay.

and carrots, the theory being that the strong pungent aroma from the onions masks the carrot smell, confusing the carrot fly. Note that certain varieties of carrots ('Flyaway' and 'Sytan') are less susceptible to attack from carrot fly.

HOE REGULARLY

This job is worth doing regularly to keep weeds in check, as there is a lot of back-breaking work later if they are left to grow. Catch weed seedlings when they are small, and they can be left on the soil surface to dry out on a warm sunny day. Not only are weeds kept under control by hoeing, but a tilth of crumbly soil is maintained on the surface of the soil. This helps to retain some moisture in the soil, reducing the need for watering.

MULCH FRUIT

Use well-rotted farmyard manure, garden compost, spent mushroom compost, or any other organic matter you can get hold of for mulching. If the soil is dry, make sure it is watered well before applying a mulch, as mulches are just as good at keeping moisture out of the soil as keeping it in. If you have the luxury of a sprinkler, leave it on one area at a time for at least two hours to give the area a good soaking, and then mulch. Rather than watering lightly over a large area, concentrate on watering small areas really well in turn, otherwise the water is just wasted. Be sure to check there are no hose restrictions in your area before using a sprinkler.

PRUNE RASPBERRIES

Unwanted shoots on raspberry canes should now be pruned; if too many new canes are allowed to develop, then the plants' energy will be channelled into developing these new canes rather than into fruit production. Thick, crowded rows are much more difficult to access and to care for, and the fruits will receive less sunshine to ripen them.

Another important point to remember is that the more congested the shoots are, the less air will be circulating through the plants, which in turn will make them more susceptible to fungal diseases. For example, grey mould (botrytis) could attack the fruits, causing them to turn brown and rot off. The more air that can circulate around the plants, the less likelihood there is of them being attacked by disease. The added bonus is that the canes that remain will also be all the more sturdy, because they have sufficient light and room to develop.

REMOVE RUNNERS FROM STRAWBERRIES

If runners are allowed to develop, most of the plant's energy goes into producing them. The crop of fruit will be poorer, and the strawberry bed will end up as a mass of tangled plants which will be difficult to weed. Putting straw or mats down to prevent the fruits being splashed with soil will also be next to impossible. If you want to maintain a few runners for new plants, pick off the flowers to

PROTECTING STRAWBERRIES

Tuck straw under strawberries and the fruits will not be damaged by splashes of mud or slugs.

sacrifice the crop so that you get really strong young plantlets.

TUCK STRAW UNDER STRAWBERRIES

Straw will protect the fruits from rotting as they rest on wet ground. It also prevents the fruits being spoiled by rain-splashed soil and slugs. However, there are few things more annoying to town gardeners than being told to use materials such as straw that are common enough in the country, but almost impossible to obtain in the city. But don't despair: the majority of garden centres stock special strawberry mats as an alternative to straw.

As the fruits develop, cover the plants with netting to stop the birds from getting them. Ensure the netting is properly secured to prevent birds getting tangled up in it. If you are concerned about birds being caught in netting, use horticultural fleece to cover the plants instead.

Strawberry mats are an alternative to straw. They will be stocked by any garden centre selling fruit plants.

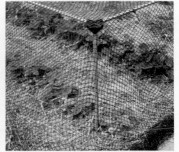

Netting will keep birds off strawberries, but make sure you check it every day to ensure that birds are not caught up in it.

MAY PROJECT

A HARDY ANNUAL BORDER

Hardy annuals are among the easiest of all plants to look after; they show quick results and flower for weeks. Most annuals need no special treatment. In fact, the poorer the soil, the more flowers you usually get. Either sow seed directly outside now that the soil has warmed up, or transplant any seedlings raised in pots. Many hardy annuals will seed themselves around the garden, giving you extra plants free.

All annuals prefer to be grown in full sun. Generally, you will get the best effects by putting taller plants at the back of the border with shorter ones at the front. However, slight variations here and there, with taller, more open plants nearer the front or middle of the border, help to make a display more interesting.

Eschscholzia californica (mixed)
This is a low-growing annual for the front of the border. The bright orange, yellow, and white flowers are very attractive against the ferny foliage.

Limnanthes douglasii 'Scrambled Eggs'
Another low-growing plant, this variety of what is commonly called the poached egg plant is fantastic for attracting bees. It self-seeds freely.

Nigella damascena 'Allsorts'
Mixed pastel colours add charm to this variety of the old cottage garden favourite love-in-a-mist. Both flowers and seed heads are good for cutting.

Tropaeolum majus Alaska Series
The highly popular nasturtium has fairly large seeds that are easy for children to handle. This variety bears red, orange, or yellow flowers and cream-speckled leaves.

BERBERIS [1]

***Berberis thunbergii* 'Helmond Pillar'**
This striking *Berberis* has a narrow
upright habit and dark red-purple
foliage, which intensifies to a bright
red in autumn. Small red-tinged pale
yellow flowers are produced in mid-
spring followed by tiny scarlet berries
in autumn.
↕ 1.5m (5ft) ↔ 60cm (24in).

CULTIVATION Grow in any good, fertile
soil in full sun. The foliage colour will be
less intense in shade. After flowering, cut
out any misshapen shoots.

ORIENTAL POPPY [2]

***Papaver orientale* 'Cedric Morris'** ♀
A showy herbaceous perennial. From
late spring to midsummer, it bears bowl-
shaped, satiny, soft pink flowers with
frilled petals, each with a black basal
mark. The bristly, jagged leaves die back
soon after flowering.
↕ 45–90cm (18–36in) ↔ to 90cm (36in)

CULTIVATION Grow in full sun, in deep,
fertile, well-drained soil. Cut back hard
after flowering, to produce fresh foliage
and a few later flowers.

CLEMATIS 3

Clematis montana **var.** *grandiflora* ♀
A rampant, deciduous climber for quick
cover. Single white flowers with cream
anthers are produced for about four
weeks in late spring and early summer.
Attractive foliage all summer.
↕10m (30ft) ↔4m (12ft)

CULTIVATION Grow in sun or part-shade
in fertile, well-drained soil, enriched with
organic matter. Site with the roots in
shade. After flowering, remove dead shoots
and prune to confine to allotted space.

GLOBEFLOWER 〔1〕

Trollius x cultorum **'Earliest of All'**
A moderately robust, clump-forming
herbaceous perennial. The bowl-shaped,
shining, clear yellow flowers arise
on strong stems from mid-spring to
midsummer. It has basal mounds of
lobed, toothed, glossy green leaves.
‡50cm (20in) ↔ 40cm (16in)

CULTIVATION Best in full sun, but
tolerant of part-shade. Grow in reliably
moist, deep, fertile soil. Lift and divide
the plants every three or four years to
rejuvenate them.

CORYDALIS 〔2〕

Corydalis flexuosa ♥ A slowly
spreading, herbaceous perennial with
delicate, fern-like, bluish-green leaves.
From late spring to summer, it produces
dense clusters of slender-tubed, brilliant
blue flowers with white throats. Dies
back after flowering.
‡30cm (12in) ↔ 20cm (8in) or more

CULTIVATION Grow in a cool site in
part- or dappled shade, in a humus-rich,
fertile, moist but well-drained soil.

EXOCHORDA [3]

***Exochorda* × *macrantha* 'The Bride'** ♡
A vigorous, mound-forming, deciduous
shrub. In late spring and early summer,
the arching stems are wreathed in white
flowers. It has attractive, light green leaves
from spring to autumn.
‡2m (6ft) ↔ 3m (10ft)

CULTIVATION Grow in full sun or
part-shade, in any fertile, well-drained
soil. Will tolerate shallow, chalky soils.
Shorten flowered shoots to strong buds
after flowering.

2

3

BRIDAL WREATH [1]

Spiraea **'Arguta'** ♀ An elegant, deciduous shrub with arching branches. In spring, clusters of tiny, bright white flowers wreathe the branches. It has attractive leaves of fresh, bright green.
‡ 2.5m (8ft) ↔ 2.5m (8ft)

CULTIVATION Best in full sun, but tolerates light, part-day shade. Grow in any fertile, moist but well-drained soil. After flowering cut back the flowered shoots to strong buds. Every three or four years, cut out one in three of the oldest flowered stems to the base to encourage strong, new growth.

AQUILEGIA [2]

Aquilegia **McKana Group** Generally robust, upright perennials; this group tend to be short-lived. From late spring to midsummer they produce flowers in varying shades of pink, yellow and white. A typical cottage garden plant, they will freely seed themselves around the garden, but the resulting seedlings will be a mixed bunch.
‡ 75cm (30in) ↔ 60cm (24in)

CULTIVATION Grow in fertile, moist but well-drained soil in sun or part-shade. Sow seeds in a container in a cold frame as soon as they are ripe.

JAPANESE WISTERIA ☐3

Wisteria floribunda '**Multijuga**' ♥
An extremely vigorous, deciduous
twining climber. In early summer, it
bears hanging chains of fragrant, pea-like,
lilac-blue flowers. Attractive, fresh green
leaves from spring to autumn.
‡9m (28ft) or more ↔ 9m (28ft)

CULTIVATION Grow in sun in any
fertile, well-drained soil. Avoid east-facing
walls. Train main stems on to supporting
wires. Prune back new growth in summer
and in late winter to control spread.

2

3

HAWTHORN 1

Crataegus laevigata **'Rosea Flore Pleno'** ♀ A very hardy, deciduous tree with a rounded crown. Clusters of double pink flowers appear in late spring. Red fruits (haws) are produced in autumn.
‡ to 8m (25ft) ↔ to 8m (25ft)

CULTIVATION Tolerates sun and part-shade and a wide variety of soils. Needs minimal pruning in winter, to maintain the shape and to cut out dead or damaged wood.

BIRD CHERRY 2

Prunus padus **'Watereri'** ♀ A vigorous, deciduous tree with a spreading crown. In late spring, it bears long, slender spires of many small, fragrant white flowers. The dark green leaves turn red and yellow in autumn. In mid to late summer, it bears small, black cherries that attract birds into the garden.
‡ 15m (50ft) ↔ 10m (30ft)

CULTIVATION Grow in any moist, but well-drained soil. Needs minimal pruning; remove badly placed or crossing branches in winter, or in midsummer if silver leaf disease is a problem in your area.

2

EUPHORBIA

3

Euphorbia × *martini* ♀ A bushy,
herbaceous perennial. From spring to
midsummer, it bears heads of yellow-
green flowers with dark red nectar glands.
The red stems and narrow green leaves
are often purple-tinged when young.
‡1m (3ft) ↔ 1m (3ft)

CULTIVATION Best in full sun, but
tolerant of dappled shade. Grow in a
light, well-drained soil enriched with
organic matter. On clay soils, dig in some
grit to improve drainage.

3

VIRIDIFLORA TULIP | 1 |

Tulipa **'Spring Green'** ♀ A fairly vigorous, bulbous perennial. In late spring, it produces very elegant, green-feathered, ivory-white flowers.
‡40cm (16in) ↔ 8cm (3in)

CULTIVATION Grow in full sun, in any reasonably fertile, well-drained soil. Add coarse grit to heavy clay soils. Plant bulbs 10–15cm (4–6in) deep in late autumn. Lift bulbs once the leaves fade, and ripen in a cool greenhouse.

LABURNUM | 2 |

Laburnum × *watereri* **'Vossii'** ♀ A small to medium deciduous tree with a spreading crown. In late spring and early summer, it produces long, hanging chains of golden yellow flowers. It has lustrous, dark green leaves from spring to autumn.
‡8m (25ft) ↔ 8m (25ft)

CULTIVATION Grow in full sun in any moderately fertile soil. Prune in late winter to remove dead and damaged wood and badly placed shoots.

ALLIUM 3

Allium **'Purple Sensation'** ♀

A bulbous perennial with long strap-shaped, grey-green leaves. In early summer it produces large, spherical umbels of star-shaped, deep violet flowers. Remove faded flowerheads before they set seed to prevent colonization of paler seedlings.
‡80cm (32in) ↔ 7cm (3in)

CULTIVATION Grow in fertile, well-drained soil in full sun; plant bulbs 5–10cm (2–4in) deep in autumn. Bulbs may aggravate some skin allergies.

2

3

BLUEBELL 1

Hyacinthoides non-scripta A vigorous, clump-forming perennial bulb. In spring, sturdy stems bear nodding, sweetly scented, violet-blue flowers amid glossy, dark green strap-shaped leaves. Dies back in summer.

‡20–40cm (8–16in) ↔ 8cm (3in)

CULTIVATION Grow in dappled shade, in any fertile soil that does not dry out in summer. Plant the bulbs 8cm (3in) deep in autumn. May self-seed to form extensive colonies.

DRUMSTICK PRIMULA 2

Primula denticulata **var.** *alba* A rosette-forming herbaceous perennial. In mid-spring and early summer, stout stems bear dense, spherical clusters of white, yellow-eyed flowers. It has handsome rosettes of mid-green leaves that are white-mealy beneath.

‡45cm (18in) ↔ 45cm (18in)

CULTIVATION Grow in sun or dappled shade in moist, fertile soil. Divide every three to four years in autumn or spring.

PERENNIAL FOXGLOVE 3

Digitalis* x *mertonensis ♀ An upright
herbaceous perennial. Tall spires of
tubular, pinkish-buff flowers rise above
the foliage in spring and early summer,
and these they attract bees. Mounds of
crinkled, deeply veined, dark green leaves.
↕90cm (36in) ↔30cm (12in)

CULTIVATION Prefers part-shade and
humus-rich soils, but tolerates most
aspects and soils if not too wet or dry.
Deadhead after flowering; it self-seeds
but seedlings are variable.

2

3

I

CAMASSIA \[1\]

Camassia leichtlinii An upright, bulbous perennial. In late spring, it bears spires of star-shaped, creamy white flowers. The grass-like leaves are ornamentally insignificant.
‡60–130cm (24–54in) ↔ 10cm (4in)

CULTIVATION Plant bulbs 10cm (4in) deep in autumn. Flowers best in full sun but tolerates light shade. Grow in deep, fertile, moisture-retentive soil. Mulch in winter in cold, frosty areas.

MEXICAN ORANGE BLOSSOM \[2\]

Choisya 'Aztec Pearl' ♀ A robust, bushy, evergreen shrub. In both late spring and late summer, it bears clusters of pink-tinted, sweet-scented, white flowers, and sometimes a few in autumn. Beautiful, aromatic leaves, divided into narrow, glossy, dark green leaflets.
‡2.5m (8ft) ↔ 2.5m (8ft)

CULTIVATION It flowers best in sun but will tolerate part-shade. Grow in any good garden soil. Trim after flowering in spring to improve the second flowering.

CLEMATIS 3

Clematis **'Markham's Pink'** ♀
A vigorous, deciduous climber. From
spring to early summer, it bears soft,
sugar-pink flowers. Pale green foliage
and silver seedheads in summer.
‡2–3m (6–10ft) ↔ 1.5m (5ft)

CULTIVATION Grow in sun or dappled
shade in fertile, well-drained soil, enriched
with organic matter. Site with the roots
in shade. After flowering, remove dead
or damaged shoots and shorten others
to confine to allotted space.

2

3

SYRINGA VULGARIS

Vigorous, deciduous shrubs or small trees. In late spring and early summer, they bear dense, conical clusters of intensely fragrant flowers. They have heart-shaped, dark green leaves from spring to late autumn. Ideal planted in a shrub border, or as specimens.
‡7m (22ft) ↔7m (22ft)

CULTIVATION Grow in any fertile, neutral to alkaline soil. Deadhead young plants, cutting back to strong buds lower down on the shrub. If necessary, prune to shape after flowering. Older shrubs can be cut back hard to renovate in winter.

TOP ROW LEFT TO RIGHT
- *S. vulgaris* 'Charles Joly' ♀
- *S. vulgaris* 'Primrose'
- *S. vulgaris* 'Président Grévy'

BOTTOM ROW LEFT TO RIGHT
- *S. vulgaris* 'Madame Lemoine' ♀
- *S. vulgaris* 'Charles X'
- *S. vulgaris* 'Katherine Havemeyer' ♀

RHODODENDRON

Rhododendrons and azaleas range from tiny, deciduous, alpine shrubs to huge, evergreen, tree-like species. Most bear spectacular flowers between early spring and early summer, but there are winter- and late summer-flowering sorts too. The best way to discover the ones you like is to visit gardens with good, clearly labelled collections.

CULTIVATION All must have an acid (lime-free), moist but well-drained, leafy, humus-rich soil. Grow in light shade with shelter from cold, dry winds. Plant with the top of the root ball no deeper than it was in the pot. Keep pruning to a minimum; shorten any overlong shoots that spoil the shape after flowering. Deadhead regularly.

TOP ROW LEFT TO RIGHT
- *R.* 'Strawberry Ice' ♀
  ‡2m (6ft) ↔ 2m (6ft)
- *R.* 'Golden Torch' ♀
  ‡1.5m (5ft) ↔ 1.5m (5ft)
- *R.* 'Beauty of Littleworth'
  ‡4m (12ft) ↔ 4m (12ft)

BOTTOM ROW LEFT TO RIGHT
- *R.* 'Freya'
  ‡1.5m (5ft) ↔ 1.5m (5ft)
- *R.* 'Narcissiflorum' ♀
  ‡1.5–2.5m (5–8ft) ↔ to 2.5m (8ft)
- *R. cinnabarinum* subsp. *xanthocodon*
  ‡6m (20ft) ↔ 2m (6ft)

WHAT TO DO IN JUNE

WEATHER WATCH

Summer is really here. There is still plenty to keep you occupied, such as cutting back and mowing, but this is a time of year when you can really begin to enjoy the fruits of your labours. So above all else, find time to sit and savour the delights of your garden.

HOT SPELLS

At last we can look forward to blissfully warm, sunny days: very warm at times, with temperatures reaching 20–22°C (68–72°F) in places. In northern areas, average temperatures will be slightly cooler, but still a respectable 16–18°C (61–64°F). Don't let young plants suffer through lack of water during any hot spells. Getting them well established in their first year is the most important consideration.

WINDS HIGHER UP

June is usually calm, with the exception of the south-western approaches, other coastal areas, and north-western coasts. As the height above sea level increases, so does the strength of the winds; this is often why wind farms, with their huge windmills, are seen on high ground and near coasts.

SUNNY DAYS

Thankfully, there are usually more sunny days than dull, overcast ones this month. Northern parts of the country get less sunshine, with the Highlands of Scotland averaging 157 hours this month and the Home Counties around 204 hours. The north-west of England usually gets around 180 hours, and East Anglia about 190 hours of direct sunshine.

VARYING RAINFALL

This is usually one of the driest months. There are occasional thunderstorms, but they tend to pass quickly and do little to replenish water in the soil. But the weather does vary from year to year, and sometimes June can be quite wet in northern and north-western parts. Average rainfall for the month falls sharply – from 114mm (4½in) in north-west Scotland down to 50mm (2in) in the north of England and 47mm (1¾in) in the south-east. On average it will rain on one day in every three in England, so you can never be guaranteed several dry days in succession.

SUDDEN SNOW FALLS

Although it has been known for freak weather conditions to produce a sudden fall of snow in June, this is an extremely rare occurrence. Certainly no snow will lie on the ground anywhere except on the very highest peaks in the Highlands of Scotland.

AROUND THE GARDEN

KEEP WATERING PLANTS

Watering needs to be done thoroughly during hot spells, concentrating on everything in the garden that needs it most: newly planted plants, young vegetables, and plants in containers. If there's a lot to do, it is no good going out every night and splashing a little water everywhere. In drought periods, divide the garden into areas, and every evening give a different one a good soaking – this should last for up to a week. This is more beneficial to the plants, because the roots will go deeper into the soil in search of water. Smaller amounts of water encourage the roots to come to the surface of the soil, causing more harm in the long run; roots near the surface make the plants even more vulnerable in dry conditions.

APPLY AND RENEW MULCHES

Mulching is good for the soil at any time of year, but is especially beneficial in warmer weather as it reduces water loss and suppresses weeds. More time enjoying your garden, and less spent watering

Chipped bark is one of a variety of ornamental mulches that can be used to minimise water loss from the soil.

and weeding, has got to be good news during summer. It's very important to make sure the soil is moist before putting down a mulch. Mulches keep out water as well as keeping it in: if the soil is dry, the mulch will simply reduce water infiltration. Don't forget that you can also "mulch" newly planted containers; there is a wide range of decorative chippings now on offer that will complement stone, terracotta, and glazed pots.

FILL GAPS IN BORDERS

It's best to fill gaps with summer bedding plants this month, then you can put in more permanent plants in the autumn. These gap-fillers will give instant colour to what may have been a bare patch of earth. If you need height among medium-sized plants, you can even drop in a whole pot or tub full of summer display plants

(but remember that it will need extra watering). Looking ahead, hardy annuals sown now will flower in late summer and autumn, extending the flowering display in the borders.

The vibrant flowers of pot marigolds (Calendula) are ideal gap-fillers, although there are many other annuals to choose from.

MOW AND TEND TO LAWNS REGULARLY

By this time of year the lawn should be cut at least once a week, and preferably twice a week if possible: the less grass taken off at each cut, the healthier the grass will remain. Mow in a different direction each time, because if you mow in the same direction on several occasions, the grass begins to grow in that direction and the mower blades, especially those on a cylinder mower, will not cut it

A neat, trimmed edge sets off both the lawn and the beds and borders around it.

If you find earthworms are bringing casts to the surface, simply brush the casts into the lawn or borders, as they are rich in nutrients.

as well. By this time the mower blades should be at the lowest setting required; for most lawns, about 1.25cm (½in), or a little higher for a lawn that takes a lot of use. If there are dry spells when the grass goes a bit brown, reduce the frequency of mowing and raise the blades a little so as not to cut it too close.

Now that grass is generating lots of clippings, don't dump them in a mass on the compost heap or they will clump together and rot down into a slimy mess, rather than good compost. This is because they are too close-textured to admit air. Keep the clippings separate until you have some looser material to mix with them. Torn and crumpled newspaper will do if the garden is not generating much suitable debris at the moment.

You could also trim the lawn edges at the same time as the grass is cut. It makes all the difference to the appearance of the garden if the edges are cut regularly. And it's less work doing the edges once a week as the trimmings are few and don't need to be cleared up.

FEED LAWNS

Use a liquid fertiliser: these fast-acting feeds are the perfect thing to give a tired-looking lawn a quick tonic. Diluted in water, following the instructions on the bottle, they are easily applied with a watering can or sprayer. One advantage these have over dry fertilisers is they don't have to be watered in should the weather remain dry.

REMOVE ANNUAL WEEDS

Hoe or hand-pull annual weeds while they are still small, as this will save a lot of work during the rest of the summer. If you choose a dry day, you can simply leave the weeds on the surface of the soil where they will wither in the sun. Any perennial weeds will have to be dug out completely, leaving no trace of the roots in the soil. If even a small piece of the root is left, it could start to grow again, effectively propagating the weed.

Weeds compete with other plants for light, nutrients, and water, so hoeing weeds off regularly will benefit ornamental plants.

Overgrown ponds must be thinned to keep them healthy. Comb a rake over the surface to remove floating weeds.

THIN OUT AQUATIC PLANTS

Put aside some time to deal with any excessive growth of aquatic plants, and generally to tidy up the pond before summer. The early part of the month is a good time to do this, as this is when the plants really start into growth. Aquatic plants that have been in place for three or four years and are rather overgrown can be lifted out and divided now if you have not already done so.

Don't worry if the the water becomes a bit murky while you're carrying out this work – it will soon settle after a few days and become clear again. If decaying leaves of water plants are left in a pond, they can stimulate the growth of algae and weeds, so try to remove as many of them as possible. Thinning overgrown plants and weeds not only benefits pond life, it makes the pond look better.

CONTINUE PLANTING AQUATIC PLANTS

Even in cold areas, tender floating plants like the water hyacinth (*Eichhornia crassipes*) can be put in the pond now that the threat of frost has passed. It's also a good time to throw in extra new floating plants for the pond if you notice that they seem a little sparse this year. They will establish quickly with the warmer weather.

Still water with little oxygen promotes algae growth; install a fountain to churn up the water and increase oxygen levels in the pond.

TREES, SHRUBS & CLIMBERS

Once deutzia (bottom left) and kolkwitzia (bottom right) have finished flowering, they can be pruned. They will benefit from having the old main stems cut low down (above).

PRUNE MATURE, DECIDUOUS SHRUBS

Once the flowers on shrubs such as deutzia, kolkwitzia, philadelphus, and weigela go over, remove any dead or damaged growth, cutting to a stem joint or leaf. Then take a worm's eye view through the thicket of stems at the base of the plant, and cut out one in three low down, selecting the oldest and thickest for removal.

Larger stems can be cut with loppers, while really tough old wood will need a pruning saw. Be careful as you pull the whole stem away through the plant, to avoid too much damage; prune away any damage that does occur. After this, feed with a general organic fertiliser and mulch with organic matter. The new growth produced over summer will flower next year.

REMOVE FADING FLOWERS

By removing the fading blooms from rhododendrons, camellias, and lilacs, the plant's energy is diverted from producing seeds to building up buds for next year's flowers. Be careful when removing the spent flowers from rhododendrons and camellias, as new shoots develop immediately below the old flowerheads. With lilacs, cut back the flowered stem to just above a pair of leaves or buds, or even small shoots, lower down the stem, in a similar way to the method used to deadhead roses.

DEADHEADING RHODODENDRONS

Remove the faded flowers very carefully between finger and thumb.

With the flower removed, you will be able to see why care is needed: new leaf buds lie just behind it.

CUT DOWN OVERGROWN LILACS

If lilacs have become overgrown and leggy, this is the time for drastic action: after you have enjoyed the flowers, but early enough to let the shrub make new growth over the summer. Saw them right down to about 45cm (18in) from the base. A mass of new shoots will regrow, from which you should thin any growing inwards across the centre of the plant. If you're lucky, you may get some flowers next year, but you may have to wait. The result, though, will be a bushier, better-shaped shrub.

After renovating a lilac shrub, new shoots will grow. Selectively thin these out to make a few good branches.

TRAIN CLIMBING AND RAMBLING ROSES

These roses produce such a lot of growth at such a rate that if you don't tie them in on a regular basis, they end up in a complete mess – trailing over other plants, catching your clothing as you go by, and generally getting in the way when you're pottering around the garden. Whenever possible, tie in the stems as close to the horizontal as possible to restrict the flow of sap.

REMOVE SUCKERS FROM ROSES

Most of the modern bush roses you'll come across are grafted, or budded, onto a rootstock which gives the plant the vigour it needs to produce all those beautiful blooms. (In addition, growers can produce a saleable, well-shaped plant much more quickly when roses are budded.)

One slight drawback with budded roses is that every so often the rootstock throws out the odd shoot, identifiable because the foliage is usually lighter in colour. It is better if these suckers are pulled off the plant at their point of origin on the roots rather than cut off. If cut off, the sucker is more likely to grow again. If it is pulled off, part of the root is damaged and it is subsequently less likely to regrow.

If your roses have a heavy infestation of aphids, use an insecticide sold for this purpose. Spray first thing in the morning or, preferably, late into the evening when there are fewer beneficial insects around. Some products available are combined treatments for common rose problems, such as black spot, aphids, and powdery mildew.

REMOVING SUCKERS FROM BUSH ROSES

1 Use a trowel to scrape away the soil and expose the top of the rootstock. The sucker should emerge from below the bud union.

2 Using protective gloves, pull the sucker away from the rootstock. Then refill the hole with soil, and firm gently.

FLOWERING PLANTS

CUT BACK ORIENTAL POPPIES

Once these finish flowering, the plants tend to look a mess. It's one good reason for siting them in the middle or near the back of a border, so that when the flowers are finished other plants will hide them. To make them look better, cut the foliage to near ground level. It may seem a bit drastic, but it has to be done. Once cut back, sprinkle a little organic fertiliser around the plants and water them in thoroughly. This will encourage new growth to appear and, if you are lucky, a few more flowers later in the summer.

TIDY HELLEBORES

You'll probably find you now have to remove old leaves and flower stems from hellebores. The old foliage has a tendency to look very tatty, and is often infected with blackspot and other diseases.

Remove the leaves at ground level and discard them. The new young foliage can often be seen growing from the centre of the plant. A feed with a general fertiliser and a mulch with organic matter will also do no harm at all.

When collecting hellebore seeds, wear gloves to collect the ripe capsules, as they might irritate your skin.

DEADHEAD FLOWERS REGULARLY

Deadheading is a task that should be carried out regularly in the garden as some of the flowers go over. With many plants — perennials, repeat-flowering roses, and hardy and half-hardy annuals — the flowering period can be extended considerably if old flowers are removed as soon as they fade. This will prevent the plants' energy going into the production of seeds, and will channel it instead into new growth and flowers later in the summer and autumn.

This phlox is among many plants that will produce more flowers if deadheaded, keeping your garden in bloom for longer.

Most deadheading can be done with secateurs, cutting back to just above strong buds lower down the stems of the plant. Some plants, such as hardy geraniums, can be quickly trimmed back hard with a pair of garden shears when the flowers fade. It may seem rather drastic action, but new foliage soon appears.

Euphorbia robbiae and *E. characias* are two plants that will look a lot tidier if the old flowerheads are removed as soon as they start going over. Make sure you wear gloves when you are pruning euphorbias, as the milky-white sap can irritate sensitive skin. Remove all of the old growth to ground level. This will encourage new growth from the base of the plant, keeping it bushy and healthy.

Deadheading lupins and delphiniums, too, as their flowers fade increases the chance of further blooms appearing later in the summer. Although they will not be as spectacular as the first flush, they are no less welcome. Cut the faded flower spikes off at ground level or back to strong new shoots.

CONTINUE STAKING TALL PERENNIALS

Nothing looks more unsightly than plants that have been battered about by rain and wind lying all over other, smaller plants in the borders. Try to stake before this happens. The earlier it is done the better, but even this month it is not too late to continue doing this task. There are many ways of supporting plants, and a whole host of products available from garden centres. The type you use will largely depend on the depth of your pockets. Bamboo canes and string are cheap, but have to be used carefully if they are not to look too rigid and prominent in the border, and you must fit eye protectors on top of the canes. Twiggy sticks are another easy means of support. The advantage of these is that the plants can grow through and hide them.

TIDY BULBS

This month, you should cut down the foliage of bulbs naturalized in grass. By now, at least six weeks should have elapsed since

Wait until at least six weeks after bulbs in grass have finished flowering before shearing off the leaves.

flowering, so the bulb foliage and the grass can be trimmed. If you cut the leaves down too soon, the bulbs will be "blind" next year. Don't be too concerned about the grass turning yellow after it has been cut where the bulbs are planted. It will soon recover with a good watering and a feed.

Bulbs that have finished flowering can be lifted, dried, and stored when the foliage has died down, but if you tend to leave yours *in situ* year after year, lift overcrowded clumps now and divide them so that they can spend the summer re-establishing.

PLANT OUT CANNAS AND LILY BULBS

Cannas started into growth in March, and lily bulbs potted up when the weather was too cold outside to plant, can now be planted out in the borders. Alternatively, simply put the whole pot in a gap in the border, either sinking it into the ground or, if the surrounding plants are tall enough to hide it,

Planted out now, cannas, such as 'Pretoria' (above), will produce bright flowers until early autumn.

just setting it on the soil surface. Left in pots, they will need extra watering, so be vigilant.

Soak and plant corms now to be rewarded by beautiful autumnal flowers, such as this Anemone coronaria *'Lord Lieutenant'.*

PLANT AUTUMN-FLOWERING ANEMONES

Anemones generally flower about three months after planting, so timing the flowering can be quite accurate. By planting some now, the tubers will give a delightful show of flowers as other plants are beginning to go over. Plant some in pots at the same time to enjoy these wonderful flowers on the windowsill. The ones to look for are *Anemone coronaria* and the de Caen types, which produce flowers up to 8cm (3in) across in glowing colours. When planting late like this, it is best to soak the tubers overnight to get them off to a good start. Plant them 5cm (2in) deep and 8–10cm (3–4in) apart. Incorporate plenty of organic matter, and the plants will repay you with a glorious display.

PLANT OUT SUMMER BEDDING

By this time of year you can plant out all bedding plants, including tender kinds like begonias, without fear of frost damage. If you have not grown your own, buy some: look out for bidens, felicia, and brachyscome as well as old favourites such as pelargoniums, salvias, and lobelia. Remove any old spring bedding, and lightly fork over the soil.

Don't spread too much fertiliser before planting, or the plants will produce lots of lush growth at the expense of flowers. Water plants well an hour or so before planting them out. This is very important

where young plants are growing in a seed tray and the roots will be disturbed when planted out. Don't forget to give them all a thorough watering after planting too.

Following this, plants must be watered at regular intervals for a few weeks and during dry spells. You can do this and conserve water by using a seephose: a permeable rubber hose which allows water to seep through its walls along its entire length. Water is concentrated at the plants' roots, instead of being sprayed through the air as with a sprinkler, where it can drift in windy conditions. The seephose can be buried slightly under the soil surface, or just snaked between the plants. It will soon be hidden when the plants grow together. If you do have to water with a sprinkler, do so very early or late in the day, or plants will be scorched in the sun.

Many bedding plants will be available from garden centres: try Felicia amelloides *(top left) or* Brachyscome iberidifolia *(left).*

PLANT HANGING BASKETS

Hanging baskets are an effective and attractive way to show off bedding plants, and they are very easy to plant up. There are many types of liner available from garden centres, and you can use almost any one of them. However, don't use sphagnum moss, as its collection can endanger rare wildlife habitats. Put together a light, free-draining compost mixture by adding some slow-release fertiliser to peat-free compost and perlite.

Place a disk of polythene at the bottom of the basket to help retain moisture. Use taller plants in the centre to give height to the display and tuck in plenty of trailing plants around them. When the plants grow, the basket will be completely hidden, and you will have a mass of flowers all summer long. Remember that hanging baskets are prone to drying out in their exposed position, so water them frequently.

CREATING A HANGING BASKET

1 Sit the basket on a large pot or bucket, line it, and fill with a 5–8cm (2–3in) layer of the compost mixture.

4 Once plants have been added around the sides, add more compost mixture and firm it well around the rootballs.

2 To make planting through the sides easier, roll up the top growth of the plants in strips of plastic, using sticky tape to secure it.

3 Cut crosses in the liner, and ease the plastic tubes through these from within the basket. Then unwrap the plants carefully.

5 Add trailing plants around the sides of the basket to spill over the edges – here, fuchsias and ivy-leaved pelargoniums.

6 Add more compost, and plant up the centre of the basket. Give the basket a good soak, and top up compost in any sunken areas.

KITCHEN GARDEN

HARVEST CROPS

Early peas will be ready to pick now. Cut down the top growth of the plants (known as the "haulm") after harvesting, but leave the roots of the peas in the soil, as these will return valuable nitrogen to it. Nodules on the roots of peas and beans are able to fix and store atmospheric nitrogen in the soil. Follow peas with a leafy crop, such as cabbages, which requires a higher nitrogen content in the soil. By practising good crop rotation in this way, you can reduce the amount of artificial fertiliser you put on the soil.

KEEP SOWING SALAD VEGETABLES

If you sow these in small quantities at regular intervals of two or three weeks, you will be rewarded by a continuous supply of fresh salad stuff over a long period, rather than a glut at one time. Keep in mind that lettuce seed will not germinate at high temperatures, so if the weather is hot and dry, you'd be wise to sow the seeds in a shady part of the garden, or sow them in seed trays and put these somewhere where they will be shaded. Transplant the seedlings when they are large enough to handle.

PLANT OUT RUNNER BEANS

Now that the threat of frost has passed, these plants can go out into ground that was prepared during the winter. Put up whatever supports you require before planting, either making wigwams or parallel avenues of canes with 60cm (24in) between the rows. Slugs love young runner bean plants; the plants can be protected by surrounding them with a collar made from an old plastic drink bottle. To ensure runner bean flowers set and produce pods, spray the flowers with water regularly and make sure they don't dry out at the roots.

Dwarf runner beans can also go out now. They don't require much support, although it may be worth inserting a few twiggy sticks around the plants, as they do often flop over even though they are dwarf. This will also prevent the pods being splashed with soil when it rains. Dwarf and climbing French beans can be treated in exactly the same way as runner beans.

PLANT TOMATOES OUTSIDE

Tomatoes can be planted in the soil at intervals of 45cm (18in), or planted two or three to a growbag. Tomatoes prefer a sunny spot against a south-facing wall if possible. Cordon plants will need staking with 1.2m (4ft) canes. When planting tomatoes outside, leave a slight depression in the soil. This helps retain water around the roots of the plants when watering them

in. It can be difficult to push canes into growbags as there is insufficient compost to hold the canes upright, so there are frames you can buy from garden centres which hold canes for use in growbags. Feed all tomatoes with a high-potash fertiliser each week from now on.

SOW ORIENTAL VEGETABLES

These can be sown at regular intervals until August. Get quick results by sowing under cloches.

Pak choi, a Chinese leaf vegetable, can be picked fresh from the garden to create crunchy stir-fries.

This way, the chances are that some of them will germinate within two or three days.

These leafy vegetables are excellent for stir-frying, so you can make delicious meals fresh from the garden in a matter of minutes. Some oriental vegetables are prone to attack from flea beetle, so it may be worth growing them permanently under cloches or covered with horticultural fleece to stop the beetles getting at the plants.

Caterpillars can destroy leafy vegetables in a surprisingly short time. Remove them when you see them, and squash any eggs.

SOW TURNIPS

Sowing these now will produce a crop in autumn. Sow the seeds in rows 15cm (6in) apart. Thin the seedlings as soon as you can handle them without damaging the young plants. Thin them to leave one plant every 10cm (4in). The turnips are best harvested when they are young, before they get to the size of a tennis ball. You can leave some roots in for longer, as their leafy tops can be cooked for winter greens.

WATCH OUT FOR CATERPILLARS

Cabbage white butterfly caterpillars will be hatching out now. You can prevent a lot of damage being done by methodically inspecting the undersides of the leaves on all of your brassicas. You will usually come across small clusters of yellow eggs here. The eggs can be squashed, but if you can't face doing that use an insecticide containing pyrethrum or lambda-cyhalothrin. This will kill off any young caterpillars. Alternatively, cover the plants with fleece as a physical barrier to prevent the butterflies laying their eggs in the first place.

CONTROL BOTRYTIS ON STRAWBERRIES

Spells of wet weather encourage the spread of grey mould (botrytis) on strawberries. Inspect fruits regularly and remove any infected ones. It's very important that you don't compost these, as they may spread the disease to other plants in the garden. There are no fungicides currently available for grey mould on strawberries, but removing infected fruits early enough should keep the problem under control. Ensure plenty of air circulates around the plants and lift developing fruits off the soil by putting straw or mats under them.

Strawberries will be producing lots of runners now. Depending on your needs, you can either remove them by pinching them out near the parent plant, or peg them down to make new plants.

Peg down a few runners in pots to increase the number of plants you have. The straw prevents soil splash, which spreads mould.

WATER FRUIT REGULARLY

To ensure a good crop of quality fruits throughout the summer, keep all fruit well watered during dry spells. Mulching with organic matter will help to retain moisture and reduce the need for water. Mulching will also keep down weeds, which compete for water and nutrients in the soil; many weeds act as hosts to pests and diseases as well.

JUNE PROJECT

MAKE A BOX OF HERBS AND LEAVES

Growing your own food is one of the most rewarding aspects of gardening. The thrill of picking homegrown produce is hard to beat. Even if you don't have a garden, you can still keep your kitchen supplied with fresh leafy vegetables. There is a huge variety of fast-growing, low-maintenance herbs and lettuces that can be grown easily in containers. No special skills are needed to make the simple wooden box shown in this project. It looks attractive and takes up very little space. You can place the box on a window sill, attach it to a wall, or leave it on the ground if you have a balcony. Plant it up with your favourite leaves and watch for quick results.

1 *The box can be tailor-made to suit the space available, so measure and cut the timber to the lengths you require.*

2 *Use screws to attach the side timbers to the end pieces of wood. Two screws at each end should be enough.*

3 *Good drainage is essential for container-grown plants. Drill 1cm (½in) holes at 10cm (4in) intervals in the base.*

4 Attach a band of copper tape around the box to deter slugs and snails, taking care not to leave gaps. As well as protecting your plants, the copper strip looks attractive.

5 Fill the box with compost and plant a range of herbs and lettuces. Ensure that the leaves don't droop over the copper strip, as slugs and snails will climb up them. Water well after planting up.

VERONICA [1]

Veronica gentianoides ♀ A mat-forming herbaceous perennial. In early summer, it produces upright stems of shallowly cupped, pale blue flowers. It has attractive basal rosettes of slightly scalloped, glossy, dark green leaves.
‡45cm (18in) ↔ 45cm (18in)

CULTIVATION Best in full sun, but tolerates light, part-day shade. Grow in moderately fertile, well-drained soil. Plants begin to lose vigour after two or three years, so divide in autumn or spring to rejuvenate.

GEUM [2]

Geum **'Borisii'** A long-flowering herbaceous perennial. From late spring to late summer, it bears long-stemmed clusters of bright, brick-red flowers with a boss of golden yellow stamens. Basal mounds of divided, fresh green leaves.
‡30–50cm (12–20in) ↔ 30cm (12in)

CULTIVATION Grow in any fertile, well-drained soil in full sun or light, part-day shade. Lift and divide the plants every three or four years to rejuvenate.

1

ALCHEMILLA 3

Alchemilla mollis ♀ A spreading, clump-forming, herbaceous perennial. Bears loose clusters of tiny greenish-yellow flowers from early summer to autumn. The hairy, soft green leaves look especially good spangled with droplets of rain or dew.
↕60cm (24in) ↔75cm (30in)

CULTIVATION Thrives in sun or part-shade. Grow in any moist, humus rich soil. Deadhead after flowering, or it will seed itself all over the garden.

2

3

ASTILBE ☐1

Astilbe **'Bronce Elegans'** ♀ A fairly vigorous herbaceous perennial of upright growth. In late summer, it produces plumes of red-pink flowers. The red-stemmed, dark green leaves make good ground cover.
‡30cm (12in) ↔ 25cm (10in)

CULTIVATION Best grown in boggy soil in sun, but will tolerate slightly drier conditions in partial shade. Cut down old foliage in late autumn. Divide every three to four years.

JACOB'S LADDER ☐2

Polemonium carneum A bushy, clump-forming, herbaceous perennial. In early summer, it bears loose clusters of shallowly bell-shaped, pale pink, yellow, occasionally dark purple or lavender flowers. It has pretty divided leaves.
‡10–40cm (4–16in) ↔ 20cm (8in)

CULTIVATION Grow in full sun or light, dappled shade in any fertile, well-drained soil. Add grit to heavy clay soils to improve drainage. Deadhead regularly to encourage more flowers.

2

CATMINT 3

Nepeta × faassenii ♀ A vigorous,
spreading herbaceous perennial. From
early summer to early autumn, it bears
fragrant, pale lavender-blue flowers with
dark purple spots. Attracts bees, moths
and butterflies. It also has wrinkled, hairy,
aromatic grey-green leaves.
↕45cm (18in) ↔ 45cm (18in)

CULTIVATION Grow in any fertile,
well-drained soil. Trim hard after the first
flush of flowers to keep plants tidy and
encourage more flowers. Rejuvenate old
plants by dividing in spring or autumn.

3

MOUNT ETNA BROOM [1]

Genista aetnensis ♀ A vigorous deciduous shrub or small tree with upright, then weeping shoots. Fragrant, yellow, pea-like flowers are borne at the stem tips in mid- to late summer. The weeping shoots are bright green and give an evergreen appearance.
‡to 8m (25ft) ↔ to 8m (25ft)

CULTIVATION Grow in full sun in light, poor, very well-drained soil. After flowering, shorten flowered shoots to strong buds on green wood; don't cut into old wood.

ABELIA [2]

Abelia 'Edward Goucher' A semi-evergreen, sun-loving shrub with arching branches. It bears a mass of trumpet-shaped, lilac-pink flowers from summer to autumn. The glossy, dark green leaves are bronzed when young.
‡1.5m (5ft) ↔ 2.5m (8ft)

CULTIVATION Best in fertile, well-drained soil in full sun, but tolerates light, dappled shade. Protect from cold winds. Prune after flowering. Deadhead and shorten to a strong bud any shoots that spoil the outline.

CRAMBE

3

Crambe cordifolia ♡ A statuesque, clump-forming, herbaceous perennial. In early to midsummer, tall strong stems arise bearing clouds of honey-scented white flowers. Forms a mound of glossy, puckered, dark green leaves that die down in late summer.

‡ 2.5m (8ft) ↔ to 1.5m (5ft)

CULTIVATION Grow in deep, fertile soil in full sun, but will tolerate part-shade. Shelter from strong winds. Is best increased by root cuttings in winter.

WEIGELA [1]

Weigela **'Looymansii Aurea'** A slow-growing, arching, deciduous shrub. In late spring and early summer, it bears bell-shaped flowers that are pale pink with a darker pink reverse. It has golden-yellow leaves from spring to autumn.
↕ to 1.5m (5ft) ↔ to 1.5m (5ft)

CULTIVATION Grow in full sun or light, dappled shade in any fertile, well-drained soil. Shorten flowered shoots to strong buds after flowering. Every three or four years, take out about one in four of the oldest shoots at the base to encourage new growth.

SHRUBBY POTENTILLA [2]

Potentilla fruticosa Princess (**'Blink'**) A small, bushy, deciduous shrub. From late spring until mid-autumn, it produces saucer-shaped, pale pink flowers that fade to white. It has dense, dark green leaves that make good ground cover.
↕ 60cm (24in) ↔ to 1m (3ft)

CULTIVATION Prefers full sun but tolerates light, dappled shade. Grow in poor to moderately fertile, well-drained soil. In early spring, cut back all stems to within 2.5cm (1in) of the old growth. The easiest way is to use a pair of shears.

1

2

BEARDED IRIS   3

Iris germanica ♥ A robust, rhizomatous
perennial. In late spring or early summer,
upright stems bear blue-violet flowers
with yellow beards. Striking fans of
sword-shaped, grey-green leaves.
‡60–120cm (2–4ft) ↔ 30cm (12in)

CULTIVATION Grow in full sun or light,
part-day shade in any moderately fertile
well-drained soil.

3

JAPANESE SNOWBALL TREE [1]

Viburnum plicatum* f. *tomentosum 'Mariesii' ♥ A spreading, deciduous shrub with distinctively tiered branches. In late spring, it produces flat "lacecap" white flowerheads. It has heart-shaped leaves that turn red-purple in autumn.
↕ to 4m (12ft) ↔ to 4m (12ft)

CULTIVATION Grow in any reasonably fertile, well-drained soil in sun or part-shade. After flowering, lightly prune any shoots that spoil the outline of the shrub.

TAMARISK [2]

Tamarix tetrandra ♥ An open, deciduous shrub or small tree. In mid- to late spring, it bears short spikes of many tiny, pale dusky pink flowers all along the arching branches. It has purple-brown shoots and small, needle- or scale-like green leaves.
↕ 3m (10ft) ↔ 3m (10ft)

CULTIVATION Grow in full sun, in moist but well-drained soil. Shelter from cold, dry winds. It is resistant to strong winds in coastal areas. After flowering, shorten flowered shoots to strong buds lower down the stems.

HONEYSUCKLE   3

Lonicera × heckrottii A vigorous, semi-evergreen, twining climber. From mid- to late summer, it bears clusters of fragrant coral-pink flowers that are orange-yellow within. It has dark green leaves with blue-green undersides and sometimes bears glossy red berries in autumn.
↕ 5m (15ft) ↔ 3m (10ft)

CULTIVATION Grow in any fertile, moist but well-drained soil. In early spring, shorten shoots to strong buds or shoots lower down the stems.

MOCK ORANGE   **1**

Philadelphus microphyllus A free-flowering, deciduous shrub. In early and midsummer, it bears single, very fragrant, pure white flowers. It has peeling, dark chestnut-brown bark and glossy leaves.
↕ to 1m (3ft) ↔ to 1m (3ft)

CULTIVATION Grow in full sun or light, dappled shade, in any moderately fertile, well-drained soil. After flowering, shorten flowered shoots to strong buds. When mature, cut back one in five of the oldest stems at the base.

ALPINE PINK   **2**

***Dianthus* 'Little Jock'** A low-growing, cushion-forming, evergreen perennial. In summer, it bears clove-scented, double, pale pink flowers with a maroon eye and fringed petals, just above the leaves. Neat mounds of grey-green foliage all year.
↕ 10cm (4in) ↔ 10cm (4in)

CULTIVATION Prefers an open, sunny spot, in sharply drained, gritty, slightly alkaline soil. On clay soils, dig in plenty of grit. Good drainage is essential.

ROCK ROSE [3]

Cistus × cyprius ♀ A sun-loving, bushy evergreen shrub. During summer, it bears clusters of white flowers with crimson blotches at the bases of the petals. Forms a neat mound of rather sticky, dark green leaves with wavy margins.
↕ to 1.5m (5ft) ↔ to 1.5m (5ft)

CULTIVATION Tolerant of poor and alkaline soils. Grow in well-drained soil in full sun; plant in spring when the risk of frost has passed. Pinch out stem tips to keep the plant bushy; don't prune hard.

ACHILLEA [1]

Achillea **'Fanal'** A clump-forming, herbaceous perennial with fragrant leaves. Throughout summer, it bears flat heads of bright red flowers with yellow centres. The flowers fade with age, but can be dried for winter flower arrangements.
‡75cm (30in) ↔ 60cm (24in)

CULTIVATION Prefers an open site in sun, but tolerates light, dappled shade. Grow in moist, but well-drained soil. Lift and divide every three or four years to maintain vigour.

LAVENDER [2]

Lavandula angustifolia **'Twickel Purple'** A spreading evergreen shrub. Dense spikes of fragrant purple flowers are borne in midsummer above narrowly oblong, grey-green leaves. Like all lavenders, the flowerheads are very attractive to bees.
‡60cm (24in) ↔ 1m (3ft)

CULTIVATION Grow in full sun in any moderately fertile, well-drained soil. In mid-spring, cut back the previous year's growth by about 5cm (2in) to strong pairs of buds. Don't cut into old wood.

COTTON LAVENDER 〔3〕

***Santolina chamaecyparissus* 'Lemon Queen'** A low-growing, grey-green evergreen shrub. From mid- to late summer, it bears pompon-like, lemon-yellow flowerheads. It has white-woolly young shoots that carry finely divided leaves with a wonderful sharp fragrance.
‡60cm (24in) ↔ 60cm (24in)

CULTIVATION Best in full sun, but will tolerate some shade. Grow in moderately fertile, well-drained soil. Dig in coarse grit on heavy clay soils. In early spring, trim plants to keep them bushy and compact.

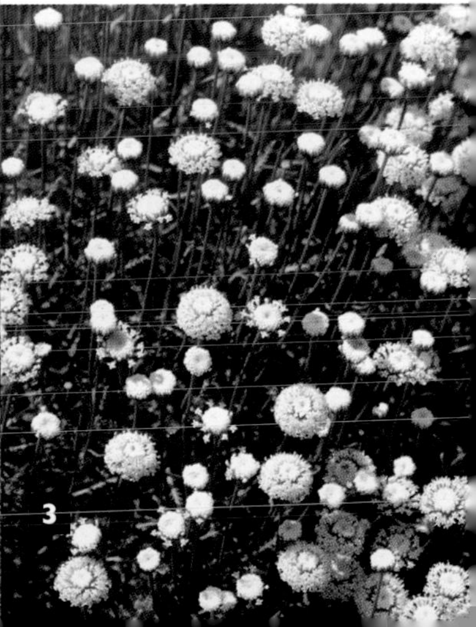

2

3

TREE LUPIN

Lupinus arboreus ♥ A bushy, vigorous, evergreen or semi-evergreen shrub with palm-like, grey-green leaves. From late spring until summer it produces pea-like, pale yellow, fragrant flowers in short, upright clusters.
↕↔2m (6ft)

CULTIVATION Grow in a light, fertile, slightly acid soil in full sun or part shade. Seeds can be sown in spring or autumn. Take cuttings in summer.

HARDY GERANIUM 2

Geranium himalayense A mound-forming herbaceous perennial. In early summer, it bears a profusion of white-centred, violet-blue to deep blue flowers, and then blooms sporadically into autumn. The lobed, soft green leaves colour well in autumn.
↕30–45cm (12–18in) ↔60cm (24in)

CULTIVATION Grow in any fertile, well-drained soil, in sun or part-shade. Trim after the first flush of flowers to encourage more in the autumn. Divide every three or four years in spring.

ORANGE BALL TREE ③

Buddleja globosa ♀ A large deciduous or semi-evergreen shrub. In early summer, it bears rounded clusters of honey-scented, orange-yellow flowers. Handsome, dark green, deeply veined leaves.
‡5m (15ft) ↔ 5m (15ft)

CULTIVATION Best grown in sun, in any fertile garden soil enriched with organic matter; it will tolerate light shade. Keep pruning to a minimum, but when mature, remove some of the oldest flowered shoots at the base, after flowering.

2

3

PAEONIA

Vigorous, long-lived, herbaceous perennials. From early to midsummer, they bear very showy, bowl-shaped, single or double flowers in white and shades of red and pink. The dark green or greyish-green leaves often colour well in autumn.

CULTIVATION Best in full sun, but tolerant of dappled shade for part of the day. Grow in deep, fertile, moist but well-drained soil that is enriched with plenty of organic matter. The stems of peonies with large flowers may need unobtrusive, grow-through supports, especially in exposed gardens.

TOP ROW LEFT TO RIGHT
• *P. lactiflora* 'Sarah Bernhardt' ♥
  ↕↔ 90–100cm (36–39in)
• *P. lactiflora* 'Laura Dessert' ♥
  ↕↔ 70–75cm (28–30in)
• *P. lactiflora* 'Kelway's Supreme'
  ↕↔ 90–100cm (36–39in)

BOTTOM ROW LEFT TO RIGHT
• *P. lactiflora* 'Bowl of Beauty' ♥
  ↕↔ 80–100cm (32–39in)
• *P. lactiflora* 'Ballerina'
  ↕↔ 90–100cm (36–39in)
• *P. officinalis* 'Rubra Plena' ♥
  ↕↔ 70–75cm (28–30in)

EARLY, SINGLE-FLOWERED CLEMATIS

These vigorous, deciduous clematis bloom in late spring and early summer, often with a second flush later in summer.

CULTIVATION Grow in fertile, well-drained soil enriched with well-rotted organic matter. They flower best with top-growth in sun and roots in shade, but darker colours bleach in sun, so these are better in part-shade. Plant with 10–15cm (4–6in) of stem below soil level to reduce danger of clematis wilt. Shade the roots with stone slabs or with nearby plants. In spring, before growth begins, cut out twiggy, dead or damaged growth and trim remaining shoots back to strong buds.

TOP ROW LEFT TO RIGHT
- *C.* 'Fireworks'
  ↕2.5m (8ft) ↔1m (3ft)
- *C.* 'Guernsey Cream'
  ↕2.5m (8ft) ↔1m (3ft)
- *C.* 'Lasurstern' ♀
  ↕2.5m (8ft) ↔1m (3ft)

BOTTOM ROW LEFT TO RIGHT
- *C.* 'Marie Boisselot' ♀
  ↕3m (10ft) ↔1m (3ft)
- *C.* 'The President' ♀
  ↕2–3m (6–10ft) ↔1m (3ft)
- *C.* 'Nelly Moser' ♀
  ↕2–3m (6–10ft) ↔1m (3ft)

WHAT TO DO IN **JULY**

WEATHER WATCH

It's summer time. The garden is full of colour and the scent from flowers such as roses and sweet peas fills the air, especially towards the end of the day. If it's hot and dry, you'll need to keep everything well watered, either in the morning or evening.

HEIGHT OF SUMMER

July is usually one of the hottest months of the year, with the highest temperatures occurring inland, away from the cooling influence of the sea. Gardening can be done at a leisurely pace.

SEA BREEZES

This is not really a month for gales or high winds, except in parts of the north-west and in coastal areas, where sea breezes can be very welcome on hot, sultry days. North-west areas average 0.2 days of gales this month, rising to 0.3 days in the north of Scotland, especially on the west coast and western islands.

SUN AND CLOUDS

The sunniest areas are along the south coast – owing to the formation of cumulus clouds over land, the skies over the sea usually remain cloud-free. Northern parts of the country are generally the cloudiest, due to the hillier nature of the terrain, and on western coasts the close proximity of low-pressure weather systems over the Atlantic may also bring in plenty of cloud cover. However, some parts of the north-east and south-west areas of Scotland compare favourably with Ireland and north-west England for hours of direct sunshine. The far northern coasts of Britain usually receive around

133 hours of sun in July, while in the south of England the average is around 213 hours.

SHORT RAINY SPELLS

July can be a dry month, but we don't escape rain altogether. The trouble is that the sudden but short spells of summer rain do little to add to soil reserves of moisture. So it makes sense to save water when we can, especially in areas more prone to drier weather. Do your watering in the early morning or evening, when it is cooler. The moisture will not evaporate as quickly as it will in the middle of the day. If you have doubts about watering restrictions, check with your local authority.

FREAK HAIL

There is no snow on the ground in July except in small isolated pockets on the highest peaks. But there are times when a freak shower of hail can make for a temporary wintry scene, and damage your plants, even in July.

AROUND THE GARDEN

PLAN FOR HOLIDAYS

July and August are usually the holiday months: prepare the garden before going away so that you don't come back either to a jungle or to a sea of dead plants. Try to "book up" a neighbour, a member of the family or a friend to call in periodically and attend to the routine tasks of watering and feeding plants and mowing the lawn. Most people are only too willing to help, though a little bribery may not be a bad idea.

Ask someone to pick and take away vegetables like beans and courgettes, which all seem to come at once. If beans and cutting flowers like dahlias, chrysanthemums, and sweet peas are picked regularly, they will continue to produce crops and blooms well into autumn. Mow the lawn, but don't mow it too close or you'll just encourage it to grow even faster. Most houseplants can be moved outside for a summer break; you can plunge the pots in the soil to lessen water loss. Automatic trickle irrigation systems are inexpensive and easy to install. They can be connected to a small computer control and set to come on whenever you want them to.

SAVE WATER

It is inevitable that if we have a few weeks of dry weather, water will be in short supply and more than likely hosepipe bans will be brought into force. So it is wise to conserve as much water as you can. Water can be collected from guttering along the house roof in a water butt. There are many types available, from plastic to genuine wooden casks; the latter are an attractive addition to the garden.

Mulch borders with any organic matter you can get your hands on, making sure the soil is moist before applying the mulch. Even old newspapers will reduce water loss from the surface of the soil. Only water plants that really need it: newly planted trees, shrubs and other plants. Newly sown or turfed lawns should be kept watered; established lawns will recover if they have gone brown.

Most importantly, give plants a good soaking when you do water them. It is better to give a few a thorough soak than to give them all a little water each day. The water-efficient way of watering plants in the border is to use the leaky pipe or seephose system. This porous pipe lets the water seep out around the roots of the plant where it's needed, avoiding waste.

MANAGE PESTS AND DISEASES

With warm weather, pests and diseases multiply rapidly. Greenfly and blackfly breed especially fast, and it can be a job to keep on top of them. If you can build up diversity in the garden by growing a variety of plants, you will attract beneficial insects and other wildlife, and a healthy balance will then develop between pests and predators.

Water butts can collect water not only from the roof of your house, but from the roofs of any sheds or greenhouses.

There may be a little bit of damage to some plants and the occasional casualty, but that is a small price to pay for the enjoyment of having so many different creatures making a home in your garden.

There are many biological controls available now for pests, and these are widely available by mail order direct from the suppliers. Try to use cultural (that is, good gardening) and biological methods of control whenever you can, even if you do not consider yourself an organic gardener.

MOW, TRIM AND FEED LAWNS

In order to keep the lawn in good condition, continue to mow and trim edges once or twice a week. During very dry weather, raise the blades of the mower and mow less often. The grass is best left a little longer during dry periods so that the plants retain more leaf area, and can therefore cope with the drier conditions better. The grass

will also not be growing as vigorously, so the frequency of mowing can be reduced. It is just not necessary to cut the lawn once a week if it's not growing fast. Leave the grass-collecting box off in very dry conditions, as the clippings on the lawn will act as a mulch, helping to retain moisture in the soil. When the grass gets going again in more moist conditions the blades can be gradually lowered to the normal height of cut.

Don't water your lawn unless it is absolutely necessary. If you have to, then do it once a week giving it a thorough soaking. Although established lawns will turn brown in very hot weather, it's just not worth wasting water on them, as the grass will soon recover when wetter weather returns. Keep the water for precious plants, or for newly established lawns.

Give the lawn a boost with a liquid fertiliser unless you did so last month. By this time of year most lawns are looking rather tired and will probably benefit from a quick boost. The effect on the lawn should be noticeable within about two or three days. There are many types of liquid fertiliser on the market, all easily applied. Follow the instructions carefully and don't overdo it. There is no point in making the solution stronger or applying more than necessary in the hope that it will speed things up a bit – it simply doesn't work like that.

INTRODUCE POND FISH

With the water in the pond warming up in spring and summer, fish get acclimatized to new conditions quickly. It's best to get them home from the garden centre (or wherever they were bought) as quickly as possible because of the limited amount of oxygen in the bag in which they are transported. When you release the fish into the pond, let them swim from the bag at their leisure.

INTRODUCING FISH TO A POND

1 Take a cardboard box with you to support the bag on the way home. The fish will have a smoother ride.

2 Float the bag in the pond for an hour or two until the water temperature inside and outside is the same.

3 Cut the bag under the water and let the fish swim out in their own time; don't force them.

MAINTAIN PONDS

During hot weather, keep an eye on the water level in ponds, especially if you have fish. Water can evaporate from the pond at an alarming rate during warmer spells. Top up with a hose as often as necessary.

At the same time, keep a watch on fish, because if the water is still and the level drops they may be starved of oxygen. Fish in difficulties will rise to the surface and gulp for air, just as we would. Spray the pond with a jet of water to put some oxygen into the water. It may be worth installing a feature such as a small waterfall or a fountain to keep the water moving and oxygen levels high.

Oxygenating plants in the pond will have to be thinned as they can take over the pond completely. Pull them out with a rake and leave by the side of the pond to dry out, and to allow any wildlife hiding in them to escape back into the pond. They can then be added to the compost heap.

TOP UP WATER FOR WILDLIFE

Birds and other wildlife need a drink during dry spells just as much as plants and we gardeners do. Regularly top up any containers

left out for the birds to ensure
they have a steady supply of water.
If you build a garden pond, make
sure the sides slope gently to allow
birds and other animals to drink
and bathe in the shallow water.

A decorative way of achieving this
is to form a beach area with pebbles
set around the edge of the pond.

*This wooden bridge joins two pebble beaches,
which allow wildlife easy pond access.*

TREES, SHRUBS & CLIMBERS

DEADHEAD ROSES

Many people, when deadheading roses, just snap the old flowerheads off. But if you want to continue the display into autumn you have to prune back to a bud in a leaf axil lower down the stem to encourage strong new shoots. Prune to an outward-facing leaf to keep the centre of the rose bush open. Wild roses should not be deadheaded as they produce

EXTENDING THE FLOWERING PERIOD

On hybrid tea roses, cut back any flowers that have gone over to a healthy sideshoot or a strong, outward-facing bud.

On floribundas, you should cut back entire trusses of flowers to a healthy sideshoot, leaf, or bud.

attractive hips in the autumn. After deadheading, give the roses a feed to boost growth and encourage more flowers later in the summer. Use a fertiliser specific to roses, or one high in potash to encourage strong shoots. A fertiliser high in nitrogen will result in soft, sappy growth which is more prone to attack from pests and diseases.

TRIM CONIFER HEDGES

Conifer hedges have received bad press in recent years, due mainly to the notoriety of × *Cupressocyparis leylandii*. Is is an excellent hedging plant, but needs regular trimming to keep it under control. Admittedly, it does grow very fast, growing 60–90cm (2–3ft) in most years. As with all other conifer hedges, it needs trimming once or even twice a year to keep it in order. If you start doing this when the conifers are small, long before they reach the height and width you require, you will build up a good, thick layer of leafy growth over the entire surface of the hedge.

REMOVE UNWANTED GROWTH FROM TREES

Many trees and shrubs often produce a mass of shoots at the base of the plant. One of the most common groups of plants with this habit are the *Sorbus* species, such as rowan and mountain ash. These shoots need to be cut away cleanly to prevent them sapping all the strength of the plant. At the same time, remove any shoots which have grown with plain green leaves on variegated plants.

Use a knife or secateurs to remove unwanted suckers flush with the trunk.

FLOWERING PLANTS

DIVIDE IRISES

Once the flowers are over, bearded and other rhizomatous irises can be divided. After several years, these irises, which form thick, fleshy rhizomes, tend to lose vigour and benefit from being divided up. This is also a good opportunity to clear weeds from within iris clumps, as these are notoriously difficult to get out – unless you lift and clean up the plants, a spot weedkiller is usually the only answer, using a sheet of card or paper to protect the iris leaves completely from contact.

Once the flowers are over, lift the clump with a fork and separate

DIVIDING IRISES

1 Lift the clump of old, knobbly rhizomes and cut off small, healthy, young pieces that each have a clump of leaves attached.

2 Pull off any dead foliage, then with a sharp knife, cut straight across the fan of leaves.

3 Replant the small divisions in a sunny spot, 8–15cm (4–6in) apart, with the rhizome just below the soil surface.

the younger pieces from the outside of the clump. Remove the younger pieces with a sharp knife, and throw away older ones. Cut off faded leaves, and cut across the remaining foliage about 15cm (6in) from the root, leaving a fan shape of trimmed leaves. This helps reduce water loss from the leaves and stops the wind catching the tall foliage like a sail and blowing the plant over.

Replant in groups of three, five, or more and water them in thoroughly. Irises must not be planted too deeply; on an exposed site, it may help to pin down the rhizomes with hoops of galvanized wire, removing these when the plants have developed their own anchoring roots.

CUT BACK FADED FLOWERS

If you don't need the seeds, continue to cut back faded flowers on perennials. This encourages new growth and more flowers later in the summer. Plants like Oriental

Once irises finish flowering, this is the time to divide them and tackle any weeds embedded within the clumps.

poppies and hardy geraniums can be cut back to ground level with a pair of shears. Taller perennials, like delphiniums, should have their faded flower spikes cut back to encourage new shoots that should produce more flowers later in the summer. All the old growth can be put on the compost heap. Give the plants a feed and a good watering if the weather is dry.

FEED LATE-FLOWERING PERENNIALS

Herbaceous perennials in general, and late-flowering ones like Michaelmas daisies (asters) and chrysanthemums in particular, will benefit from a sprinkling of a general organic fertiliser now to give a boost to their growth for the rest of the summer. Hoe or lightly rake it in, and if the weather is dry, water it in as well.

DRY OUT BULBS

Bulbs which were heeled in within trenches for the foliage to die back can be dug up and stored until they are required for planting in the autumn. Make sure that the bulbs are thoroughly dry and free from any diseased material for the winter, so that they do not rot in store. Remove all the dead foliage and flowering stems if they are still on the bulbs. Inspect the bulbs for any signs of disease or rotting, and remove and discard any that are affected. Lay the bulbs out in a single layer to dry off completely for a few days in a greenhouse, garage, or spare room, and then store in boxes or trays in a cool, dry, airy place.

PLANT AUTUMN-FLOWERING BULBS

These bulbs will flower through September, October and, if the weather is reasonable, also into November. The flowers appear without foliage, because the leaves have died down during the summer – leaves will appear in the spring. Choose either colchicums or the autumn-flowering crocus: *Crocus speciosus* with blue-purple and white flowers, *C. kotschyanus* with lilac-pink flowers, and *C. sativus*, with dark-veined lilac flowers. Plant them in full sun to a depth of 10cm (4in).

Nerines are wonderful plants from the warmer climes of South Africa, and are very eyecatching indeed. Like colchicums and crocuses, the flowers appear before the leaves, with tall stems bearing up to nine blooms with pink

curling petals. As they come from a warm country they will need a warm, sunny, sheltered spot, preferably at the base of a south-facing wall or fence, and well-drained soil.

From the point of view of hardiness, *Nerine bowdenii* is the most widely known and easiest to grow, but even this will need some protection in colder areas. In northern parts and very exposed, chilly gardens it may be best to grow nerines in a cold greenhouse or conservatory. As with all bulbs, the general rule when it comes to depth of planting is to plant the bulb to at least twice its own depth. If you have a heavy clay soil, put a layer of coarse sand or grit in the bottom of the hole and sit the bulbs directly on this. It will help to improve the drainage.

The flowers of Colchicum byzantinum *(top left) and* Crocus kotschyanus *(bottom left) appear without leaves in the autumn.*

DRYING CUT FLOWERS

1 Cut everlasting flowers such as statice as the flowers start to open. Cut low down to get the full length of stem.

2 Tie the flowers in small bunches and hang them upside-down in an airy place, out of full sun which will bleach the colour.

CUT AND DRY EVERLASTING FLOWERS

Flowers of plants like statice, bracteantha, and rhodanthe can be cut for drying and used for decorative displays in the home during the winter. They have to be picked just before they reach their peak, which is when they are almost fully open. They will open slightly more as they dry out. Tie them in bunches and hang them up in an airy place to dry out. Don't attempt to speed up the drying process by putting the flowers in a warm place, as they will simply shrivel up.

FINISH PLANTING OUT SUMMER BEDDING

These plants can be planted out in baskets, containers, and borders. Gaps in the borders can be filled with larger plants grown yourself or bought from the garden centre. The sooner this job is done the better, as the plants will have time to settle in and flower for the rest of the summer.

MAINTAIN ANNUALS AND PERENNIALS

This will help keep the display going well into the autumn. Deadhead old flowers regularly to prevent the plants setting seed unless, of course, you want to collect seeds from some plants. Do bear in mind, though, that hybrid plants such as "F1 hybrids" will not come true to type from seed.

Plants like pansies and petunias tend to get straggly at this time of year, and picking off individual spent flowers from these plants can be tedious. An easy way to deadhead them is to cut them back with secateurs or a pair of shears. Cut them back quite hard, give a quick tonic with a high-potash fertiliser, and new growth will soon be produced with flowers later in the summer.

MAINTAIN CONTAINERS

Watering and feeding containers regularly will extend the colourful display into autumn. Watering may have to be done twice a day during

A watering lance, a handy hose attachment, makes watering hanging baskets less of a chore.

hot spells. Containers need plenty of water even when it rains: the mass of roots inside the container and the foliage on top make rain penetration almost impossible. Deadhead the plants regularly to keep them looking good and prevent them from setting seeds. Plants crammed together in containers can sometimes begin to look a bit straggly towards late summer, so occasionally prune off any straggly shoots and any that are crowding out other plants – you could make cuttings of these.

KITCHEN GARDEN

WATER VEGETABLES REGULARLY

If vegetables are not watered regularly they will usually bolt and start producing seeds, making the plants almost inedible. It is such a waste, after all the hard work put into earlier cultivation, to see vegetables bolting because of a lack of water. The easiest way to water is by using leaky-pipe or seephose laid along the rows, or buried just below the soil. This directs the water where it's most needed, preventing splashing, especially from large-leaved plants such as all the brassica (cabbage) family. The most efficient time to water is at night.

WATER RUNNER BEANS REGULARLY

You should water at the roots to help the flowers set and form pods. Many gardeners also recommend spraying the flowers with water each day. Add a small

A seephose oozes droplets of water along its entire length. It can be wound between plants to attain an even distribution.

handful of hydrated lime to a full 10-litre (2-gallon) watering can and apply this along the row of runner beans at the base of the plants – it will help the flowers to set and produce more pods. Always wear gloves and a face mask when handling lime, as it can be harmful if ingested.

CONTINUE WEEDING

Keep down weeds by continuing to hoe between the rows. Do this regularly and the weeds will never become a problem. Hoe on a dry day and the weed seedlings will shrivel up in the warm sun, saving you having to cart them off to the compost heap. Mulching the soil with a layer of dry grass mowings will also suppress weeds.

KEEP HARVESTING VEGETABLES

Most vegetables taste better when they are young, so harvest them as soon as they are ready. If you do this, you are likely to get more crops out of your land than if they are left to grow to maturity, becoming coarser and less palatable. A succession of young vegetables spread throughout the seasons is far better than a glut of one kind all at once.

BEGIN HARVESTING SHALLOTS

Shallots need dry, sunny weather to ripen properly. Lift the bulbs carefully, levering them out of the ground with a fork when the leaves turn yellow. In sunny weather they can be left on the surface of the soil to dry out. Or, to allow plenty of air to circulate around the bulbs, you could always erect a temporary support.

This drying rack can be created by attaching chicken wire between four posts. It helps air circulate around the shallots.

Bang four low stakes into the ground, and stretch a piece of chicken wire between the posts to create a "hammock". Put the shallots on this and they will dry out quickly. If rain is forecast, cover them with a piece of polythene. And if the weather is very wet, keep the shallots under cover, in a cold frame with the lid on, or just lay them out in a greenhouse or shed with good light.

You can harvest garlic planted last year in exactly the same way as for shallots. If the bulbs have been healthy and shown no sign of virus (which usually shows up as yellow spots and streaks in the foliage), then some of the cloves can be kept for replanting.

HARVEST EARLY POTATOES

To see if potatoes are ready, lift one plant and see how big the crop is. If there aren't many potatoes there that are more than marble-sized, leave the rest of the plants to develop further. To encourage the tubers to swell, water the plants once a week, giving them a good soaking.

HARVEST GLOBE ARTICHOKES

Harvest as the scales begin to open. This is a striking architectural plant that can be grown in ornamental borders as well as in the vegetable garden. The bold foliage makes a perfect contrast to other finer-leaved plants in the garden. If the flowerheads are left on, they open up to reveal the most beautiful thistle-like flowers.

Pick and eat the flower buds of globe artichokes just as the scales begin to open.

HARVEST ONIONS

You'll know they're ready when the leaves begin to turn yellow and flop. It is often recommended that the leaves of onions be bent over to encourage the onions to ripen. However, this actually tends to happen quite naturally. Ease the bulbs from the soil with a fork and leave them on the soil for a few days if the weather is warm and dry.

As with shallots, you can make a chicken wire support for them, allowing air to circulate freely around the bulbs and drying them off quickly. Once dry, onions can be stored in several ways. Tie them up to make an onion string, or put them into an old pair of tights, and hang them up – or just lay them in a single layer in boxes.

SOW AUTUMN AND WINTER SALADS

Corn salad (or lambs' lettuce) and rocket can be sown now. Both are happy in most situations. Claytonia (winter purslane) prefers lighter, sandy soils. Sow the seeds thinly in

Claytonia, or winter purslane, has a peppery, cress-like taste.

drills about 23cm (9in) apart. These crops don't need to be thinned out; they can just be cut as required and will grow away again.

You can also sow oriental vegetables now if you haven't already – they make an interesting addition to autumn salads. They are also attractive to look at, so can be grown in with ornamental plants in borders as well as in the vegetable garden. Look out for Chinese radish, mizuna greens, pak choi, and spinach mustard. Sow in rows 30cm (1ft) apart and thin to 15–30cm (6–12in) between plants.

FINISH PLANTING OUT WINTER BRASSICAS

The weather is usually dry now, so to make watering the plants in a bit easier, take out a deep drill with a draw hoe and put the plants in with a dibber or a trowel, planting in the drill. A watering can or hose can then be run along the rows, with the drill keeping the water where it is needed. Remember to put collars at the base of the stems to prevent the cabbage root fly from laying its eggs there. And grow them under fleece to protect them from the cabbage white butterfly, which lays its small yellow eggs beneath the leaves.

SOW SPRING CABBAGES

Sowing should take place at intervals of a week to 10 days. This vegetable is particularly welcome when there is little else to be harvested from the vegetable garden. Sow the seeds thinly in drills 15cm (6in) apart, watering the drills before sowing if the soil is dry. Follow the directions on the back of the seed packet. Cover them with fleece to stop pigeons eating the emerging seedlings and flea beetles making small holes in the leaves. When the young plants have made two or three true leaves, they can be transplanted to their cropping places.

PICK AND DRY HERBS

Pick herbs regularly to maintain a supply of fresh, young shoots. It's almost like pruning the plant: the more you pick, the more young shoots (with the best flavour for cooking) will be produced. If herbs are not picked regularly they tend to become rather spindly. But if they have been neglected they can be brought back to bushiness again. Most herbs will benefit from being trimmed over occasionally with a pair of garden shears. This will encourage a flush of new growth.

Sage, rosemary, and thyme can be cut now and hung up to dry. Do this in an airy place outdoors, such as a shed or garage, where the ice-making compartment of the fridge and use them as required. In some cases, you can simply add the ice cube to the dish you are cooking.

STOP CLIMBING BEANS

When climbing beans reach the top of their supports, pinch out the tip of the leading shoot. This encourages plants to make more sideshoots lower down, so that more beans will be produced.

Make sure you pick beans regularly, because if the pods are left on the plants too long they become tough and stringy and are not very palatable. But perhaps more important is that the more you pick them, the more beans will be produced throughout the summer because plants will continue cropping for longer. Of course, if you are exhibiting runner beans you will want to grow pods that are as straight and long as possible. The longest pods are achieved by growing show varieties such as 'Enorma'.

The woodier herbs such as sage and rosemary retain their pungent flavours well when dried.

the herbs will be protected from rain. A lot of people hang them up in the kitchen to dry, but here they can get covered in dust and grease from cooking, and this makes them less appealing to use, as well as damaging their flavour.

Another easy way to store herbs is to freeze them; greener, softer herbs like parsley and chives can be cut up small and put into ice cube trays. Fill with water, put in

BLANCH ENDIVES

This will turn the foliage white and make it more palatable. The easiest way to do this is to cover each plant with a plate or large upturned pot, making sure you cover up any drainage holes in the bottom of pots so the plants are in total darkness. They should be ready to harvest after about ten days of blanching.

STOP OUTDOOR CORDON TOMATOES

Wait until they have made four trusses of fruit to do this. Outdoor tomatoes in this country will not carry or ripen any more fruit than this because of our relatively short summers. Pinch out the growing tip one leaf beyond the topmost flower truss. This allows plant foods to travel up the stem to the

BLANCHING ENDIVES

1 Place an upturned plate over the heart of the plant to exclude the light.

2 In a week or two, the inner leaves will have become pale and sweet to eat.

Remove the sideshoots of cordon tomatoes in order to concentrate the plant's energy on fruit production.

PICK AND PRUNE RASPBERRIES

Summer-fruiting raspberries should ripen for picking this month. If you have a surplus, they freeze very well, either singly or, to save freezer space, cooked gently to reduce to a puree.

When you've picked all of the fruit, prune the summer-fruiting raspberries. The old fruited canes will be easily identifiable if they were tied to the supporting wires. If not, the wood of these canes is more brown in colour, there will be the remains of fruit clusters, and the leaves will probably look a bit tatty. By contrast, the younger canes that have been produced during the summer will have fresh green foliage and the stems will still be green.

Start by untying the old canes from the supporting wires and then cut them out to ground level.

topmost truss, setting and ripening the tomatoes. Keep feeding the plants with a high-potash fertiliser for a good crop, and remove any sideshoots from the leaf axils on cordon-grown varieties. Bush and trailing varieties can be left to their own devices; they fruit on sideshoots and there is no top truss of flowers.

TIDYING RASPBERRY CANES

1 Prune out the old fruited canes of summer-fruiting raspberries by cutting them down to ground level.

2 Secure the new canes of summer-fruiting raspberries, which will fruit next year.

You can now tie in the new canes, spacing them about 10cm (4in) apart. Make sure that you only tie in good, strong canes; any weak ones need to be pruned out completely. Any canes growing far out from the rows should be dug up or they will continue to creep outwards. The old canes which have been pruned out can be shredded and used as a mulch in other parts of the garden. Shredders can be bought or hired from your local hire shop.

REMOVE OLD FOLIAGE FROM STRAWBERRIES

Once fruiting has completely finished, you should remove the old leaves, as they can become diseased and are of little use to the plants. Remove them by going over the plants with a pair of shears. Any straw which was put around the plants to keep the fruits from being spoiled should be removed too. Lightly fork over the soil between the plants and take out any weeds. The plants

STRAWBERRIES AFTER CROPPING

1 *After the last fruits have been picked, trim all the leaves with shears and put them on the compost heap.*

2 *Remove straw mulches or strawberry mats, clear debris from the crowns of the plants, then weed and gently fork the soil.*

should produce new foliage over the next few weeks. The old leaves and straw can be consigned to the compost heap.

PREPARE FOR NEW STRAWBERRY PLANTS

After three years, the yield from strawberry plants tends to decline, and the plants sometimes get virus disease. Therefore it is better to replace plants after three seasons of cropping. If the old plants have shown any signs of virus, dig them up now, and buy in new plants from reputable fruit nurseries, where you will be able to get healthy new stock which is certified to be free of virus.

Choose a new patch in which to plant the strawberries. Start by preparing the ground well, incorporating plenty of organic matter to improve the soil structure and retain moisture in the soil. It's worth carrying out this preparation work thoroughly, as you are more likely to be rewarded by a healthy crop in the end.

JULY PROJECT

SIMPLE TOPIARY

Trees and shrubs trained into the formal shapes known as topiary can make a strong impact in the garden and provide a year-round structure. The cone shapes shown here, for example, add vertical emphasis to a well-filled border.

Evergreens such as box (*Buxus*), bay (*Laurus nobilis*), and yew (*Taxus*) are among the most commonly used plants for topiary. They are often slow to get established, but this can be an advantage when it comes to routine trimming. Once the desired shape is achieved, a single, annual trim is all that is needed.

Creating topiary shapes is much easier if you use the correct tools and keep the blades sharp and clean. Long-handled shears give the most accurate control for trimming, while small topiary shears are best for intricate work.

1 **Choose a healthy plant** that is roughly the shape you want to create. For example, to make a sharp-pointed cone, you will need a tree or shrub with a strong leading stem.

2 **Using shears, lightly trim** your plant to shape. To minimize the risk of errors, cut away only a little at a time. Stand back at frequent intervals to appraise your work.

3 **Keep walking** around the plant, studying the shape to make sure it is symmetrical. Initially, you can use canes to guide your work, but this should not be necessary once the shape is established.

4 **Routine maintenance** involves trimming at least once a year, but two or even three trims a year will ensure a tighter-knit plant. Midsummer and early autumn are ideal times for clipping.

HOLLYHOCK [1]

Alcea rosea **Chater's Double Group**
A short-lived perennial of vigorous,
upright growth. In summer, it bears
peony-like flowers, ranging from white,
yellow, apricot and red to lavender and
purple. They attract butterflies and bees.
Handsome leaves for most of the year.
‡ to 2.5m (8ft) ↔ 60cm (24in)

CULTIVATION Flowers best in sun, but
tolerates dappled shade. Grow in any
fertile, well-drained soil. Stake in exposed
sites. Treat as annuals or biennials to limit
hollyhock rust.

SUNFLOWER [2]

Helianthus **'Music Box'** This fast-
growing, free-flowering annual bears
flowers up to 12cm (5in) across. The
flower colour varies from creamy yellow
to dark red, including some bicolours.
It is a fairly compact making it suitable
for any border.
‡ 90cm (36in) ↔ 30cm (12in)

CULTIVATION Grow in fertile, humus-
rich, moist, but well-drained soil in full
sun. Sunflowers need long, hot summers
to flower well. Seeds can be sown outside
in spring.

CALIFORNIA POPPY 3

Eschscholzia californica ♥ A mat-forming, hardy annual with finely cut greyish-green leaves. From summer to autumn, it bears satiny orange, yellow, white or red cup-shaped flowers; these are followed by long, curving seed pods. ‡30cm (12in) ↔ 15cm (6in)

CULTIVATION Grow in poor, well-drained soil in full sun. Sow the seeds outdoors in early spring and thin out when the seedlings are large enough to handle. Deadhead regularly.

VERBENA [1]

Verbena bonariensis ♀ A tall, airy, frost-hardy perennial. From midsummer to autumn, wiry, branching stems bear heads of lilac-purple flowers. It has attractive, toothed, dark green basal leaves.
↕ to 2m (6ft) ↔ 45cm (18in)

CULTIVATION Grow in any moderately fertile soil in full sun. It may not survive cold wet winters, so provide a dry winter mulch. Take stem-tip cuttings in late summer. Overwinter young plants under glass.

BORDER PHLOX [2]

Phlox paniculata 'Eva Cullum'
An upright herbaceous perennial. From summer to mid-autumn, it bears bright pink flowers with darker pink centres and a heady scent. Excellent for cutting. Fresh green leaves from spring onwards.
↕ 1.2m (4ft) ↔ to 1m (3ft)

CULTIVATION Grow in fertile, moist soil in sun or light dappled shade. Divide every three to four years in autumn or spring to maintain vigour. Take basal cuttings in spring, or root cuttings in autumn or winter.

1

PETUNIA ⟨3⟩

Petunia **'Purple Wave'** Vigorous, spreading, half-hardy perennials usually grown as annuals. From early summer until late autumn, this cultivar bears masses of small, trumpet-shaped, vibrant magenta-pink flowers. Cuttings can be taken and plants grown inside to flower in winter and early spring.
‡45cm (18in) ↔ 30–90cm (12–36in)

CULTIVATION Grow in full sun in light, well-drained soil. Shelter from strong winds. Deadhead to prolong flowering.

MORNING GLORY   1

Ipomoea tricolor **'Heavenly Blue'**
A fast-growing, twining, frost-tender annual climber with heart-shaped, bright green leaves. From summer until autumn, it bears white-throated, funnel-shaped, deep sky-blue flowers. It is usually discarded after flowering.
‡to 4m (12ft) ↔ 15cm (6in)

CULTIVATION Prefers a warm, sheltered site, in moderately fertile, well-drained soil. It needs sun, but also shade from strong midday sun. Sow seeds in spring at 18°C (64°F); grow on in warmth and set out when risk of frost has passed.

DAYLILY   2

Hemerocallis **'Gentle Shepherd'**
A moderately vigorous, semi-evergreen perennial. The ivory-white flowers with green throats appear over long periods in midsummer. The slender, arching green leaves often persist through winter and make good ground cover.
‡65cm (26in) ↔ 1.2m (4ft)

CULTIVATION Prefers full sun, but tolerates light, dappled shade. Grow in fertile, moist but well-drained soil. Mulch in autumn. Divide every three or four years, in spring, to maintain vigour.

1

SHIRLEY POPPY [3]

Papaver rhoeas **Shirley Series**
Free-flowering hardy annuals. During
summer, they bear bowl-shaped, single
or semi-double papery flowers in white
and shades of yellow, pink, orange, and
red. They have hairy stems with downy,
light-green leaves.
↕ 90cm (36in) ↔ 30cm (12in)

CULTIVATION Grow in sun in any poor
to moderately fertile, well-drained soil.
Sow seeds in spring in the flowering site.
Self-seeds freely, but seedlings are variable.

2

3

VERBASCUM [1]

Verbascum **'Cotswold Queen'** An upright, moderately vigorous perennial. From early until late summer, erect spires bear saucer-shaped yellow flowers with red-purple centres. It has striking basal rosettes of wrinkled, grey-green leaves.
‡ 1.2m (4ft) ↔ 30cm (12in)

CULTIVATION Best in full sun in poor, well-drained, preferably slightly alkaline soil. Too rich a soil produces soft, floppy stems that then need staking. May be short-lived, so divide in spring or autumn, or take root cuttings in winter.

ANNUAL COSMOS [2]

Cosmos bipinnatus **Sensation Series** An erect, freely branching, half-hardy annual. Large pink or white flowers are produced through summer and autumn; they are good for cutting. It has attractive feathery foliage all summer.
‡ to 90cm (36in) ↔ to 45cm (18in)

CULTIVATION Best in full sun, but tolerates dappled shade. Grow in any well-drained, moderately fertile soil. Sow seeds under glass in early spring, or in the flowering site in late spring. Deadhead regularly.

2

DELPHINIUM [3]

Delphinium **'Bruce'** ♀ A classic
herbaceous perennial. From early to
midsummer, it bears tall spikes of violet-
purple, semi-double flowers with dark
brown eyes. It also has attractive, deeply
lobed, mid-green foliage.
‡ 1.8m (6ft) ↔ 60–90cm (24–36in)

CULTIVATION Grow in full sun in
fertile, well-drained soil enriched with
plenty of organic matter. Needs staking
in exposed gardens. Cut back in autumn
when foliage has withered.

3

ZINNIA [1]

Zinnia elegans Dreamland Series **'Dreamland Scarlet'** Compact, half-hardy annual. From early summer to autumn, vivid scarlet, long-lasting flowers are borne above a carpet of mid-green leaves. It is discarded after flowering.
↕25cm (10in) ↔ 25cm (10in)

CULTIVATION Grow in sun, in any moderately fertile, well-drained soil. Sow seeds in warmth in early spring. For a longer succession of blooms, sow some in the flowering site in late spring. Deadhead regularly to keep more flowers coming.

CORNFLOWER [2]

Centaurea **'John Coutts'** A spreading, clump-forming herbaceous perennial. In summer, it bears fragrant, deep rose-pink flowers that attract bees and butterflies. The divided, grey-green leaves are grey-white beneath.
↕60cm (24in) ↔ 45cm (18in)

CULTIVATION Grow this drought-tolerant plant in full sun in any well-drained soil. Regular deadheading results in more flowers later in the season. Divide every three to four years to maintain vigour.

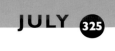

TOBACCO PLANT ⬜3

Nicotiana sylvestris ♀ An elegant, upright biennial or short-lived perennial. Loose heads of sweetly-scented, white, trumpet-shaped flowers are borne in summer above large, dark green leaves. ‡1.5m (5ft) ↔ 60cm (24in)

CULTIVATION Grow in light, dappled shade in any fertile, moist but well-drained soil. Tolerates full sun in reliably moist soils. Sow seeds under glass in early spring. Plant out only after the threat of frost has passed.

BELLFLOWER $\quad$ 1

Campanula takesimana 'Elizabeth'
A beautiful *Campanula* with rosettes of
heart-shaped, toothed, mid-green leaves.
In mid- and late summer it bears pendent,
bell-shaped cream flowers, flushed reddish
purple outside and spotted red inside.
‡35–40cm (14–16in) ↔ 40cm (16in).

CULTIVATION Grow in fertile, neutral
to alkaline, moist, but well-drained soil,
in sun or part shade. Cut back after
flowering to encourage a second flush
of flowers.

LOVE-IN-A-MIST $\quad$ 2

Nigella damascena 'Miss Jekyll' ♀
An elegant, self-seeding annual. During
summer, it produces sky-blue flowers,
surrounded by a ruff of slender leaves.
It has finely divided, feathery foliage.
The attractive seed pods can be dried
for indoor arrangements.
‡50cm (20in) ↔ 20cm (8in)

CULTIVATION Grow in any moderately
fertile, well-drained soil in full sun. Sow
seeds in the flowering site in spring
and thin seedlings to 23cm (9in) apart.
May also be sown in autumn for earlier
flowers. Protect with cloches in areas
that have very cold wet winters.

SATIN FLOWER 3

Clarkia amoena An upright, hardy annual that thrives in poorer soils. Throughout summer, it bears clusters of satin-textured, lilac to red-pink flowers. ↕75cm (30in) ↔ 30cm (12in)

CULTIVATION Best in sun in slightly acid, moist but well-drained soil, but tolerates light shade. Rich soils encourage leafy growth at the expense of flowers. Sow seeds in the flowering site in spring or autumn. Protect late-sown seedlings with cloches overwinter.

2

3

LOBELIA 1

Lobelia erinus 'Crystal Palace'
A dense, compact herbaceous perennial
grown as a half-hardy annual. From
summer to autumn, it produces masses of
dark blue flowers above mounds of dark
green foliage. Discard after flowering.
‡10cm (4in) ↔ 10–15cm (4–6in)

CULTIVATION Prefers an open, sunny
site but will tolerate light dappled shade.
Grow in any fertile, moisture-retentive
soil. Sow seeds in late winter. Plant out
when risk of frost has passed.

PERUVIAN LILY 2

Alstroemeria 'Friendship' ♀ A clump-
forming, upright herbaceous perennial.
For many weeks in summer, it bears pale
yellow, lily-like flowers with pink tinges
on the outer petals; the inner petals are
brighter yellow with dark streaks. The
flowers are excellent for cutting.
‡90cm (36in) ↔ 60cm (24in)

CULTIVATION Ideally grow in full sun,
but it tolerates light shade. Plant carefully
in late summer or early autumn in any
moist but well-drained soil. In cold areas,
apply a dry winter mulch.

SOLANUM 3

Solanum crispum 'Glasnevin' ♀
A vigorous, evergreen or semi-evergreen, scrambling shrub or climber. Throughout summer, it bears fragrant, deep purple-blue flowers at the stem tips, followed by pale yellow fruit. It has handsome dark green leaves for most of the year.
‡ to 6m (20ft) ↔ to 6m (20ft)

CULTIVATION Grow in full sun, or light, part-day shade, in neutral to slightly alkaline, fertile, well-drained soil. After flowering, shorten sideshoots to three or four buds.

2

3

HEBE [1]

Hebe **'Eveline'** A fast-growing, half-hardy evergreen shrub with glossy, lance-shaped, rich-green leaves. From late summer until late autumn, it bears hanging clusters of small pink flowers.
↕ to 1m (3ft) ↔ to 1m (3ft)

CULTIVATION Grow in fertile, well-drained, neutral to alkaline soil in sun or dappled shade. Shelter from cold winds. It may not survive outdoors in very low temperatures; bring pot-grown plants into a cold greenhouse for the winter. Trim lightly to shape in spring.

SPIDER FLOWER [2]

Cleome hassleriana **'Colour Fountain'** An eye-catching, half-hardy annual. Throughout summer, it bears dense heads of scented flowers with delicate petals in shades of pink, violet-pink, or white. Pretty, divided leaves of fresh green.
↕ 1.2m (4ft) ↔ 45cm (18in)

CULTIVATION Best in sun but tolerates light, dappled shade. Grow in light, free-draining soil. Sow seeds under glass in warmth in spring and plant out when the threat of frost has passed. Cut or deadhead regularly to prolong the flowering period.

ASTRANTIA 3

Astrantia major An upright herbaceous perennial. In early and midsummer, it bears heads of tiny green, pink, or purplish-red flowers surrounded by white bracts. The flowerheads can be used for dried arrangements.

↕ to 90cm (36in) ↔ 45cm (18in)

CULTIVATION Ideally, grow in full sun, but it will tolerate light shade. Plant in a humus-rich soil that doesn't dry out. Cut down dead stems when flowering is over. This plant self-seeds quite prolifically.

ROSA

Diverse in size, habit, and flower form, bush and shrub roses are vigorous, deciduous, and flower freely from summer to autumn. They bear single to fully-double flowers, either singly or in clusters. Many are richly scented and are excellent as cut flowers.

CULTIVATION Grow in full sun in deep, fertile, moist but well-drained soil. Apply a balanced fertiliser and mulch in late winter or early spring. Deadhead regularly. In general, prune bush roses quite hard in spring to encourage plenty of new growth and flowers. Shrub roses require little pruning, except to remove older shoots and keep them within bounds; again, prune in spring.

TOP ROW LEFT TO RIGHT
- *R.* Eglantyne ('Ausmak') ♥
  ↕1.2m (4ft) ↔ 1.5m (5ft)
- *R.* 'Chinatown' ♥
  ↕1.2m (4ft) ↔ 1m (3ft)
- *R.* Amber Queen ('Harroony') ♥
  ↕50cm (20in) ↔ 60cm (24in)

BOTTOM ROW LEFT TO RIGHT
- *R.* Graham Thomas ('Ausmas') ♥
  ↕1.2m (4ft) ↔ 1.5m (5ft)
- *R.* 'William Lobb' ♥
  ↕2m (6ft) ↔ 2m (6ft)
- *R.* Blue Moon ('Tannacht')
  ↕1m (3ft) ↔ 70cm (28in)

ROSA

The key difference between climbers and ramblers is that climbers usually have stiffer stems and can be trained into a strong framework from which their shoots develop. They are better on walls than ramblers, which send up long, flexible stems from the base making them easy to train up arches, pillars, and pergolas. Ramblers tend to have smaller flowers in clusters, and bloom only once in summer.

CULTIVATION Grow in full sun in deep, fertile, moist but well-drained soil. Apply a balanced fertiliser and mulch in late winter or early spring. Deadhead regularly to encourage more flowers.

TOP ROW RAMBLERS, LEFT TO RIGHT
- *R.* 'American Pillar'
  ↕5m (15ft) ↔ to 4m (12ft)
- *R.* 'Bobbie James' ♀
  ↕10m (30ft) ↔ 6m (20ft)
- *R.* 'Albertine' ♀
  ↕5m (15ft) ↔ 4m (12ft)

BOTTOM ROW CLIMBERS, LEFT TO RIGHT
- *R.* Handel ('Macha') ♀
  ↕3m (10ft) ↔ 2.2m (7ft)
- *R.* 'Danse du Feu'
  ↕2.5m (8ft) ↔ 2.5m (8ft)
- *R.* 'Golden Showers' ♀
  ↕3m (10ft) ↔ 2.5m (8ft)

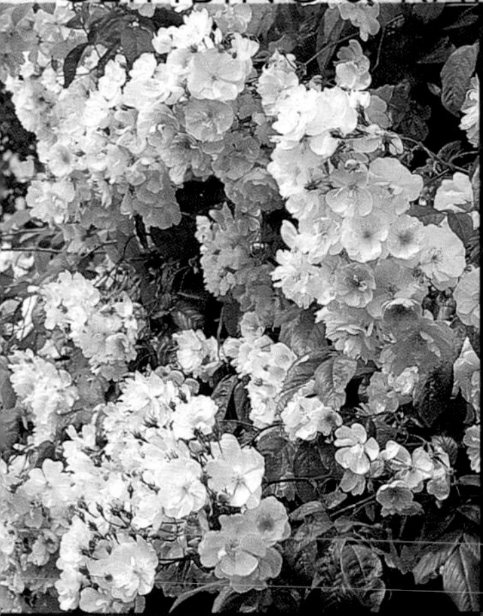

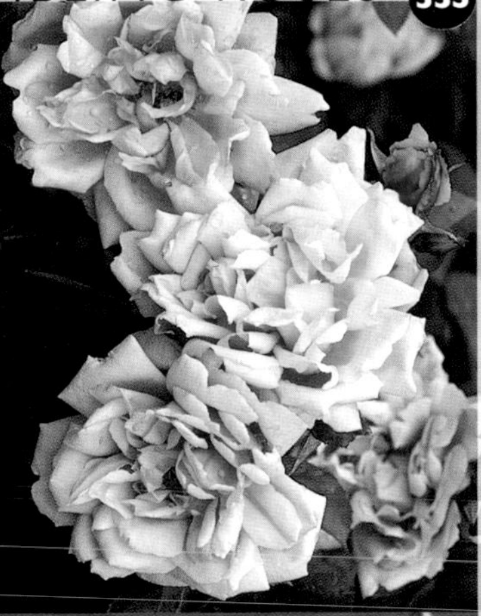

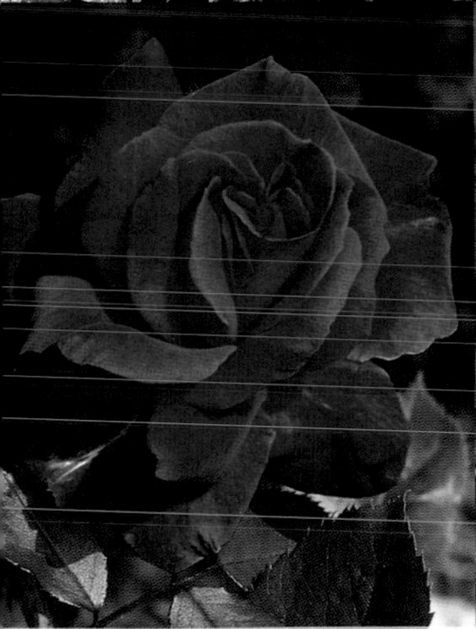

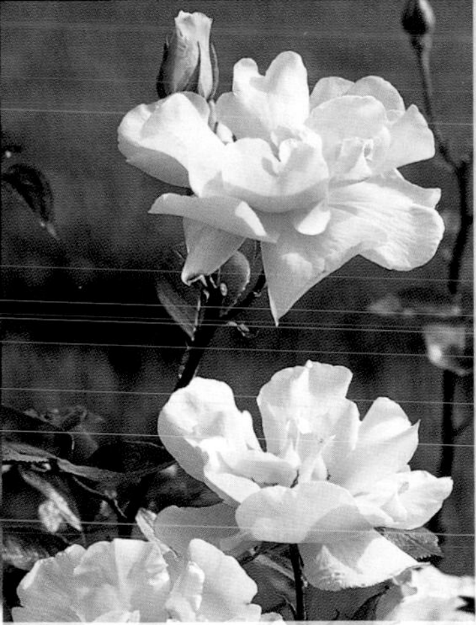

WHAT TO DO IN AUGUST

WEATHER WATCH

You will certainly get some hot, sultry days this month, so be prepared to water your garden regularly and make preparations if you are going away. Take time to enjoy your garden, but don't neglect the routine jobs such as weeding and deadheading.

SULTRY DAYS

August temperatures are similar to July's, often with hot days occasionally interspersed with thundery showers. Daily minimum temperatures are usually around 11–13°C (52–55°F) in the south, and 8–10°C (46–50°F) in the north. Maximum temperatures can, of course, be more than double this on bright, sunny days. High ground is always slightly cooler and coastal areas are kept fresher by sea breezes.

STRONG WINDS

There are few gales in any parts of the country now, but there can be strong winds in coastal areas, especially in the north and west.

Up to 0.5 days of gales may be experienced in the western isles of Scotland and some regions of north-west England may have up to 0.4 days of gales.

SUNSHINE HOURS

Generally, August is a slightly duller month than July, with more marked differences in the number of sunshine hours up and down the country – northern parts of Britain getting around 140 hours while southern parts on average enjoy 190 hours of direct sun. The amount of sunshine will always vary according to locality, being influenced by height above sea level and proximity to the coast, and the local topography.

VARYING RAINFALL

The amount of rainfall this month varies depending on the area. The south coast typically receives around 50mm (1in) of rain; inland regions experience around 60mm (2¼in), due to a higher frequency of thunderstorms as the clouds break over higher ground. In the Midlands, thunderstorms occur on average on 15 days a year, but in the west and north this is reduced to around eight days a year.

NO SNOW

There is generally no snow anywhere in the country save on the highest mountains, where patches may linger in isolated pockets for most of the year.

AROUND THE GARDEN

BEWARE OF PESTS AND DISEASES

Warm, dry weather encourages diseases such as powdery mildew (a white coating on stems and leaves). Preventative fungicide sprays can be used, but if you ensure that the plants do not come under any stress — for instance, lack of water — they will stand up to any problems much better. There will be the usual army of aphids about;

these can be kept in check by squashing by hand. If you have a bad infestation of aphids, control them by using a specific pesticide available from garden centres, and spray in the evening when fewer beneficial insects are around.

MINIMISE SLUG DAMAGE

In damp summers, slug damage to plants in the garden can be rather dispiriting. The lusher and greener foliage is, the more they like it. But there are ways to combat the onslaught without resorting to pellets. First of all, birds, ground beetles, and frogs all eat slugs, so the more they can be encouraged into the garden the better. Put

When spraying with pesticides, coat both surfaces of leaves. Ensure there are no children or pets in the vicinity when you do so.

Slugs like dark, cool, moist hiding places, so you will often find them hiding in leaf litter.

crushed eggshells or grit. Slugs don't like the coarse surface, and so are less likely to reach the plants.

CONTINUE WEEDING BORDERS

Watch out for any self-sown seedlings while you do this – it is surprising what you can find. Most hybrids and many cultivars of plants will not reproduce true from seed, but the seedlings that do emerge can throw up all sorts of variations in flower colour, plant growth habit and even leaf colour. You never know when you might discover a winner of a plant in your own back yard.

down pieces of slate or wood in the border for the slugs to creep under. These traps can then be turned over, exposing the slugs to any birds in the vicinity – or just pick them up and dispose of them.

Beer traps also work well, or try inverted hollow grapefruit or orange halves placed about the border. Even hollowed-out potatoes are often used as decoys by vegetable gardeners trying to protect a potato crop. Plants that are particularly prone to slug attack can be surrounded with a layer of

GROUP CONTAINER PLANTS

Make sure containers will be cared for if you are going on holiday. Group containers together in the shade before you go: this will make it easier for the person watering, as well as benefiting the plants. Under normal circumstances this is not to be recommended:

KEEP PONDS IN CHECK

Top up pondwater regularly, as water evaporates quickly in hot weather. At the same time, look over plants around the pond and remove any fading flowers and yellowing leaves. This will improve the appearance of the pond and the borders surrounding it. Leaves left to rot in the water also increase its nutrient content, which in turn encourages the growth of algae. If you find you have a real problem with algae, consider installing a fountain to keep the water moving.

Before you go away, group your containers together in a shady spot to maintain a humid atmosphere around the leaves.

crowded growth tends to encourage diseases. However, it's fine for a week or two. Hanging baskets can be taken down and grouped with the others by perching them on buckets or upturned pots.

Water levels can fall dramatically at this time of year, so remember to top up ponds, especially if you're going away on holiday.

When applying lawn feed, four pots moved around the lawn can be used to measure square areas by eye.

APPLY LAWN FEED

Use a fertiliser with a high phosphate content to do this. In late summer, it is not advisable to apply a high-nitrogen fertiliser to a lawn, as it will promote vigorous growth which will not stand up to the rigours of the winter. Fertilisers high in phosphates will instead promote root growth, and this will toughen up the grass for the winter ahead. These fertilisers are usually sold as autumn lawn feeds and are readily available. Apply all fertilisers strictly according to the manufacturer's instructions. Using a wheeled fertiliser spreader will take the guesswork out of applying the feed, and saves the chore of marking out the area to do it by hand. These wheeled applicators can be hired from your local hire shop.

Don't water unless absolutely necessary. There is no point in watering established lawns, as they will soon recover whenever rain does come. Grass has remarkable powers of recovery.

CONTINUE MOWING

Keep mowing regularly, raising the blades if the weather is very hot and dry. The frequency of mowing can be reduced in hot, dry weather, as the grass won't be growing much at all in these conditions.

Leave grass clippings on the lawn in dry weather – take the grass box off the mower and the clippings will act as a mulch for the grass, helping to retain moisture in the soil and returning organic matter at the same time.

TREES, SHRUBS & CLIMBERS

FEED AND WATER CONTAINER PLANTS

Shrubs and trees growing in containers need looking after just as much as temporary summer bedding plants: feed and water them regularly. Woody plants in particular should be fed with a high-potash fertiliser to encourage ripening of the wood, and not the production of soft, sappy growth which may be damaged during the winter.

DEADHEAD ROSES

Remove the fading flowers to prevent plants putting energy into producing seeds. Instead, that energy will go into new growth and more flowers. Even when deadheaded now, modern roses can still produce new shoots that will grow vigorously and flower before the end of the season. It is

not uncommon these days, with our milder winters, to see roses blooming into November or even later. Prune them back to at least one or two leaves below the base of the flowered shoots, to a healthy, outward-facing bud. You may have to prune harder than this to find a good bud, but don't be afraid to do so. The harder you prune, the more strongly the new shoot will grow.

PRUNE RAMBLING ROSES

Pruning of woody plants, most especially roses, is sometimes portrayed as being very complex, and this may make you hesitant when it comes to doing the job. But pruning rambling roses is in fact very easy. All you have to remember is that these roses will produce flowers on wood that was

Rambling roses, such as Rosa *'Albertine', are best pruned in summer when you can see the different types of shoots more easily.*

produced the previous year. All sideshoots that have flowered can be pruned back to one or two buds from the main stems. Any new, strong growths can be tied in to replace older shoots, and any very old stems can be pruned out to the ground, thereby encouraging more new shoots to develop from the base of the plant.

TRIM LAVENDER

At this time, you want to remove the old flower spikes, which you may well have already done if you like to cut lavender for drying. If not, just go over the plants with a pair of hand shears, cutting off the old flower spikes and about 2.5cm (1in) of the leafy growth at the tips of the shoots. This will encourage sideshoots to grow, keeping the plants bushy and compact.

Keep in mind that lavender rarely grows again from old wood.

Prune the flowered sideshoots on rambling roses hard to encourage more next year.

If plants have become old and straggly, it is best to either take cuttings from them, or to remove the old plants altogether and buy in new plants. If your soil has a high clay content, incorporate plenty of coarse grit before planting new lavenders. This will improve drainage, which they will enjoy.

TRIM HEDGES

Most hedges can be given their final trim towards the end of the month as they will not grow much after this, although conifers may need another going-over. If you want a level top to the hedge, fix a post at either end and tie twine between them at the required height. Trim the sides of the hedge first, working from the bottom up whether using either a powered hedge trimmer or hand shears. The reason for working upwards is that as you cut, the trimmings will fall away, and you will be better able to see where you are going. Make the hedge wider at the base and narrower at the top. This way it

Prune the stems of Aucuba japonica *to well within the plant's outline in order to hide the cut marks.*

will stand up to the weather better. The top can be trimmed last using the twine as a guide.

You may have trimmed conifer hedges last month; if not, do it now. It is often recommended that conifer hedges only be trimmed with shears, because powered hedge trimmers bruise the growth. This can happen, but frankly, the damage is so minimal that it doesn't really make any difference at all. Even if they are damaged it

Keep the blades of the shears parallel to the hedge to ensure that you achieve a neat, horizontal finish.

When using hedgetrimmers, keep the blade parallel to the hedge, and adopt a wide, sweeping action.

soon disappears when the hedge regrows. The key point with conifer hedges is never to let them get beyond the height and width you want, as they won't regrow if cut back into hard, old wood. The only exception is yew: it can be cut back to very old wood and will still grow again.

Large-leaved hedges such as spotted laurel (*Aucuba*), however, cannot be trimmed with shears or hedge trimmers, because these would cut through the large leaves, causing the edges to go brown. The way to cut these hedges is with a pair of secateurs. Put posts and string across the top as described for other hedges, and trim the sides first in the same way, starting at the base and working up. It can be a tiresome task, especially if you have a large hedge, but it is well worth the effort as the hedge will look so much better with no browned-off foliage.

FLOWERING PLANTS

REMOVE EARWIGS FROM PLANTS

Chrysanthemums and dahlias are terrific plants for displaying a mass of flowers throughout late summer and autumn until the first frosts. They also last well as cut flowers.

Dahlias are often referred to as the cut-and-come-again flower, as the more you cut them, the more flowers you get.

But they both have one problem, and that is that the flowers are irresistible to earwigs. It can be off-putting, to say the least, to put these flowers in a vase and then find earwigs crawling around the room. The best way to control these pests is to put upturned pots filled with straw on the top of canes among the plants, or if you can't get straw, shredded-up newspaper. Earwigs love to crawl into dark places during the day. In the morning you can empty the pots of earwigs and dispose of them in any way you see fit.

Trap earwigs by placing an inverted flower pot filled with dried grass or straw on top of a cane. Remove the earwigs daily.

CUT BACK WAYWARD PERENNIALS

If perennials have collapsed or spread over the lawn and other plants in the border, they should be cut back. In wet weather, a lot of taller-growing perennials, especially achilleas, tend to flop over and smother other, smaller plants. Trim them back from the smaller plants to give the latter a chance to recover and flower. The cut-back plants may also grow again and produce some flowers in the autumn.

You may find that perennials that have spread over the lawn will have killed off the grass in that area. Trim them back, and give the bare grass a good watering and a dose of lawn fertiliser, and it will very quickly regrow.

Hardy geraniums which were not cut back earlier should be cut back now to make them look neater. Again they will produce new growth which may flower later in the autumn. Feed and water them to encourage growth.

Perennials encroaching on lawns may kill off the grass below. Cut back the plant, and rejuvenate the grass with water and fertiliser.

CONTINUE WATERING

Keep watering and feeding bedding plants in hanging baskets, tubs, and other containers. Watering may have to be done several times a day when the weather is very hot. Feed at least once a week with a high-potash fertiliser to encourage the plants to bloom well into autumn.

If bulbs are planted now, Lilium candidum will produce pure white, trumpet-shaped flowers in midsummer next year.

PLANT MADONNA LILIES

Most lilies are planted from November until the spring, but the madonna lily (*Lilium candidum*) is best planted this month as it is dormant. It will start into growth next month. The most likely source of these exquisite bulbs is from a bulb specialist by mail order. Most advertise in the gardening press.

Plant the bulbs in a warm, sunny spot in well-drained soil. These lily bulbs must not be planted as deeply as you would plant other lilies. Cover the bulbs with no more than 2.5–5cm (1–2in) of soil. Always feed them after flowering.

COLLECT SEED FROM HARDY ANNUALS

Seed can be collected from most hardy annuals except the F1 hybrids, which will not come true to type. Often they don't produce any seeds at all. Harvest the seeds on a dry sunny day, and place into paper bags. Once indoors, tip the seeds onto a sheet of paper and sort out the seeds from the chaff. This can be a tedious job, but it's well worth doing to get clean seeds: any debris left in with the seeds when they are stored may cause them to rot. An old flour sieve can be useful. Store the seeds in labelled paper envelopes in a cool, dry place; an airtight box in the bottom of the fridge is ideal.

These pretty, papery heads each contain several ripe honesty seeds. Collect them up and store in the fridge.

DEADHEAD ANNUALS

Deadheading prevents the plants' energy being used to produce seeds and will extend the flowering period well into autumn. However, no matter how regularly you deadhead, some of the earlier-sown hardy annuals will be over later in the month. These can be cleared away and consigned to the compost heap. Gaps in the borders can be filled with larger plants in pots, either planting them or plunging the pots in the ground to be lifted easily in the autumn.

TAKE FLOWER CUTTINGS

This is the traditional month for taking cuttings from pelargoniums, fuchsias and other tender perennials. They can, of course, be taken at other times from spring through until autumn. But if they are taken later than September, then don't pot them up until the spring. Cuttings are very easy to take, although taking pelargonium cuttings differs slightly.

All cuttings should be removed from the parent plant by cutting off strong, non-flowering shoots just above a bud, leaving a cutting about 10cm (4in) long. Trim the lower leaves off and then trim the cutting tip immediately below a leaf joint. With all pelargoniums remove the stipules – the little papery flaps – at the base of the leaf stalks. Pelargoniums do not need hormone rooting solution; they root perfectly well without it.

All other kinds of cuttings benefit from being dipped in hormone rooting solution. Insert the cuttings around the edge of small pots containing cuttings compost (half peat-free compost, half perlite or vermiculite), and cover all kinds with polythene except pelargoniums; the fine hairs on the leaves of these trap moisture and may cause cuttings to rot. Place the pots on the windowsill or in a shady part of the greenhouse. The cuttings will root in about four weeks, when they can be potted on to overwinter under cover.

TAKING SEMI-RIPE CUTTINGS

1 Choose a shoot that is soft and green at the tip, and cut it just below a leaf joint. Trim off the soft part at the top just below a leaf, and discard. This reduces moisture loss.

2 After making a shallow cut 1.5cm (½in) long on one side of the stem base, dip this end of the stem in hormone rooting powder. Tap to remove any surplus.

3 Insert the cuttings down to the point of their lower leaves in cuttings compost. Firm the soil around them, label, then water well with tap water.

4 Cover the entire pot with a polythene bag. Don't let the bag touch the leaves: place sticks at the side of the pot to hold the bag away and prevent rotting.

KITCHEN GARDEN

KEEP HARVESTING YOUNG CROPS

It is important to harvest crops while they are still young, as this is when vegetables have a much better flavour. As they age, the flavour and texture become coarser. If both marrows and courgettes are harvested regularly, it encourages the plants to produce more flowers and fruits,

Keep harvesting courgettes when they are young and fresh, as they taste the best at this point; it will also encourage more to grow.

and the crop will continue well into autumn. Summer cabbages should be ready to eat now, too; cut them before pests get to them first.

HARVEST AND FREEZE BEANS

There is no doubt that fresh vegetables taken direct from the plant to the kitchen and cooked within a short time have the best flavour of all, but there are times when you get a glut of some crops and can't cope with them all. Freezing is one way round the problem, and most vegetables, including French and runner beans and podded broad beans, can be frozen. No matter how often you pick beans, there always seem to be buckets of them remaining towards the end of the season. The perfect way to avoid waste is to freeze them. They will provide a welcome vegetable throughout the winter.

Onion bulbs can be left on the soil to dry in prolonged dry, sunny periods.

KEEP HARVESTING ONIONS

You'll know your onions are ready when the foliage collapses. It is often recommended that you bend over the tops of onions to ripen them, but this usually happens naturally so there is probably no need to do it. Choose a dry day if you can; gently ease the onions out of the soil with a fork to break the roots' hold on the ground. It's important that the onions are dry when stored. If the weather turns wet, cover the onions with cloches or a sheet of polythene, or lay them out in a shed.

HARVEST EARLY APPLES AND PEARS

You can tell when apples and pears are ready to harvest as there are usually a couple of them on the ground. However, a more reliable method is to cup them in your hand and gently twist. If ripe, they should part from the tree with the stalk intact. If they don't come loose easily, leave them there for a few more days. Early apples and pears don't store well and they are best used soon after picking. Severely damaged fruits should be consigned to the compost heap.

To test for ripeness, cup the fruit in your palm and give it a quarter-twist.

AUGUST PROJECT

MAKING COMFREY FERTILIZER

Good-quality soil is at the heart of every successful garden, and even a naturally rich one will benefit from some help from the gardener. It is quite easy to make your own organic fertilizer at home, saving you money and helping the environment at the same time.

Liquid feed is particularly easy to apply and can be made using comfrey (*Symphytum officinale* or *S. × uplandicum*). The leaves can be harvested through summer and autumn to make into a nutritious fertilizer. Take care where you plant comfrey, as it regrows from small pieces of root, and is hard to eradicate once established.

1 **Pick the leaves** in the morning when they are freshest and place them in a bucket that holds about 8 litres (14 pints). Weight them down with a piece of rock or concrete and cover the bucket.

2 **After about three weeks,** remove the bucket lid and check how much liquid has been produced. If there is none, replace the weight and lid and leave for a further week.

3 **Strain the liquid** through a piece of muslin or cheesecloth. For root feeding use a dilution of 2 tablespoons per litre (1¾ pints) of water; for foliar feeding use 1 tablespoon per litre (1¾ pints) of water.

SOIL IMPROVERS

Green manure crops improve soil fertility and structure and suppress weeds. Such crops are not harvested but simply dug into the soil.

• Hungarian grazing rye, sown in autumn, smothers weeds while it grows and locks nutrients in the soil.

• Mustard, sown from March to September, is very fast-growing and gives structure to the soil.

• Winter tares are sown in spring or autumn. They give good weed control and fix nitrogen in the soil.

SWEET PEA [1]

Lathyrus odoratus **Bijou Group**
A compact selection of this familiar hardy
annual that climbs with twining tendrils.
From summer to early autumn, it bears
slightly scented flowers, with small, wavy
petals, in shades of pink, blue, red or
white. Many taller-growing cultivars are
available. Flowers are good for cutting.
‡ to 45cm (18in) ↔ to 45cm (18in)

CULTIVATION Grow in sun in fertile,
well-drained soil enriched with plenty
of organic matter. Sow seeds under
glass in late autumn or late winter, or
in the flowering site in spring. Deadhead
regularly to prolong flowering.

MARGUERITE [2]

Argyranthemum foeniculaceum
A frost-tender, subshrub that forms a
compact flower-covered bush. It bears
single, white, daisy-like flowerheads
with yellow centres, continuously from
summer to autumn. Fine, blue-grey
leaves all year.
‡ to 80cm (32in) ↔ to 80cm (32in)

CULTIVATION Prefers full sun, but
tolerates light shade. Grow in well-drained
soil. Pinch out stem tips to keep plants
bushy and deadhead regularly. In cold
areas, overwinter under glass.

ANGEL'S FISHING ROD 3

Dierama pulcherrimum A graceful,
upright, evergreen cormous perennial.
In summer, it produces tall stems bearing
bell-shaped, pale to deep magenta-pink
flowers on very slender stalks. Grass-like,
grey-green leaves for most of the year.
↕1–1.5m (3–5ft) ↔60cm (24in)

CULTIVATION Best in full sun in fertile,
well-drained soil. Keep well watered in dry
weather. Plant corms 5–7cm (2–3in) deep
in spring. Divide every three or four years.
Divisions may take a season to flower.

2

3

TASSEL FLOWER 1

Amaranthus caudatus A bushy, erect perennial, usually grown as a frost-tender annual. From summer to autumn, it produces long, hanging tassels of crimson-purple flowers. Its lush light green leaves have red or purple stems. The flowers are good for dried arrangements.
‡1–1.5m (3–5ft) ↔ 45–75cm (18–30in)

CULTIVATION Grow in full sun in humus-rich soil in a sheltered spot. It tolerates poor soils. Sow seeds under glass in early spring and plant out when the threat of frost has passed.

OSTEOSPERMUM 2

Osteospermum jucundum ♀ A sun-loving, evergreen perennial with silvery leaves. From late spring to autumn, it bears mauve-pink to magenta, daisy-like flowerheads. The dense mat of leaves make good ground cover.
‡10–50cm (4–20in) ↔ 50–90cm (20–36in)

CULTIVATION Grow in sun in any well-drained soil. Deadhead regularly to prolong flowering. May not survive cold wet winters, so take stem cuttings in late summer; overwinter young plants under glass.

TROPAEOLUM 3

Tropaeolum speciosum ♥ Exotic-
looking, herbaceous perennial climber.
From summer to autumn, the slender
stems form swags of long-spurred,
vermilion flowers. It has very attractive,
lobed, bright green leaves.
‡ to 3m (10ft) or more ↔ to 3m (10ft)

CULTIVATION Grow in moist,
reasonably fertile, preferably slightly
acid soil, with its roots in cool shade
and head in sun. It can be difficult to
establish, as the long fleshy white roots
are fragile; plant carefully.

SALVIA   1

Salvia coccinea **'Lady in Red'** ♥
Vivid, upright perennial, often grown
as an annual, which needs some winter
protection. From summer to autumn, it
bears slender open spikes of luminous red
flowers. It has heart-shaped, toothed and
veined, dark green leaves.
↕40cm (16in) ↔30cm (12in)

CULTIVATION Grow in full sun in any
moderately fertile, well-drained soil. May
not survive cold, wet winters, so take
softwood cuttings in spring or summer
and overwinter young plants under glass.

BUTTERFLY BUSH   2

Buddleja davidii A vigorous deciduous
shrub with arching branches. From
summer to autumn, it bears dense, arching
spires of lilac-pink flowers. Attractive
mid-green to grey-green foliage. It
is excellent for attracting butterflies.
↕3m (10ft) ↔5m (15ft)

CULTIVATION It tolerates dappled
shade but flowers best, and attracts more
butterflies, in full sun. Grow in any fertile,
well-drained soil, rich in organic matter.
Prune back the previous year's growth to
a woody framework in early spring.

1

2

HYDRANGEA   **3**

Hydrangea paniculata 'Grandiflora' ♀
A fast-growing, deciduous shrub. In late
summer and early autumn, it produces
large, conical heads of white flowers that
flush pink with age. Handsome dark
green leaves. Flowers are good for drying.
‡3–7m (10–22ft) ↔ 2.5m (8ft)

CULTIVATION Grow in fertile, humus–
rich, moisture-retentive soil in part-shade
or sun. Shelter from cold, dry winds.
Needs minimal pruning, but for larger
flowers, in late winter, cut back all
sideshoots to within 5–8cm (2–3in)
of the main stems.

3

PERENNIAL NEMESIA   1

Nemesia caerulea A woody-based, slightly tender perennial. Clusters of yellow-throated, pink, pale blue, lavender or white flowers appear from early summer through to autumn. It has dark green leaves.

↕60cm (24in) ↔ 30cm (12in)

CULTIVATION Grow in a sheltered site in full sun in moderately fertile, well-drained soil. It may not survive very cold winters. If pot-grown, it can be brought into a greenhouse in autumn. Otherwise, take stem cuttings in summer and overwinter young plants under glass.

CONEFLOWER   2

Echinacea purpurea 'White Swan' A hardy, upright herbaceous perennial with clumps of narrow, roughly hairy basal leaves. From midsummer until early autumn, it bears large, single white flowers with orange-brown centres.

↕60cm (24in) ↔ 45cm (18in)

CULTIVATION Best in full sun, but tolerates light, part-day shade. Grow in fertile, humus-rich, well-drained soil. Cut back the flowering stems as the blooms fade to encourage a second flush of flowers.

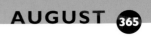

RHODOCHITON 3

Rhodochiton atrosanguineus ♀

A frost-tender, herbaceous perennial climber. From summer to autumn, it bears hanging, tubular, deep red-purple flowers with a "skirt" of rose-pink calyces. It has attractive, heart-shaped rich green leaves.
‡3m (10ft) ↔ 75cm (30in)

CULTIVATION Grow in sun or light shade, in humus-rich, moist but well-drained soil or potting compost. Trim in summer, if necessary, to keep it within bounds. Bring under glass for the winter.

BEE-BALM [1]

Monarda **'Mahogany'** A vigorous, clump-forming, herbaceous perennial. From midsummer until autumn, it bears whorls of wine-red flowers at the stem tips; they appear in profusion above the aromatic, red-veined, dark green leaves, and are very attractive to bees.
↕90cm (36in) ↔45cm (18in)

CULTIVATION Best in sun, but will tolerate light, dappled shade. Grow in any fertile, well-drained soil that doesn't dry out in summer. Divide overcrowded clumps in spring.

BEDDING VERBENA [2]

Verbena × *hybrida* **Sandy Series** These cultivars have a compact and erect habit of growth with flowers ranging in colour from rose-pink with white eyes, through magenta and scarlet, to white; colour mixtures are also available. Although they are perennial, they are generally grown as annuals.
↕↔25cm (10in).

CULTIVATION Grow in moderately fertile, moist but well-drained soil, in full sun. Sow seed indoors in early spring. Deadhead to encourage more flowers.

1

INDIGOFERA

3

Indigofera heterantha ♀ A medium-sized, deciduous shrub with arching branches. From early summer until autumn, it bears slender, upright clusters of purple-pink, pea-like flowers. It has elegant grey-green leaves.
↕ 2–3m (6–10ft) ↔ 2–3m (6–10ft)

CULTIVATION Grow in full sun in fertile, moist but well-drained soil. In late winter or early spring, trim overlong, badly placed, or damaged shoots. In areas with severe winters, prune all stems back hard to a woody framework in spring.

FUCHSIA 1

Fuchsia **'Auntie Jinks'** A trailing variety of these popular half-hardy shrubs. From early summer until late autumn, it bears masses of single flowers with pink-red tubes, cerise-margined white sepals and purple corollas.
‡ 15–20cm (6–8in) ↔ 20–40cm (8–16in)

CULTIVATION Tolerates sun or light shade. Grow in fertile, well-drained soil or potting mix, and plant out when the threat of frost has passed. Bring indoors for the winter. Deadhead regularly, and cut back hard in spring.

SCABIOSA 2

Scabiosa **'Butterfly Blue'** A clump-forming, spreading herbaceous perennial with divided, grey-green leaves. From mid- to late summer, it bears wiry-stemmed, lavender-blue flowers that attract butterflies and bees.
‡ 40cm (16in) ↔ 40cm (16in)

CULTIVATION Grow in any moderately fertile, well-drained soil in full sun, or light part-day shade.

2

MONTBRETIA 3

Crocosmia × crocosmiiflora 'Jackanapes'
A moderately vigorous, upright cormous
perennial. In late summer, it produces
arching sprays of orange-red and yellow
flowers. Handsome, sword-shaped leaves
for most of the year.

↕40–60cm (16–24in) ↔8cm (3in)

CULTIVATION Ideally grow in full sun,
but it will tolerate part-shade. Plant the
corms 8–10cm (3–4in) deep in fertile
soil. On heavy clay, plant on a layer of
coarse grit. Lift and divide every three
or four years, in spring.

3

HARDY GERANIUM [1]

Geranium psilostemon ♀ A clump-forming herbaceous perennial. From early until late summer, it bears sprays of upturned, brilliant magenta flowers with black centres and veins. The leaves are tinted crimson in spring and red in autumn; they make good ground cover.
‡60–120cm (2–4ft) ↔ 60cm (24in)

CULTIVATION Grow in sun or light shade, in any well-drained, fertile soil. Deadhead regularly to encourage continuous blooming.

JAPANESE ANEMONE [2]

Anemone × hybrida 'Elegans' ♀ A vigorous, spreading, herbaceous perennial of upright growth. From late summer until late autumn, it bears single, light pink flowers that become paler as they age. The lobed, dark green leaves make good ground cover.
‡75–120cm (30–45in) ↔ indefinite

CULTIVATION Prefers a moist, humus-rich soil and thrives in sun or dappled shade. It is invasive, but easily controlled by digging out unwanted pieces.

I

SMOKE BUSH   3

Cotinus coggygria f. *purpureus*
A mound-forming deciduous shrub.
Plumes of tiny purplish pink flowers
become smoky grey by late summer,
giving rise to the common name. The
oval light green leaves turn to orange
and finally flaming red in autumn.
‡5m (15ft) ↔ 5m (15ft)

CULTIVATION Grow in any moderately
fertile, moist but well-drained soil. For
larger, brighter coloured foliage, prune
back hard in spring, but allow the plant
to become established before doing so.

2

3

MALLOW ☐ 1

Lavatera × *clementii* **'Barnsley'**
A very robust, bushy, semi-evergreen
shrub. Throughout summer, it produces
open funnel-shaped, red-eyed, white
flowers that flush soft pink with age. It
has attractive lobed, grey-green leaves.
‡2m (6ft) ↔ 2m (6ft)

CULTIVATION Prefers an open, sunny
site. Grow in any reasonably fertile, well-
drained soil. Shelter from cold winds in
exposed gardens. In spring, cut back hard
to good buds low down on the shrub
and apply a balanced fertilizer.

ZONAL PELARGONIUM ☐ 2

Pelargonium **'Apple Blossom
Rosebud'** ♀ A frost-tender, evergreen,
fleshy-stemmed perennial. From summer
to autumn, it bears large clusters of white
flowers with pink margins. Rounded,
pale green leaves.
‡40cm (16in) ↔ 25cm (10in)

CULTIVATION Grow in fertile, well-
drained soil or compost in full sun.
Set out when risk of frost has passed.
Give a high-potash fertilizer weekly,
and deadhead regularly. Take stem cuttings
during spring or summer and overwinter
under glass.

2

GAZANIA

3

Gazania **Chansonette Series**
Half-hardy perennial often grown as
an annual. Throughout summer, it bears
daisy-like, dark-zoned flowerheads in
bronze, orange, rose-pink, salmon-pink,
or red. The glossy, dark green leaves have
silky white hair beneath.
‡20cm (8in) ↔ 25cm (10in)

CULTIVATION Sow seeds in warmth in
spring and plant out young plants when
the risk of frost has passed. Grow in full
sun in light, well-drained soil. Deadhead
regularly to prolong flowering.

3

PENSTEMON

Vigorous, frost-hardy, evergreen or
semi-evergreen perennials of upright
growth. From summer to late autumn,
they bear bell-shaped, foxglove-like
flowers in white and shades of red,
pink, lilac, and maroon. They form
dense clumps of fresh green leaves.

CULTIVATION Best in sun, but also
tolerant of dappled, part-day shade.
Grow in fertile, well-drained soil.
Incorporate grit into heavy clay soil to
improve drainage. Deadhead regularly.
May not survive cold wet winters, so
take stem cuttings in late summer and
overwinter under glass.

TOP ROW LEFT TO RIGHT
- *P.* 'Burgundy'
  ‡90cm (36in) ↔ 45cm (18in)
- *P.* 'Stapleford Gem' ♈
  ‡60cm (24in) ↔ 45cm (18in)
- *P.* 'Chester Scarlet' ♈
  ‡60cm (24in) ↔ 45cm (18in)

BOTTOM ROW LEFT TO RIGHT
- *P.* 'Alice Hindley' ♈
  ‡90cm (36in) ↔ 45cm (18in)
- *P.* 'Maurice Gibbs' ♈
  ‡75cm (30in) ↔ 45cm (18in)
- *P.* 'Apple Blossom' ♈
  ‡60cm (24in) ↔ 60cm (24in)

LATE-FLOWERING CLEMATIS

The late-flowering clematis include large- and small-flowered cultivars, as well as species, that extend the flowering season from midsummer well into autumn.

CULTIVATION Late-flowering clematis are grown as for early-flowered clematis (*see p. 284*) but are pruned differently, since they flower on the current season's shoots. Simply cut back all of the previous year's stems to strong buds 23–45cm (9–18in) above the ground, just as the buds begin to break in spring. If some of the new shoots are trimmed lightly when they reach 30–50cm (12–20in) long, they flower later and extend the season.

TOP ROW LEFT TO RIGHT
- *C.* 'Hagley Hybrid'
  ↕2m (6ft) ↔ 1m (3ft)
- *C.* 'Ville de Lyon'
  ↕2–3m (6–10ft) ↔ 1m (3ft)
- *C.* 'Paul Farges' ♚
  ↕7–9m (21–28ft) ↔ 3m (10ft)

BOTTOM ROW LEFT TO RIGHT
- *C.* 'Jackmanii' ♚
  ↕3m (10ft) ↔ 1m (3ft)
- *C.* 'Comtesse de Bouchaud' ♚
  ↕2–3m (6–10ft) ↔ 1m (3ft)
- *C.* 'Abundance' ♚
  ↕3m (10ft) ↔ 1m (3ft)

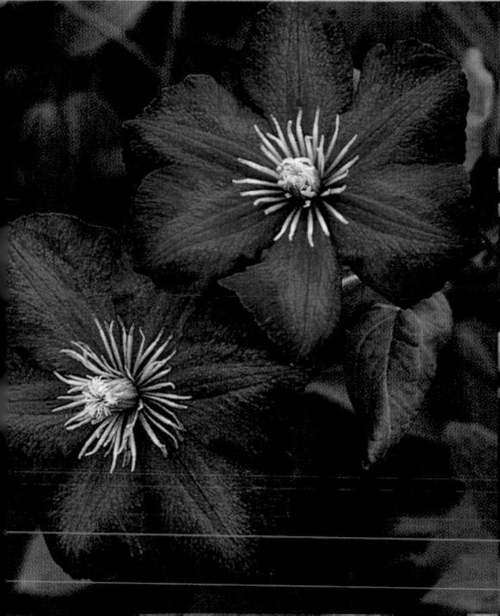

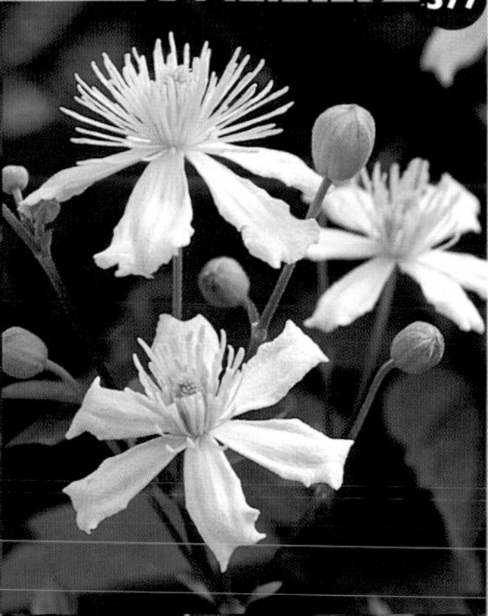

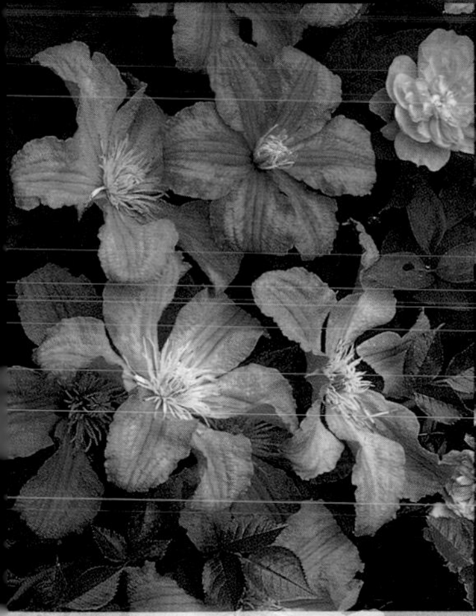

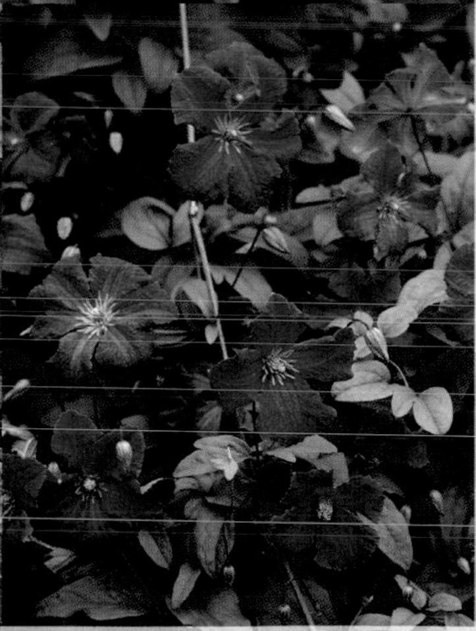

WHAT TO DO IN **SEPTEMBER**

WEATHER WATCH

At this time of year you will be gathering in the harvest and watching autumn colours develop – a hint of the glorious shades to come. With winter approaching, you can start to think about shaping and planting your garden for next year.

SHORTENING DAYS

There can be occasional warm days in September, but on the whole it is cooler in all parts of the country and the first night frosts can be expected in exposed areas. But the warm autumn days should be relished as the days get shorter and there is less time to work in the garden. Good weather will prolong the flowering display until well into autumn.

A WINDY MONTH

September can be a windy month, but after a sultry summer this usually comes as something of a relief. Gales increase in frequency as autumn approaches and low-

pressure systems move in from the Atlantic: areas most likely to receive the first of the autumn gales are the western isles and the west coast. Although most prevailing winds come from the west, these can change rapidly to colder directions – either the north or east.

DIRECT SUNSHINE

It is surprising just how much direct sunshine there can be this month, although this will depend on cloud cover. Parts of the north and west can experience over 100 hours of direct sunshine and the south and east as much as 150 hours. Days with clear, blue sky, bright sunshine and just a hint of a chill in a gentle breeze are a pure delight in autumn.

INCREASING RAINFALL

If we are fortunate, we can enjoy an Indian summer that lasts well into the next month, but we can't expect this to happen every year. The amount of rain falling generally increases in September. Again, the wettest areas will be the north and west parts of the country. The south and east will receive the least rain, with around 47–51mm (1¾–2in) falling on average, while the north and west can have anything from 90mm (3½in) to over 200mm (7¾in) of rain in north–west Scotland.

REMOTE SNOW

Snow rarely falls in Britain before the months of November or December. Only on the higher peaks, such as Ben Nevis in Scotland, does the snow remain on the mountain top right through the summer.

AROUND THE GARDEN

GET A COMPOST BIN

It is essential to add plenty of organic matter to the soil to maintain it in good heart. Growing plants intensively, as we tend to do in small gardens, means that a lot of goodness is taken out of the earth in a relatively small area. It is therefore necessary to put something back in order to continue to get the best out of the garden. You can contruct your own bin, but there are also plenty of bins available to buy; both homemade and bought bins will provide you with somewhere to store all of your autumn debris. Remember to use a good mix of different materials, whilst excluding woody and diseased material, to make the best compost. If you grow vegetables, they should generate a great deal of useful composting material.

This compost bin has an open front for easy access, and cardboard between the double-layer of wire netting to provide insulation.

Straw packed between the double layer of wire netting makes an alternative insulation layer. A slatted front contains the compost.

A beehive box is easy to contruct, and tiers can be added as the compost builds up. Plastic sheeting keeps rain off and heat in.

You could also purchase a compost bin from your garden centre. Plastic ones are both resistant to rot and inexpensive.

START TO CLEAR GARDEN DEBRIS

Clear any debris in borders, consigning it to the compost heap or burning it if it is diseased. Damage from pests and diseases will be slowing down at this time of year, but it is still necessary to be on the lookout to prevent pests overwintering and becoming a problem next year. Yellowing leaves on plants should be removed as they will encourage mildew and botrytis.

Any pests like aphids that are still around can be dealt with by squashing them. Shoot tips that have become heavily infected with mildew or are overwhelmed by aphids can become distorted under the attack. Trim these back to healthy growth and burn the prunings. Don't just add them to the compost heap, or you're in danger of spreading the problem.

REMOVE THATCH FROM LAWNS

Over time, a layer of dead grass and other debris accumulates in any lawn; this is called thatch. Left in the lawn over the years it restricts air movement around the grass and can cause problems with surface drainage, encouraging moss and other weeds to colonize the lawn. Remove this thatch from now until autumn.

Use a garden fork to aerate your lawn every couple of years. In clay soils, you might need to do this more often.

Scarify your lawn to remove the thatch. Make sure moss is dead before doing this, as raking live moss will spread the problem.

The most back-breaking way to remove thatch is to drag it out with a spring-tined rake. Rake out both the dead grass and moss. This can be very hard work, so if you have a large lawn, you might find it easier to use a powered scarifier (which can be hired). Be warned: the lawn will look an absolute mess after scarifying, but it will do it the world of good and the grass will soon recover.

Immediately after aerating, apply a gritty top-dressing to improve drainage and increase the nutrient content.

AERATE AND TOP-DRESS LAWNS

Like any other plant, grass needs air, and the surface of the lawn can get very compacted over the course of the summer with constant use and cutting every week. To relieve this compaction, aerate the lawn with a fork pushed into the ground, to a depth of 15cm (6in) at 15–18cm (6–9in) intervals over the whole area.

Top-dressing immediately after aerating keeps holes open and revitalizes the upper layer of soil. Use a mix of three parts of sieved garden soil, two parts of sharp sand, and one part sieved garden compost. Spread a 1–2cm (½–1in) layer over the lawn and work it in with a stiff broom or the back of a rake. It will look a bit of a mess for a couple of weeks, but the grass will soon grow through again.

Allow the top-dressing to dry, then use a stiff broom or the back of a brush to work it into the grass and air holes.

FEED AND RESEED LAWNS

At this time of year, you need one of the low-nitrogen fertilisers sold as autumn lawn feeds in garden centres, as you don't want to encourage soft, sappy growth.

Small bare patches on the lawn can be easily repaired by sowing seed. Rake out any thatch and then roughen the surface slightly with a fork to make a fine tilth and level it. Put the grass seed in a bucket and mix in an equal quantity of old potting compost or sieved garden compost. Spread this mix evenly over the bare patch and tamp it down with the back of a rake. To encourage quick germination, cover the area with polythene pegged into the ground. Keep the patch watered if it gets dry, and the seed should germinate in two to three weeks. Remove the polythene as soon as the seeds begin to germinate.

Patches of broad-leaved weeds can be treated with a selective lawn weedkiller.

Apply an autumn lawn feed evenly over the whole lawn – read the instructions on the packet for details of how much to use.

Sprinkle seed on any bare patches – ensure the seed type matches your grass. Use about half the amount you would for a new lawn.

KEEP THINNING AQUATIC PLANTS

Oxygenating and floating plants can grow so well that they almost take over the pond, so these will need thinning out if there are other plants growing in the water. After removing them, always leave them by the side of the pond for a few days to allow any wildlife hiding in the plants to get back into the pond. While you're at it, you can also divide poolside plants such as irises and astilbes that have finished flowering if they are becoming congested.

COVER PONDS WITH NETTING

Done early, this will prevent leaves falling into the pond. If leaves accumulate and rot in the pond they give off gases as they decompose, and these can be lethal to fish and other wildlife.

Prevent autumn leaves from falling into your pond by netting it, as rotting leaves can cause harm to wildlife.

Use the finest mesh you can get, otherwise smaller leaves will still get in. Secure it around the edge of the pond with bricks or pegs used for securing horticultural fleece. Pegs can also be made from fencing wire. If any leaves have fallen in the pond already, fish them out before netting.

TREES, SHRUBS & CLIMBERS

PLANT CONTAINER-GROWN SHRUBS

At this time of year the soil is still quite warm and moist, so the roots of the shrubs can become established before winter sets in, and the plants will get off to a flying start come spring. Because the soil is relatively moist there is no need to pay so much attention to watering in the early stages, saving on water and time.

PLANTING A CONTAINER-GROWN SHRUB

1 Dig a hole twice the width of the shrub's rootball. Sit the shrub in the hole, and lay a cane across the hole to check it is at the same depth it was in the container.

2 Backfill around the shrub with your hands. As you firm in with your heel, create a saucer-shaped depression around the shrub so water will collect at the root area.

MOVE EVERGREENS

Autumn and early spring are good times to relocate evergreen shrubs, as the soil tends to be relatively warm at these times. Dig around the plant as far from the base as you can, and as deep as possible, which should enable you to remove a good root system. If you're moving a large shrub, ask someone for help in order to avoid back strain.

3 Cut out any dead or damaged stems, and prune inward-growing stems back to a healthy, outward-facing bud or shoot. Water well, then mulch.

START PRUNING CLIMBING ROSES

Only do so when the flowers fade; if they are still going strong, wait until next month. To prune, first remove dead or diseased wood. Then look for new shoots, especially from the base of the plant, for tying in. If there aren't many new basal shoots, prune all the sideshoots from the existing framework of branches to two or three buds. Remove entirely any very old stems, pruning them to near ground level. New shoots can be tied in to replace these.

STOP FEEDING CONTAINER PLANTS

Shrubs and trees in containers will, if fed, produce soft growth now which will be damaged in winter, so stop feeding them with general fertilisers now. One last feed with sulphate of potash – or rock potash if you want to be organic – will benefit them by ripening the wood, building up their resilience to the rigours of winter.

FLOWERING PLANTS

PLANT NEW PERENNIALS

This is a good time of year for planting new perennials, as the soil is moist and still warm enough for the plants' roots to become established before the winter sets in. Garden centres should have a good selection of flowering and foliage herbaceous perennials available. It's fun spending time choosing plants that will grow well in your garden. Perennials are generally inexpensive – and, of course, the plants can be lifted and divided, and cuttings can be taken in years to come, so each plant then costs almost nothing.

PLANTING NEW PERENNIALS

1 Begin by digging holes for the new plants. To the bottom of each one, add some garden compost and a handful of bonemeal.

2 Give the plants a good soak for an hour or two before you want to plant, then carefully ease the rootball out of the pot.

3 If you find the plant has become tight and compacted in its pot, tease out the rootball slightly before planting.

Choose plants carefully, ensuring they are right for your garden and for the position they are intended for. It's a waste of money to buy something simply because it is appealing, only to find it struggles or even dies because it was a bad choice. Be on the lookout for plants with strong healthy growth, with the rootballs showing plenty of roots, but not so packed that the plants are pot-bound. If you don't want to turn the plant out of its pot (though no good nursery should mind you doing this) then at least make sure no roots are thrusting through the drainage holes at the bottom.

Water the plants well before and after planting. If the plants are dry when you buy them, plunge them in a bucket of water to ensure that the rootball is moist right through.

4 Set the plant at the same depth as before, and then fill in around it with soil, firming it well with your fingers.

5 Water the plant thoroughly: half a watering can for each plant is not excessive if the weather has been very dry.

6 Mulch around the plant with garden compost, chipped bark, or leafmould to reduce evaporation from the soil.

CUT DOWN AND DIVIDE PERENNIALS

Most perennials look rather tatty when the flowers go over, so cut them down and make the borders look tidier. Clumps which are becoming old and bare in the centre can be lifted and divided. Some plants, such as sedums, thrive when divided every year and others, like peonies, resent being disturbed. It's very difficult to give generalised advice. There are so many perennials available now that it is well worth treating yourself to a good reference book on the subject.

Clumps which need dividing can be lifted with a fork and placed on a sheet of polythene on the lawn. Divide large clumps with two forks inserted into the centre of the clump back to back, pushing them apart. Smaller pieces

DIVIDING HERBACEOUS PERENNIALS

1 Cut down old stems to expose the crown. Dig around the clump and lever it out with a fork. Shake off surplus soil so the roots show.

2 Insert two forks back to back, and push the handles apart to split the clump. Repeat until the segments are the right size.

can be pulled apart by hand. Revitalize the soil with plenty of organic matter and plant the smaller pieces in groups of three, five, or more if you have the space.

If you haven't time to divide clumps of herbaceous perennials now, it can be done throughout autumn and into spring as long as the soil conditions are good enough to work. If you can't get on with the work, at least make

notes about the plants to be divided or moved. Sometimes, no matter how expert we think we are, some plant associations just don't work. Colour combinations are easy to plan using photographs, but getting the heights and relative vigour of neighbouring plants right can be slightly more tricky. However, the one advantage of growing herbaceous perennials is that they can always be moved if this happens and they don't take many years to get established.

SUPPORT ASTERS

Tall-growing clumps of asters need support or they will be blown down in windy conditions. Wire supports available from garden centres do a good job, but have to be put in place while plants are young and can grow through them. Alternatively, put three or four canes around the plant and wind string around them to enclose the stems. If done carefully, the canes and string will be almost hidden by foliage.

3 Replant these segments in well-prepared ground at the same level as before. Firm and level the soil, and water.

POT UP BULBS FOR CHRISTMAS

Pot up prepared hyacinths and other bulbs such as 'Paper White' narcissi for flowers at Christmas. If you are planting them in bulb bowls that have no drainage holes, use bulb fibre; otherwise, any proprietary potting compost will suffice.

Dwarf bulbs in pots are particularly appealing, as the beauty of these miniatures can really be appreciated at close quarters. There are plenty of daffodils to choose from, among them *Narcissus tazettus*, with yellow and white scented flowers; *N.* 'Jack Snipe', with creamy yellow petals, and *N. minimus* with yellow flowers. Other dwarf bulbs you could try include species tulips, such as *Tulipa tarda*, chionodoxas, crocus, and dwarf iris.

Plant several bulbs in a bowl or pot, and cover with compost leaving just the nose of the bulbs uncovered. Then 'plunge' the containers outside, covering them

Plant hyacinth bulbs so they are almost touching. They will provide a welcome floral display for the festive season.

with compost, or put them in a cool, dark place. After six weeks, start inspecting the bulbs and when they have made about 2.5cm (1in) of growth they can be brought inside.

PLANT SPRING BULBS IN GRASS

Plant daffodils and narcissi before the end of this month. Daffodils look particularly good when they are planted in drifts, naturalised in grass. Bear in mind, though, that the grass will have to be left uncut for at least six weeks after the flowers are over, to allow the bulb to build up its flower bud for the following spring. Dwarf varieties also look good in rock gardens or in raised beds, where the flowers can be appreciated more easily.

Buy bulbs early, and you will almost always get the best choice, particularly among sought-after bulbs like alliums. There are so many more bulbs to choose from than the ubiquitous daffodils and crocuses: it's worth being a little experimental. Keep an eye out for chionodoxas, ornithogalum, scillas, puschkinia and *Iris histrioides*, for example, as well as corms of the many varieties of *Anemone blanda*. Grape hyacinths (*Muscari*) are essentials, too, for pretty, low-growing clumps of the most vivid blue flowers.

DAFFODILS TO TRY

'Broadway Star'

'Cassata'

'Ambergate'

'Rip van Winkle'

'Jumblie'

'Tahiti'

Don't forget to put some bulbs in amongst your spring bedding plants, as they'll produce a stunning show when spring comes. If you have problems with mice taking your bulbs (they are particularly fond of crocuses), pegged-down chicken wire can give some protection.

If you are planting the bulbs in a border where you don't need to lift them, it's a good idea to mark them with a label; you may well forget where they are after the flowers and foliage have died down, and it's all too easy to dig them up again.

With the exception of the very tiniest alpines, all bulbs can be planted in turf, where they look particularly pleasing. In the case of colchicum bulbs, the flowers appear before the leaves and they can look rather startling on their own, so naturalise them in grass amongst other plants to tone them down a little.

For smaller bulbs or corms like miniature daffodils and crocus, the

PLANTING BULBS IN GRASS

To plant small bulbs in grass, make H-shaped cuts and lift flaps in the turf, planting beneath.

To plant large bulbs in grass, make individual holes with a planter, spacing the bulbs randomly.

simplest way to plant them is to lift a piece of turf and place the bulbs in groups on top of the soil, folding down the turf afterwards. With larger bulbs like daffodils and tulips, it's easier to use a bulb planter rather than digging individual holes for each one. To achieve an informal drift of bulbs in grass, scatter a handful of them over the area, and plant the bulbs wherever they fall.

As ever, the general rule when planting all bulbs is to plant them two to three times their own depth. If you're not sure how deeply a bulb should go, it's always better to plant a little too deeply than too shallowly. In heavy clay soils, it's worth adding some grit to the planting hole before you sit the bulbs in it – this will aid drainage. It's definitely worth investing in a bulb-planting tool if you have a large quantity of bulbs to plant: they do make the job much easier. Leave tulip bulbs until late October or November before planting.

PLANT BULBS IN CONTAINERS

There is no need to renew the compost in your containers when summer bedding has been pulled out, as bulbs will thrive perfectly well in old compost. The most important time to feed bulbs is after they flower, when they are building up the flower bud to flower the following year.

Pack the bulbs in as close as possible, planting them to approximately two or three times their depth. For a really striking show in the spring, use one kind or colour of bulb for each container. There are some bulbs, such as daffodils, which are resilient enough to be planted in several tiers in one pot. If you do choose to plant your bulbs in layers, put the largest ones at the bottom and the smallest at the top to fill out the display.

SOW HARDY ANNUALS

Some hardy annuals can be sown outside now for flowering next year. Rake the soil to a fine tilth, then mark out informal areas with a stick or sand poured out of an empty wine bottle. Take out shallow drills within each marked area, and water them if the soil is dry. Sow the seeds thinly and cover with dry soil. When the seedlings are approximately 2.5cm (1in) high, thin them out to about 10cm (4in). In spring you may have to thin them again. Look on the back of seed packets for those annuals that can be sown outside now; they include marigolds (*Calendula*), cornflowers (*Centaurea*), poached-egg plants (*Limnanthes*), California poppies (*Eschscholzia*), and poppies (*Papaver somniferum*).

Sown now, plants such a cornflowers (far left), poached-egg plants (left), and California poppies (above) will flower from next May.

SPRING BEDDING PLANTS TO TRY

Digitalis purpurea f. *albiflora*

Bellis perennis

Erysimum cheiri 'Blood Red'

Anchusa 'Loddon Royalist'

PLANT OUT SPRING BEDDING

This is the time to plant out spring-flowering biennials, either bought, or transplanted from where you have been growing them in nursery rows through the summer. Clear old summer bedding away once the flowers have gone over, and remember to incorporate organic matter into the soil if it is needed. Afterwards, rake the soil level, and mark out informal drifts with a stick.

Plant groups of each kind of plant in each drift for the best effect. Make sure the crown of plants is level with the soil, and that you firm them in well. Then water them in to settle the soil around the roots.

If you were not able to grow your own biennials, garden centres should have a selection available from now on. Plants to look for are wallflowers, forget-me-nots (*Myosotis*), bellis, canterbury bells (*Campanula medium*), sweet Williams (*Dianthus barbatus*), foxgloves (*Digitalis purpurea*), anchusa, Iceland poppies (*Papaver nudicaule*), ornamental cabbages, and winter-flowering pansies.

CLEAR OUT POTTED SUMMER BEDDING

Once summer bedding plants in containers have come to the end of their time they can be cleared out, and spring bedding plants can be planted in their place.

Remove some of the old compost and put in some fresh material – preferably a John Innes potting compost as it will retain more nutrients and, being heavier, will prevent containers blowing over in windy weather. The choice of plants and colour schemes is entirely personal, so let your imagination run riot. If you haven't raised your own spring bedding like wallflowers, forget-me-nots, and bellis yourself, garden centres will have a wide range of plants from which to choose. Remember to plant bulbs in with the spring bedding too.

KITCHEN GARDEN

LIFT MAINCROP POTATOES

Lift them on a warm sunny day, and leave them on the surface of the soil for an hour or two to dry out. Store undamaged ones in paper sacks tied at the neck. Potatoes must be stored in darkness, otherwise they turn green and become poisonous. It's also important to protect them from frost.

Harvest potatoes as they reach maturity, and leave them exposed for a few hours to dry out. Discard any damaged produce immediately.

GET ONIONS UNDER COVER

Lift and dry any onions still in the ground, and bring them into a cool, dry storage area before damp weather sets in. In mild autumns especially, if onions are left in the ground after the leaves have gone over, they often start to regrow, and they are then less useful in the kitchen and no good for storing. You'll know the bulbs are ready to store when the skins become papery and they make a rustling sound when handled.

PICK PUMPKINS, MARROWS & SQUASHES

Leave them in the sun for several days (or put them in a greenhouse if the weather is wet) so that they can ripen and dry off before they are put into storage in a cool, dark place. They should keep until well after Christmas. Clear the old plants away as soon as the fruits have been picked, as they will by now almost certainly have been attacked by mildew.

Pumpkins and squashes should be harvested with a long stalk. This will harden as the fruit dries, protecting the stem from rotting.

Pumpkins benefit from being harvested in advance. Leave them in the sun for a few days to harden the skins and dry off the stalks.

PLANT AUTUMN ONION SETS

The sooner these go in and get growing before winter sets in the better. Varieties to look for are 'Radar' and 'Swift'. Plant them 8cm (3in) apart in drills, deep enough to just cover the tip of the sets. Apply a general organic fertiliser now, and again in spring to boost their growth.

SOW WINTER LETTUCE

Sow lettuce seeds in shallow drills in the usual manner, then cover with cloches. The seeds should germinate fairly quickly; when the seedlings are large enough to handle, thin them out to approximately 15cm (6in) apart. You can harvest them from January onwards. A good old reliable favourite is 'Winter Density'.

PLANT GARLIC

Autumn is the traditional time for planting garlic, as it needs a period of cold weather to grow well. To get good-quality crops, buy bulbs specially cultivated for planting. Plant in a sunny site in well-drained soil. On heavy soil, dig in some horticultural grit to aid drainage. Break each bulb into individual cloves, and plant each one 8–10cm (3–4in) apart, with 30cm (24in) between rows. Plant so that the tips of the cloves are just below soil level.

If you decide to plant your garlic in modules, choose a tray with large cells to accommodate the chunky cloves.

To get the plants off to a quicker start, plant them in module trays with large cells and keep these in a cold frame for the winter, or place them at the base of a sheltered wall. The plants can then be put in the ground in the spring.

PLANT OUT SPRING CABBAGES

Spring cabbages sown last month can be planted 15cm (6in) apart in rows 30cm (24in) apart. Harvest every other plant as spring greens, leaving the others to heart up. Cover the plants with netting or fleece or the pigeons will have them eaten to the ground as soon as your back is turned.

There is still a little time to sow a fast maturing variety like 'Duncan' or 'Pixie' if you do so under cover. To get them off to a good start, sow the seeds in modules, so that when it comes to planting them out the roots are not disturbed and the plants can be moved easily without a check to their growth.

LAY TOMATO PLANTS ON STRAW

It is rare in our short summers to ripen the whole crop from outdoor tomatoes. By laying the plants down and covering them with a cloche, you can maximise the ripening effect of the late sunshine. Any fruits left unripe can be used to make green tomato chutney – or, place them into a drawer and put a banana in with them. The gases given off by the banana help the ripening process. Remember to check the harvested tomatoes carefully for any signs of rot or disease – throw away any that look unhealthy.

Lay cordon tomatoes down on clean straw and cover with cloches to finish ripening.

PLANT NEW STRAWBERRIES

If your plants are healthy and show no signs of disease, plant out some of their runners, which you may have pegged down into pots. But if there are any signs of virus, which usually shows up as streaks through the foliage, then start afresh with strawberries from a specialist fruit grower, where you know the stock has been certified free from virus. Establish the plants on ground that has not grown them for a few years. You can move a strawberry bed in stages – if you have three rows of fruit growing in the vegetable garden, renew one row each year. Plant the new row to one side of the

If you want to increase the number of strawberry plants, peg out some of the runners, provided the parent plant is disease-free.

existing rows and remove the last old row on the other side. Do this each year and you will work your way down the vegetable plot, planting new strawberries in fresh ground each year.

Water new strawberries well: planting them now enables them to establish before the winter, but if they go short of water, they will not fruit well next year. Plants under stress from lack of water are also more prone to attack from pests and diseases. Strawberries are not a permanent crop like other fruits so, if you can, grow them in the vegetable garden where they can be rotated like the other crops.

PICK AUTUMN RASPBERRIES

Towards the middle and end of September, autumn-fruiting raspberries come into their own. These late-fruiting varieties are delicious, as they are often more concentrated in flavour than their summer counterparts. Once you have picked the last fruits, leave the canes unpruned until late winter or early spring. However, you can still finish cutting out any remaining fruited canes of summer-fruiting raspberries.

CONTINUE TO HARVEST TREE FRUIT

Cooking varieties of apples and pears will be ready for picking towards the end of this month. Handle fruits gently, as the skins are easily bruised, which adversely affects their keeping qualities.

Store only unblemished fruits; damaged ones should be used right away, or at least kept away from the main storage area. Wrap large crops of apples individually in paper, and lay on trays in a single layer. Store smaller quantities in polythene bags. Make a few holes in the bags with a skewer to let out gases given off by the fruits that will hasten ripening. Pears are best left unwrapped, standing on slatted benches. Pick early dessert pears while they are still hard and let them ripen indoors.

SEPTEMBER PROJECT

PLANTS FOR A COLD GREENHOUSE

A greenhouse doesn't have to remain empty throughout the winter because of prohibitive heating costs. There are many plants that will grow happily in a cold greenhouse, needing no more than a little protection from rain and frosts. Just remember to leave the vents and doors open to allow good circulation of air and avoid a build-up of damp.

Almost any hardy plant can be grown successfully in a cold greenhouse, including small shrubs, many perennials and hardy annuals, alpines, bulbs, and more. A few examples are given here, but the choice is yours. The extra shelter and encouragement you give these plants is likely to be rewarded next spring, when they flower earlier than they would have done if grown outdoors.

Centaurea cyanus (Cornflower)
This attractive hardy annual is a cottage garden favourite and very easy to grow. Sow seeds in pots in the autumn and enjoy a mini wildflower meadow in spring.

Chrysanthemum carinatum
Another easy-to-grow hardy annual, this chrysanthemum comes in a range of colours. Try growing three or four mixed plants in a medium-sized pot.

Helleborus x sternii
By growing hellebores indoors, you can
protect this beautiful plant from being
ruined by soil splashes every time it rains.
There are many cultivars to choose from.

Cyclamen coum
Hardy cyclamen are ideal in a cold
greenhouse. They can be grown from
seed and will flower over the winter
months when little else is in bloom.

Sedum spathulifolium
A dwarf alpine sedum makes a delightful
pot plant for indoors, where you can
appreciate its miniature flowers at close
quarters. Grow in free-draining compost.

Camellia japonica
Camellias are the perfect candidates for
growing indoors. Although they are hardy
plants, frost usually has a disastrous
effect on their flowers.

AGAPANTHUS

Agapanthus **'Blue Giant'** A tall, clump-forming, herbaceous perennial with large, strap-shaped, deep green leaves. It bears rounded clusters of bell-shaped, rich blue flowers from mid- to late summer.

‡1.2m (4ft) ↔ 60cm (24in)

CULTIVATION Best in sun, but will tolerate light, dappled shade. Grow in moist but well-drained soil. In cold areas, mulch in winter to protect fleshy roots from frost.

DAHLIA

Dahlia **'Bishop of Llandaff'** ♀
A tuberous, frost-tender perennial. From late summer until late autumn, it produces semi-double, velvety, glowing red flowers. It also has very attractive dark red leaves.

‡1.1m (3½ft) ↔ 45cm (18in)

CULTIVATION Best in full sun in fertile, well-drained soil enriched with well-rotted organic matter. Plant in early summer when all risk of frost has passed. In frost-prone climates, lift tubers and store in a cool, dry place over winter.

CONEFLOWER 3

***Rudbeckia laciniata* 'Herbstsonne'** ♛
A vigorous herbaceous perennial. From midsummer until early autumn, it bears daisy-like, bright yellow flowers with cone-shaped centres. It has attractive, prominently veined, glossy green leaves. ‡to 2m (6ft) ↔ 90cm (36in)

CULTIVATION Best in full sun, but tolerates light, dappled shade. Grow in a fertile, preferably heavy soil. After three or four years, lift and divide in spring or autumn to rejuvenate.

SEA HOLLY [1]

Eryngium × *tripartitum* ♀ An upright, prickly, herbaceous perennial. From midsummer until early autumn, it bears branching stems of violet-blue flowers with narrow, grey-blue bracts; they are good for drying. Basal clumps of shiny, slightly spiny, dark green leaves.
‡60–90cm (24–36in) ↔ 50cm (20in)

CULTIVATION Grow in full sun in poor, dry gritty soil. It may need protection from excessive winter wet, especially in cold or exposed gardens.

GOLDENROD [2]

Solidago 'Goldenmosa' ♀ A bushy, herbaceous perennial. In late summer and early autumn, it bears feathery, conical plumes of yellow-stalked, bright yellow flowers. It has wrinkled, mid-green leaves. The flowers are good for cutting.
‡75cm (30in) ↔ 45cm (18in)

CULTIVATION Grow in full sun in any poor to moderately fertile soil. Every three or four years, lift and divide in spring or autumn to maintain vigour. Cut off the flowers as they fade to prevent them seeding.

[1]

HELENIUM [3]

Helenium **'Moerheim Beauty'** ♥
This upright perennial, with strong
branching stems, produces a succession
of eye-catching, daisy-like flowers from
early to late summer; their prominent
dark brown centres are complemented
by vivid, copper-red petals.
‡90cm (36in) ↔ 60cm (24in).

CULTIVATION Grow in fertile, moist but
well-drained soil in full sun. May need
support in windy areas. Deadhead to
prolong flowering. Divide every 2–3 years.

GUELDER ROSE   **1**

***Viburnum opulus* 'Compactum'** ♥
A sturdy but slow-growing deciduous
shrub. In late spring and early summer,
it produces showy, flat, "lacecap" clusters
of white flowers at the stem tips. In
autumn, the glossy, bright red fruits
nestle among the red autumn leaves.
‡ to 1.5m (5ft) ↔ to 1.5m (5ft)

CULTIVATION Thrives in any reasonably
fertile, well-drained soil in sun or dappled
shade. It needs little pruning other than
to shorten any shoots that spoil the shape
after flowering.

TURTLEHEAD   **2**

Chelone obliqua A vigorous, upright,
herbaceous perennial. From late summer
to mid-autumn, it bears dark pink or
purple flowers with yellow beards on the
lower lip. It has attractive, lance-shaped,
boldly veined leaves.
‡ 40–60cm (16–24in) ↔ 30cm (12in)

CULTIVATION Grow in full sun or
part-shade. A deep fertile soil which
retains moisture is ideal; it will tolerate
heavy clay soils. Mulch well in spring
before growth begins.

CARYOPTERIS `3`

Caryopteris × clandonensis **'Kew Blue'**
An arching, deciduous shrub. From late
summer to early autumn, it bears spires
of deep blue flowers. The dark grey-
green leaves are silvery beneath.
‡1m (3ft) ↔ 1.5m (5ft)

CULTIVATION Flowers best in full sun
but tolerates light dappled shade. It
prefers light, fertile, well-drained soil.
In cooler areas, plant against a warm,
sheltered wall. In early spring, cut back
to a permanent woody framework.

`3`

MICHAELMAS DAISY [1]

Aster novi-belgii **'Peace'** A reliable, tall, clump-forming perennial. During autumn it produces clusters of mauve flowers up to 7cm (3in) or more across. The dark green leaves are attractive all through summer.
‡1.2m (4ft) ↔ 90cm (36in)

CULTIVATION Grow in fertile, well-drained soil in sun or part-shade. Plants are better for lifting and dividing every two or three years. Divide in spring or autumn. Asters can be susceptible to powdery mildew.

SEDUM [2]

Sedum spectabile **'Brilliant'** ♀
A clump-forming, herbaceous perennial. From late summer until late autumn, it bears large, flat heads of many tiny, star-shaped, bright pink flowers. The fleshy, slightly scalloped, grey-green leaves are handsome throughout spring and summer.
‡45cm (18in) ↔ 45cm (18in)

CULTIVATION Best in fertile, well-drained, neutral to slightly alkaline soil in sun. Divide in spring, every three or four years, to maintain vigour.

1

COSMOS

3

Cosmos atrosanguineus The chocolate
Cosmos is an unusual, beautiful perennial
with a spreading habit. It is tuberous with
reddish-brown stems and spoon-shaped,
dark green leaves. During midsummer
and autumn, it bears solitary, cup-shaped,
chocolate-scented, dark maroon flowers.
‡75cm (30in) ↔ 45cm (18in).

CULTIVATION Grow in moderately
fertile, moist, but well-drained soil in full
sun. Deadhead to prolong flowering. In
cold areas, mulch for winter protection,
or bring indoors.

2

3

ORNAMENTAL GRASSES

Striking, architectural plants, with arching or upright stems, feathery or tufted flowerheads, and subtly shaded seedheads. Grasses catch the light and bring constant movement and grace to the garden; many remain attractive well into winter. It is important to make sure the grasses you select are suitable for your garden. If in doubt, check the label or ask for advice.

CULTIVATION Most grasses thrive in sun or part-shade in light, well-drained soil, and are drought-resistant once established. They require little further attention apart from cutting down old foliage, where needed, in early spring. All the grasses featured here can be propagated by division.

TOP ROW LEFT TO RIGHT
- *Alopecurus pratensis* 'Aureovariegatus'
  ‡1.2m (4ft) ↔ 40cm (16in)
- *Arundo donax* var. *versicolor*
  ‡1.8m (6ft) ↔ 60cm (24in)
- *Hakonechloa macra* 'Aureola' ♀
  ‡35cm (14in) ↔ 40cm (16in)

BOTTOM ROW LEFT TO RIGHT
- *Helictotrichon sempervirens* ♀
  ‡to 1.4m (4½ft) ↔ 60cm (24in)
- *Stipa gigantea* ♀
  ‡2.5m (8ft) ↔ 1.2m (4ft)
- *Pennisetum alopecuroides* 'Hameln'
  ‡1.2m (4ft) ↔ 1.2m (4ft)

WHAT TO DO IN
OCTOBER

WEATHER WATCH

Autumn colours are at their best this month in gardens, parks, and woodlands with only a short time to appreciate them before the leaves begin to fall. Now is the time to plant trees and shrubs, gather the remaining crops, and collect and store seeds.

AUTUMN CHILL

There is a significant drop in temperatures now. The nights are drawing in and, if the weather is clear, overnight frosts are increasingly likely. But October can have warm, sunny days, too. A still, frosty start to a bright, sunny day definitely increases the intensity of autumn leaf colour in deciduous trees and shrubs.

HIGH WINDS

The number of gales tends to increase now that we are well into autumn. This is a pity, because high winds blow the leaves off the trees, spoiling the beautiful autumn display in a matter of days. Gales are now most likely in western coastal areas and will occur on average 3–4 days in the month. Southern and eastern areas generally get between 0.1 and 1.3 days in the south-west.

DECREASED SUNSHINE

The amount of direct sunshine is now on the decrease, but there can be some fine days in October. The northern Highlands compare favourably with parts of central England: around Wick on the north coast of Scotland the average is 88 hours of sun and in Nottingham, 86. The south coast fares better, averaging 107 hours of sunshine this month.

MORE RAINFALL

October inevitably brings more rain for all parts of the country, especially in the north and west. The north of England and central Scotland receive similar amounts of rainfall, ranging from 93mm (3½in) in north-west England to 115mm (4½in) in the Glasgow area. The farther north you go the more rain falls, with Highland areas getting about 216mm (8½in) this month. The driest places are East Anglia and north-east England. where typical October rainfall is 47–67mm (1¾–2½in).

SNOW ON HIGH GROUND

Snow begins to fall this month, but only on high ground in the north. Northern areas of Scotland and Ireland have on average 0.1 days of snow on ground above 30m (100ft). In the north-east this may increase to 0.3 days on ground above 300m (1000ft). In these areas, make the best of good weather before winter sets in.

AROUND THE GARDEN

CLEAR FALLEN LEAVES

Rake up fallen leaves from the lawn and amongst plants in the borders regularly. Fallen leaves left lying around plants can encourage slugs and snails. It seems to be something of a tradition to burn leaves in the autumn, but this is a waste of a valuable commodity. As an alternative, create a container for autumn leaves in which they can be left to decompose for a year or two. The result will be the most wonderful organic matter, known as leafmould, to use as a mulch or a soil conditioner. Leaves can be mixed with other material and put on the compost heap, but if you want leafmould, then they will need a heap of their own.

Contruct a container with four stakes and some chicken wire netting: bang the four posts into the ground to make a square, and nail the netting round the posts. The leaves will look tidier and cannot blow all over the garden.

Sweep autumn leaves from the lawn regularly: if left in a thick layer for even just a few days they will spoil the grass.

KEEP AN EYE OUT FOR PESTS AND DISEASES

Pests are generally on the decline this month, now that the weather is turning cooler, but diseases such as botrytis and mildew are still fairly prevalent with the more moist weather in autumn. Practising good garden hygiene will go a long way to avoiding problems. Don't leave a lot of rubbish lying around; either compost it or put it in the bin. Diseased material can be burned or binned, but it should never be composted. It's also important to clear weeds, as they act as host plants to many pests and diseases.

It's not worth using chemical sprays for mildew and botrytis at this time, as they are much more effective as a preventative measure early in the year. Plants such as courgettes and marrows are particularly prone to both of these diseases at this time of year. Burn all of the infected parts of the plants as they come to the end of their cropping time.

Create a homemade bin for leaves. This cage is simple to make and will stop piles of leaves being blown about.

Larger leaves take longer to rot down, but after about eighteen months you should have good friable leafmould. Use it as a mulch or dig it into the soil as you would do with garden compost.

If you haven't enough room to make a wire enclosure, or enough leaves to make it worthwhile, then put them into black polythene bags with a few holes punched in them and tie them up. You will have good leafmould in the same length of time.

REDUCE FREQUENCY OF MOWING

Established lawns should be mown less frequently now as growth slows down. You should also raise the height of the cutting blades. Grass which is cut too short over the winter will not stand up to the poorer weather conditions, and will be more likely to become infested with moss and weeds, because it is weaker.

You should also continue to rake out thatch, aerate, and top-

If the grass becomes patchy, reseed damaged areas using seed that is the same type as the rest of the lawn.

dress lawns, and reseed any bare patches that develop. This autumn overhaul will make a tremendous difference to the lawn after a summer of hard use. For large lawns, powered machines can be bought or hired to help with all of these jobs.

REDUCE FEEDING OF FISH

Now the days are getting shorter, fish are becoming less active, so feeding should be reduced. Any food not eaten by the fish will just decompose in the water. Apart from being a waste of food, large amounts of rotting food in the water may cause harm to the fish.

TIDY PONDS

Any fallen leaves in the water should be fished out, and any yellowing leaves from plants like waterlilies can be removed at the same time. The dead growth on marginal plants can be cut back too. Remove any blanket weed and thin out oxygenating plants;

Use a sharp knife to remove any yellowing or dead leaves from aquatic plants until there are only healthy, green stems remaining.

in modest quantities, they can be added to the compost heap.

Unless an Indian summer is allowing you to continue the enjoyment of your water feature, remove submersible pumps and lighting systems from the pond and store them over the winter.

Leave weed you have removed by the side of the pond for a few days so wildlife living within it can return to the water.

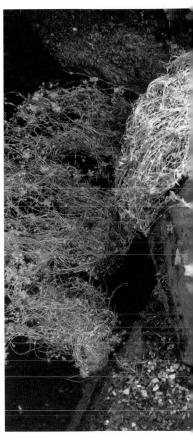

TREES, SHRUBS & CLIMBERS

PREPARE FOR PLANTING TREES AND SHRUBS

If you want to plant bare-root trees and shrubs next month, prepare the ground now. For long-lasting plants that give the garden structure, don't skimp on preparation, as it is not so easy to make up for this once plants are in.

If planting a whole border, dig over the area, removing roots of perennial weeds. Don't leave even tiny portions of roots as they will grow again. Dig in plenty of organic matter. If the soil has not been cultivated before, "double-dig" it. Start by taking out a trench at one end of the area and transport the soil to the other end in a barrow. Then break up the soil at the bottom of the trench with a fork, without bringing the poorer subsoil to the surface. Mix plenty of organic matter into the trench.

When making the next trench, throw the soil forward onto the first trench, covering the organic matter. Continue the process until the area has been dug. The soil you transported to the end at the beginning goes in the last trench.

For planting individual trees and shrubs in an existing border, take out a hole big enough to hold the roots. If a stake is required, drive it into the hole before planting, so as not to damage the plant's roots. Fork over the bottom of the hole to break up the subsoil, and mix in some organic matter. Plant to the same depth as before (easily seen by the darker mark low down on the main stem). Work soil back in among the roots and fill in, firming with your boot as you go. Rake the soil level, and water in. Finally, tie the trunk to the stake using an adjustable tree tie.

KEEP PLANTING CONTAINER CLIMBERS

Plant hardy climbers that will survive their first winter. All are planted in the same way as container-grown trees and shrubs, then tied into their support. Dig a deep hole and work in some organic matter – leafmould and a little bonemeal is ideal, as they will condition the soil without adding too much nitrogen.

Plant climbers with the surface of the rootball level with the soil surface, with the exception of clematis. Most clematis varieties are prone to a disease called clematis wilt: when a plant suddenly wilts for no apparent reason. To overcome this, plant clematis deeper than normally suggested for most plants. Plant so that the top of the rootball is about 15cm (6in) below soil level. If it is then affected by wilt, cut it down completely. The portion of stem below ground may have unaffected buds that send up new shoots.

PLANTING A CLEMATIS

1 Set the plant at an angle, leaning towards the support, with the top of the rootball 15cm (6in) below ground level.

2 Fill the hole, firm the plant in, and cover the root area to keep the roots cool, using roof tiles (as shown), pebbles, or a thick mulch.

PLANT DECIDUOUS AND EVERGREEN HEDGES

Evergreen plants for hedging should be put in as soon as you can do so; if this is not possible, then it's best to wait until spring (*see pp.22–23*). Deciduous hedging can be planted all through the winter provided soil conditions allow (*see pp.140–141*).

Prepare a trench 90cm (36in) wide along the length of the proposed hedge. Deciduous hedging such as beech is usually planted around 45cm (18in) apart, and conifers about 90cm (36in) apart. Plant firmly to the same depth as they were previously planted, and water them in well.

If you live in an exposed area, it is advisable to protect conifers using a screen of plastic mesh stapled or nailed between strong posts for the first year after planting, as this is when they are at their most vulnerable. Water new hedges regularly while they get established, and feed with an organic fertiliser when spring comes.

PLANT CONTAINERS FOR WINTER COLOUR

Don't limit your choice of plants for containers to bedding plants: many evergreen shrubs provide colour and interest all year round. Variegated shrubs are particularly

This hanging basket contains winter-flowering heathers, pansies, and ivy to give a cheerful display from now until summer.

good value – keep an eye out for *Euonymus japonicus* 'Marieke' and 'Aureopictus'. There are also varieties of variegated box, and dwarf conifers in a range of shapes and colours. Other plants to brighten containers through winter include hardy cyclamen and heathers, which also have a wide range of foliage hues.

PRUNE TALL SHRUBS

Tall shrubs such as lavateras and *Buddleja davidii*, which are pruned hard in the spring, should now be cut back by about a half their height in order to neaten up their appearance and to prevent wind rock during winter. Tall plants are very prone to being blown about in windy conditions, which causes them to rock to and fro at the base. Eventually, a hole will form in the soil at the base of the plant's stem; when it rains, water collects here and is likely to cause the stem to rot. When the weather turns cold, the water can freeze, damaging the roots further.

Flowering shrubs like this lavatera can put on a lot of top growth in summer. Cut back by half to reduce the effect of wind rock.

Check all newly planted trees and shrubs regularly; if they are loose, firm them in again, and provide a stake to hold the plant steady if necessary. If your soil is a heavy clay don't firm too heavily, as air will be driven out of the soil. This can be even worse for the plant, as it causes the roots to die.

PRUNE CLIMBING ROSES

If you didn't complete pruning of your climbing roses last month, it's important to get the job finished now, and to get them tied in before autumn gales pick up. Rose stems are stiff compared to those of other climbers, and can be snapped by high winds.

Climbing roses such as Rosa 'Climbing Iceberg' will produce healthy blooms from next summer if pruned and tied in now.

PRUNING A CLIMBING ROSE

1 Cut dead, diseased, or weak growth down to the ground or to a healthy bud. Leave any wood that is merely old.

In addition, don't forget to rake up rose leaves to prevent black spot spores from overwintering in the soil. This is a job that has to be done on a regular basis, and the leaves should then be burned or put into the bin. On no account should you add these leaves to the compost heap, as the heat generated might not be sufficient to kill off the blackspot spores. In a small garden, it is difficult to make a large enough compost heap to generate enough heat to

kill off all harmful organisms, and it is not worth risking the spread of disease through the rest of the compost.

TRIM CONIFERS IF NECESSARY

Leyland cypress in particular can regrow after trimming in late summer; it can now be trimmed again for the final time. It's important not to cut into old wood, as the majority of conifers will not regenerate.

2 Prune off any sideshoots to about two-thirds of their original length, cutting to a bud facing in the correct direction.

3 Tie in newly-pruned stems horizontally along the support, to encourage the formation of flowering sideshoots.

FLOWERING PLANTS

DRY ATTRACTIVE SEEDHEADS

Many plants, such as *Acanthus spinosus*, poppies, achillea, eryngiums, teasel, and globe artichokes, have beautiful seedheads which can be cut and dried for decoration in the home over winter. Cut the seedheads off with plenty of stem, and hang them up in an airy place to dry out.

CUT BACK PERENNIALS

Tidying perennials that have finished flowering will make the garden look much tidier and discourage diseases from attacking old growth. If the flowers have finished but the foliage is still green and attractive, leave it until it is really blackened by the frosts. Cutting everything down can leave unsightly gaps in the borders, which should be avoided until as late in autumn as possible.

Any soft growth cut down, such as that of hardy geraniums, can be consigned to the compost heap. Other growth which is semi-woody will take longer to break down on its own. But the process can be speeded up by shredding the material, rather than burning it, which is the more usual practice.

Let plants such as this teasel dry naturally. This will have a better effect than hastening drying in a warm room.

Shredded material can be added to the compost heap to rot down further, or used as a mulch on the borders in spring.

LIFT AND DIVIDE PERENNIALS

Older clumps of overgrown perennials are easily spotted, as the young vigorous growth is at the outside of the clump while the centre is bare. You can divide from now until spring as long as soil conditions allow. If the soil is so wet that it sticks to your boots, then keep off it; likewise later on if it is frozen. Late-flowering perennials like asters (Michaelmas daisies) are best left until the spring before being divided.

Lift the clumps and separate larger ones with two forks pushed into the centre of the clump back to back, pushing the handles apart to separate the roots. Smaller pieces can be separated out by hand. Replant the new pieces after revitalizing the soil with organic matter. Water in well after planting.

PLANT HERBACEOUS PERENNIALS

The soil will probably not be warm and moist for a good deal longer, so this might be your last chance to do this. Prepare the soil by incorporating lots of organic matter and some bonemeal. There are many perennials to choose from these days, and attractive displays can be made for little financial outlay. Perennials last for many years if propagated regularly, by dividing them up and replanting, collecting seed and sowing it, and by taking cuttings and growing them on. Note that with seed you will not necessarily get exactly the same plant; there will almost always be some slight variation.

Perennials always look best when they are planted in groups of three or more plants, but if your budget is limited, buy one of each of the varieties you want, and then propagate them yourself using whichever methods are most appropriate, so building up the numbers over two or three years.

DIVIDING CROCOSMIAS

1 Once flowers are over and the leaves are fading, lift congested clumps carefully with a fork, trying not to damage the roots.

2 Crocosmias form exceptionally tight, crowded clumps; it may help to lay them down and play a hose over them first.

3 You may need a knife to start separating the clumps; then they can be pulled apart into small sections and the leaves cut off.

4 Lay all of the divisions out, about 15cm (6in) apart, before you plant them, so you don't lose track of where you are.

LIFT AND DIVIDE CROCOSMIAS

If your crocosmia bulbs have formed overgrown clumps, you can lift and divide them exactly as you would perennials. Lifting and dividing congested clumps will ensure that the plants maintain their vigour and produce healthy blooms come summer.

LIFT AND STORE BULBS

When the leaves of gladioli start to go yellow, it is time to lift and store corms before frost damages them. Cannas must be lifted by early next month wherever you are. These have a thick, fleshy root rather than a true bulb, and can be treated as any tender perennial: trimmed, cleaned up and potted into peat-free compost, and stored somewhere cool and dry.

In sheltered gardens and warm regions, slightly tender summer-flowering bulbs like galtonias may survive *in situ*, but in cold areas bulbs such as these, plus eucomis, and certainly tigridias, should be lifted, dried, and stored in pots or boxes of dry sand. Lift, clean up, and dry the bulbs just as you would spring-flowering bulbs.

This is also the time to lift and store dahlias. Cut the plants from their supports, and cut the stems back to approximately 10cm (4in) from ground level. Label each plant just in case you lift it and forget which variety it is.

Once gladioli leaves start yellowing, lift the bulb-like corms gently with a trowel. Leave them to dry, and then cut back the foliage.

Use a garden fork to dig carefully around the plant so as not to damage the tubers underground. Shake off as much of the old soil as you can; you can also hose or rinse off the tubers to get rid of the last of the soil.

Dahlia stems are hollow, and if moisture collects at the stem base while the tubers are in store it can cause them to rot. Turn the tubers and stems upside down for a couple of weeks in a cool, dry place to allow any moisture to drain out.

Following this, box up tubers in peat-free compost, making sure that their crowns (the point where the stems meet the tubers) are not buried in compost. Small embryo buds are located here, and if they are buried they might rot off.

Cover the compost surface with something loose and dry like bark chippings, and keep in a cool, frost-free place. They can be started into growth in spring and will provide cuttings to increase your stock before being planted out.

LIFTING AND STORING DAHLIAS

1 Cut down the top growth from the plants (here, blackened by an early frost). Lift the tubers and shake or rinse off soil.

2 Stand them upside-down in wooden trays in a cool, dry place so that they dry thoroughly.

KEEP AN EYE ON FORCED BULBS

Examine bulbs that are being forced in darkness to see if any top growth has been made. If it has, it's time to bring them into the light in a cool place. But before you do this, knock them out of their containers to see how good a root system has been made. If there are not many roots, it's a good idea to put them back in the dark for a few more weeks so that they can build up a better root system.

3 Store them for winter in boxes of dry, peat-free compost. Make sure the stem is above the surface and space out in spring.

PLANT BULBS

Tulip bulbs can be planted towards the end of this month and the next. Tulips are more prone to disease than other bulbs, so are planted later. As with other bulbs, the depth of planting for tulips should be about two to three times their own depth.

You should also finish planting all spring-flowering bulbs before winter sets in. The bulbs will start to grow now, sending out roots into the soil. Planting them late just means they will flower a bit later than others – perhaps no bad thing to give continuity.

This month and the next are also an ideal time to plant lily bulbs. Plant them in well-prepared soil in sun or partial shade. If your soil is heavier than average, sit the bulbs on a layer of coarse grit to aid drainage. Plant the bulbs at two and a half times their own depth. Lilies can also be grown in pots to make graceful summer patio plants. Some of them are powerfully scented, too.

If planting lilies in pots, put them in ordinary multipurpose compost and on a layer of grit, from now until late winter. Leave the pots outside to allow a good root system to form. When new growth has been made, you can take some pots inside, and the lilies will flower early, in spring. After flowering, the bulbs can be planted in the garden.

FINISH PLANTING SPRING BEDDING

Get this job done before the soil cools too much, especially if you have a heavy clay soil. In some parts of the country, summer bedding plants may still be flowering, but you will have to take the bull by the horns and get them out if you want to plant spring bedding. On light, sandy soils you may get away with planting spring bedding later, as these soils warm up quicker in the spring. If planting late, add some fertiliser high in phosphates like bonemeal, seaweed meal, or hop manure rather than a general feed to encourage root growth, which is what we want at this time of year. Soft growth is more easily damaged during winter.

POT UP HALF-HARDY FUCHSIAS

Half-hardy fuchsias should be potted up if necessary and taken under cover, either storing them with other tender perennials, or keeping them in a cool room. The leaves will still drop off now, but these plants will start into growth and produce the earliest shoots for cuttings. Keep the plants cool and dry, but don't let them dry out completely. Give enough water to keep them alive. It's difficult to say how often plants kept over winter should be watered, as it depends on how warm the plants are kept. It really is a matter of experience and practice.

Half-hardy fuchsias like Fuchsia 'Swingtime' *need a rest period over winter if they are to bear healthy flowers in summer.*

KITCHEN GARDEN

DIG OVER GROUND AFTER CLEARING

The sooner soil cultivation in the vegetable garden can be done the better. Heavy clay soils benefit from being broken up and exposed to winter weather conditions. Rain, snow, and frost play a vital part in breaking down soil, enabling us to make good seed and planting beds in the spring. Dig for short periods at a time, and intersperse with other jobs to prevent damage to your back.

To dig a large area of the vegetable garden, take out a trench at one end of the plot and barrow the soil to the other end. Put organic matter into the bottom of the trench. Then take out the next trench with your spade and throw the soil forward into the first one, covering the organic matter. Do this over the whole area and fill in the last trench with the soil taken out at the start.

EMPTY COMPOST BINS

Use the well-rotted compost from your bin for mulching and digging in to improve the soil. Well-made garden compost will do the soil a power of good, and using it up will free the compost bin for more material; it may take a little longer to rot down at this time of year but it should be ready to use in the spring. If you haven't got much compost, it is better to give it all to a small area, rather than trying to spread it too thinly over all of the ground. You should try to incorporate organic matter into at least a third of the vegetable garden each year.

COVER GROUND WITH POLYTHENE

This will keep the worst of the rain off. From now onwards we can expect more rain, and later in the winter, perhaps snow. To enable us to get on with preparing the soil in the new year it helps to cover at least part of it; then you can get up to date with cultivating before the busy seed-sowing and planting season in the spring.

Weeds have a tendency to grow under the polythene in milder weather, but these can be easily removed if caught early. It is quite surprising how much water will be kept off the land by covering it, and how early you can start

planting and sowing by replacing the sheeting with cloches in late winter and early spring.

PICK THE LAST OF THE RUNNER BEANS

No matter how quickly you pick runner beans, there comes a point when they seem never-ending. If they are not too big, freeze them. Overgrown pods can be composted, as they will be old, stringy, and not appetising at all. If you want to collect your own seed, leave some pods on the old plants until they turn brown. Otherwise, cut the plants from their supports and compost them, but leave the roots in the ground. Runner beans, like broad beans and peas, return valuable nitrogen to the soil and this is a resource which should not be wasted. In the crop rotation system, beans can be followed by leafy crops such as brassicas which have a high demand for nitrogen. By doing this, less nitrogen will have to be applied to the soil in the form of synthetic feeds.

Protect your soil from heavy winter rain by covering it with polythene, held in place with bricks or long pieces of wood.

FINISH LIFTING POTATOES

Leave potatoes on the surface of the soil for a couple of hours to dry out, or in a greenhouse if it is a damp day. They must be dry before putting them into storage. Store only undamaged potatoes, using those that are damaged first. Only ever store in paper or hessian sacks, as storing in polythene bags will make the potatoes sweat, and this will encourage rotting. Any potatoes that are turning green should be discarded.

HARVEST HERBS

Indoor pots of herbs, such as parsley and mint, will provide you with valuable additions to winter meals. Dig up a few roots of each and remove yellowing leaves. Put each piece in a small pot of compost, water in, and stand on a bright windowsill in the kitchen. You will then have fresh, tasty herbs at your fingertips all through the winter.

Basil grown outdoors will not survive now. If grown in pots, you could bring them into a greenhouse or conservatory – alternatively, harvest all the leaves and freeze in ice cube trays topped up with water.

REMOVE YELLOW LEAVES FROM SPROUTS

Old yellowing leaves on Brussels sprouts – and other winter brassicas such as cabbages, cauliflowers, and broccoli – are of no use to the plants; they encourage diseases

Place potatoes in paper or hessian sacks, and cover over to ensure no light gets to them, as this will turn them green.

Remove yellow leaves from Brussels sprouts and compost them to discourage disease and make the garden look tidier.

such as botrytis and grey mould, reducing the overall crop yield. If there are early sprouts that are ready to pick – they should be about about 2.5cm (1in) in diameter – snap them off by pulling sharply in a downwards motion.

FINISH PLANTING GARLIC

If the soil is too wet to plant outside, grow the cloves in modules and plant out in late winter or early spring. Put one clove in each cell,

with the tip of each clove just sticking out of the compost. They don't need any warmth, so keep them outside under the shelter of a wall, just to keep the heaviest of the rain off them.

FINISH PLANTING SPRING CABBAGES

This is the latest month for planting spring cabbages, and the sooner it is done, the better. Remember to net the plants or the birds will have the lot overnight.

FINISH PLANTING AUTUMN ONION SETS

Plant them 8cm (3in) apart in well prepared soil. Japanese onion sets can also be planted, a little later than seeds are sown, now and next month. Japanese onions from both sets and seeds can be harvested before other onions, from June next year.

SOW BROAD BEANS OUTSIDE

Take out a shallow trench about 5cm (2in) deep with a spade, and space out the seeds at intervals of 15cm (6in), as they are quite large. Cover with soil and tamp it down with the back of a rake. Cover with a cloche or fleece, principally to stop mice digging them up, but also to protect from frost in cold parts of the country.

The seeds will germinate fairly quickly and then grow slowly through the winter, producing a crop of succulent beans in early summer the following year.

FINISH PICKING MAINCROP APPLES

Varieties like 'Spartan' and 'Sunset' and the cookers will be ready for harvesting around now. Pick when they are ripe and only store sound fruit. Damaged fruit can be used straight after picking, provided it is ripe. Ripe apples should part from the tree with very little effort. If they don't, leave them on the tree

Store apples in a clean plastic or wooden crate. Ensure that they don't touch, as rot can spread quickly when the fruits touch.

for a little longer. Stored properly they will last through winter. Apples can be eaten straight from store, but pears need a few days in a warm room to ripen fully.

PRUNE BLACKCURRANTS IF NECESSARY

If you want to get the job done, you can begin pruning your blackcurrants now. However, if you can hold off, there are a couple of reasons to put it off.

Firstly, in winter it will be easier to see what you are doing with no foliage on the plants. And secondly, if you prune them as soon as the fruits have been picked, the plants will still be in full leaf. The foliage manufactures plant food, and as early pruning takes off a lot of leaves, it reduces the plants' capacity to manufacture this food.

PREPARE FOR NEW FRUIT TREES

This is a good time to look through specialist fruit nursery catalogues and choose new fruit trees. Ordering bare-root trees to plant during the dormant season is cheaper than buying container-grown ones.

The sooner you order trees, the better the chance of getting the varieties you want. There will be a wide selection available, all on different types of rootstock. What this means is that the top part of the tree that bears the fruit has been grafted at a very early stage onto the roots of a different tree.

The chosen rootstock will affect the vigour, and thus the eventual size, of your fruit tree, and also the age at which it bears fruit. Various rootstocks are available and each one gives a different size of tree. Good catalogues will give you plenty of information about the rootstocks they use, and how large trees will eventually grow.

Choose a mild, dry day to prepare the ground for the trees. If you're planting several trees together, dig over the whole area whilst incorporating plenty of organic matter. If only one or two trees are being planted, prepare generously sized individual holes to accommodate the roots without cramming them in. Break up the bottom of the hole to loosen the subsoil, without bringing any of it to the surface. Put plenty of muck into the hole and work it into the bottom. It might be beneficial to purchase low stakes and tree ties now so that you have them to hand when planting.

OCTOBER PROJECT

SAVING SEEDS

It is fascinating to grow plants from seed collected in your own garden. There is a tremendous sense of satisfaction in raising plants this way. However, it is important to know when seeds are ready for harvesting, so it is wise to keep a regular check on developing seed pods. Most will usually turn brown and papery when the seeds are ripe, but different plants will vary in this respect. If you are unsure whether they are ripe enough, gently tap the seed head and if some seeds fall out they are ready to collect.

Always harvest on a dry, still day and take a paper bag, or seed tray lined with paper, to prevent seeds dropping and spreading indiscriminately.

_**1**_ **Ripe seed**, such as Angelica (above), falls easily into the hand with a gentle tap when ripe. Use a paper bag to collect the seed. Alternatively, cut the dry head from the plant and place in a tray.

_**2**_ **Spread harvested seed** on a piece of absorbent kitchen paper and place in a warm, well-ventilated spot for a few days. This will ensure that the seeds dry thoroughly before storing.

_**3**_ **Glass or plastic jars** with air-tight lids are ideal for storing seeds – or you can keep them in sturdy paper envelopes. Label clearly with the name of the plant and when the seed was collected.

HARVEST BERRIES

Pick fresh berries when ripe and soft, and dry berries when they start to shrivel. Separate the seed from the pulp. Berry seeds are best sown straight away rather than dried and sown the following season.

BOSTON IVY ☐1

Parthenocissus tricuspidata ♥ A very vigorous, deciduous, self-clinging climber. It has lobed, bright green leaves from spring onwards; these turn brilliant red and deep purple in autumn.
‡ to 20m (70ft) ↔ to 20m (70ft)

CULTIVATION Grow in any fertile, well-drained soil in sun or shade. Guide young plants into the support until they cling for themselves. Prune in late winter, if necessary, to confine to bounds.

AUTUMN CROCUS ☐2

Colchicum cilicicum Upright, low-growing, cormous perennials. In autumn, it bears funnel-shaped, purplish-pink flowers. They appear before the leaves, which are not ornamentally significant.
‡ 10cm (4in) ↔ 8cm (3in)

CULTIVATION Best in an open site in full sun, but will tolerate light shade. In late summer or early autumn, plant corms 10cm (4in) deep in fertile, well-drained soil. If grown in grass, allow the foliage to die down naturally before mowing.

CHINESE LANTERNS 3

Physalis alkekengi ♀ A spreading, rhizomatous, herbaceous perennial. Nodding, bell-shaped, creamy white flowers are produced in midsummer. In late summer and autumn, inflated, papery red lanterns enclose orange-red fruits. They are often used in dried flower arrangements.

‡60–75cm (24–30in) ↔ 90cm (36in)

CULTIVATION Grow in full sun in any well-drained soil. Cut stems for drying just as the lanterns begin to colour.

2

3

AMELANCHIER [1]

Amelanchier lamarckii ♥ A small deciduous tree with both spring and autumn interest (*see also* April, *p.181*). The young leaves are bronzed as they unfold, turning to green in summer and then to blazing shades of orange and red in the autumn.

‡10m (30ft) ↔ 12m (40ft)

CULTIVATION It will tolerate light, dappled shade, but autumn colour is best in full sun. Grow in lime-free (acid) soil that is moist but well-drained and enriched with plenty of organic matter. It generally needs pruning only to shorten wayward branches.

KAFFIR LILY [2]

Schizostylis coccinea 'Sunrise' ♥ An exotic but hardy evergreen perennial. From late summer to early winter, it bears spikes of glossy, salmon-pink flowers. These are good for cutting. The narrowly sword-shaped, bright green leaves persist for most of the year.

‡60cm (24in) ↔ 30cm (12in)

CULTIVATION Grow in a fertile, moist but well-drained soil. Shelter from cold winds. It benefits from an organic mulch in winter, especially in very cold areas.

ROWAN 3

Sorbus commixta A compact, broadly
conical, deciduous tree. In late spring,
it bears heads of tiny white flowers. In
autumn, clusters of orange-red berries
festoon the branches, and the divided
leaves turn yellow to red and purple.
The berries attract birds into the garden.
‡10m (30ft) ↔7m (22ft)

CULTIVATION Grow in any fertile,
moist but well-drained, neutral to acid
soil. Little pruning is necessary; remove
crossing or damaged branches in winter.

2

3

ACTAEA [1]

Actaea simplex **Atropurpurea Group
'Brunette'** ♀ A robust, upright,
herbaceous perennial. From early to mid-
autumn, it bears spires of fragrant, pink-
flushed white flowers that open from
purple tinted buds. The attractive, dark
purple leaves form dense ground cover.
↕ 1.2m (4ft) ↔ 60cm (24in)

CULTIVATION Grow in moist, fertile,
humus-rich soil in part-shade. May need
staking in exposed gardens.

NERINE [2]

Nerine bowdenii ♀ A moderately
vigorous, perennial bulb. In autumn, it
bears rounded heads of funnel-shaped,
faintly scented pink flowers. The strap-
shaped leaves emerge after flowering.
↕ 45cm (18in) ↔ 8cm (3in)

CULTIVATION Grow in full sun in
sharply drained soil in a warm, sheltered
site. Provide a dry winter mulch in cold
areas. Plant in summer with the tip of
the bulb just at soil level.

CHRYSANTHEMUM 3

Chrysanthemum **'Talbot Jo'** An upright, hardy herbaceous perennial. It bears masses of single pink flowers in early autumn. They make excellent cut flowers. Aromatic grey green leaves.
‡1.3m (4½ft) ↔ 75cm (30in)

CULTIVATION Grow in full sun in fertile, well-drained soil. Plant out in late spring; pinch out the growing tips to encourage plentiful flowers. Except in very cold areas, it can be left outdoors in winter; protect the crown with a deep dry mulch.

2

3

SALVIA 1

Salvia uliginosa ❦ A delightful clump-forming perennial with lance-shaped, mid-green leaves that become progressively smaller up the slender, branching stems. From late summer to mid-autumn it bears terminal clusters of clear blue flowers.
‡2m (6ft) ↔ 90cm (36in).

CULTIVATION Grow in any moist, but well-drained soil in full sun. Protect from excessive winter wet. In spring, lightly trim shoots that spoil the shape of the plant.

STAG'S HORN SUMACH 2

Rhus typhina ❦ A vigorous, suckering, deciduous shrub or small tree. In summer, it bears spires of yellow-green flowers that give rise, on female plants, to dense clusters of hairy, deep crimson-red fruits. In autumn, the divided leaves turn a brilliant orange-red.
‡5m (15ft) ↔ 6m (20ft)

CULTIVATION Gives the best autumn colour in sun, but tolerates light shade. Grow in any moist but well-drained soil. Can be pruned hard in spring to within two or three buds of the base for larger, lusher leaves.

HEDGEHOG ROSE 3

Rosa rugosa A robust, deciduous shrub of dense, prickly growth. In summer, it bears single, spicily fragrant magenta or white flowers with a boss of yellow stamens. Each flower produces a large, bright, tomato-red hip.
↕ 1–2.5m (3–8ft) ↔ 1–2.5m (3–8ft)

CULTIVATION Grow in any fertile, moist but well-drained soil in sun or part-shade. Every three or four years, in winter, cut out one or two old shoots to the ground. Shorten wayward shoots at any time.

2

3

ACER PALMATUM

Deciduous, mostly mound-forming shrubs or small trees with lobed or finely cut leaves. All are highly valued for their delicate foliage and vibrant autumn colours. Most have small, beautifully tinted spring flowers and winged fruits in autumn.

CULTIVATION Grow in full sun, or dappled shade, in leafy, moist but well-drained soil. Mulch annually in autumn. Shelter from cold winds and spring frosts, which may damage new growth. Remove badly placed shoots in winter to develop a well-spaced network of branches. Keep pruning to a minimum on established plants.

TOP ROW LEFT TO RIGHT
- *A. palmatum* 'Bloodgood' ♥
  ‡5m (15ft) ↔ 5m (15ft)
- *A. palmatum* 'Chitose-yama' ♥
  ‡2m (6ft) ↔ 3m (10ft)
- *A. palmatum* 'Corallinum'
  ‡2m (6ft) ↔ 3m (10ft)

BOTTOM ROW LEFT TO RIGHT
- *A. palmatum* 'Sango-kaku' ♥
  ‡2m (6ft) ↔ 3m (10ft)
- *A. palmatum* 'Garnet' ♥
  ‡2m (6ft) ↔ 3m (10ft)
- *A. palmatum* 'Linearilobum'
  ‡2m (6ft) ↔ 3m (10ft)

MALUS

Deciduous, mostly vigorous small trees
that are ideal as specimens for smaller
gardens. In autumn, they bear crab
apples in colours ranging from yellow
to red; the leaves turn yellow and
orange too. In spring, they bear masses
of blossom ranging from white to
pink and purplish reds (*see p.184*).

CULTIVATION Grow in any fertile,
well-drained soil in sun; they tolerate
light shade, but purple-leaved variants
are best in sun. Prune in winter to
remove misplaced shoots or dead or
damaged wood.

TOP ROW LEFT TO RIGHT
• *M.* 'Butterball'
  ‡8m (25ft) ↔ 8m (25ft)
• *M.* 'Marshal Ôyama'
  ‡8m (25ft) ↔ 6m (20ft)
• *M.* 'Veitch's Scarlet'
  ‡8m (25ft) ↔ 8m (25ft)

BOTTOM ROW LEFT TO RIGHT
• *M. pumila* 'Cowichan'
  ‡8m (25ft) ↔ 8m (25ft)
• *M.* x *zumi* 'Professor Sprenger'
  ‡7m (22ft) ↔ 7m (22ft)
• *M.* 'John Downie' ♛
  ‡10m (30ft) ↔ 6m (20ft)

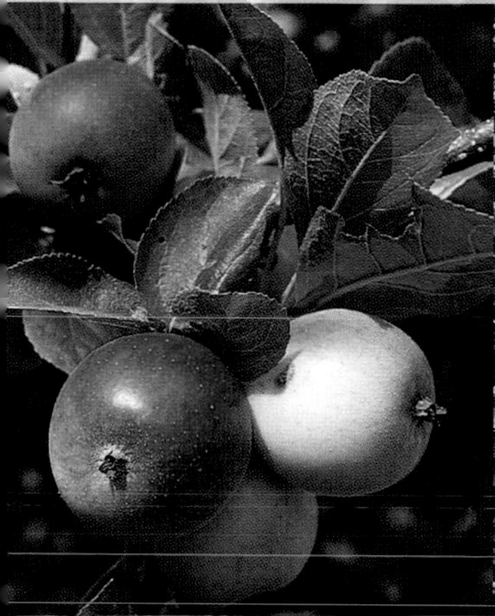

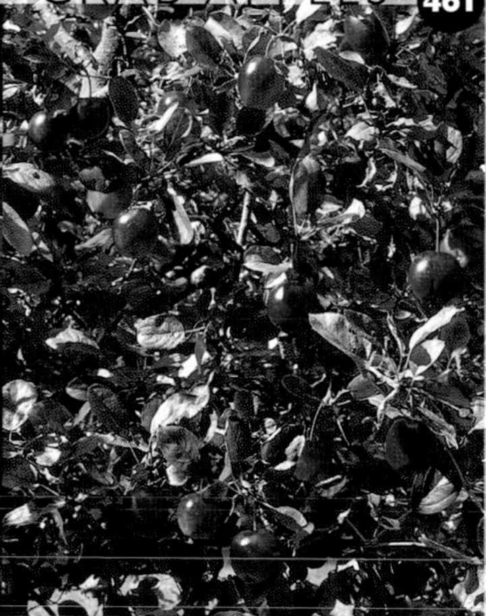

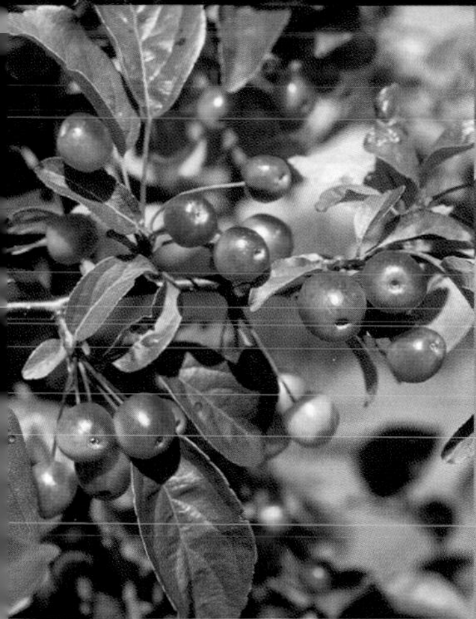

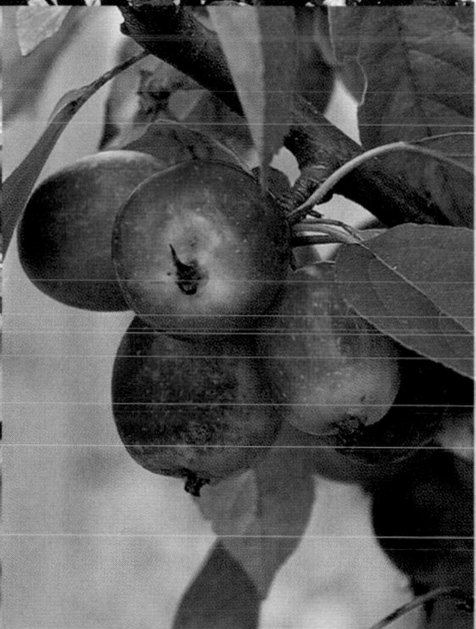

WHAT TO DO IN NOVEMBER

WEATHER WATCH

November can be damp and raw. Flowers may be scarce in the garden, but there are berries, evergreen foliage, and trees with decorative bark to add interest on the dullest of days. Warm yourself up by tidying the garden and preparing for the winter ahead.

COOLING DOWN

Some November days can be particularly wintry, especially if there is low cloud cover. Frosts may occur quite frequently at night now; the likelihood is greater when the weather is calm and clear. Cold winds, especially those from the east, will make it feel much colder than it really is.

AUTUMN GALES

Gales increase this month, now that we've reached the middle of autumn. In England, most gales hit the south-west, with on average two days of gales being driven in from the Atlantic. Inland, conditions are generally calmer, but eastern coastal areas can turn very cold when the wind comes

from mainland Europe. However, the worst gales are suffered on the west sides of Scotland and Ireland – up to five days in some parts.

BRIGHT SPELLS

It is surprising how much direct sunshine there can be this month, although this depends on cloud cover. Parts of the north and west can experience over 100 hours of direct sunshine, and the south and east as much as 150 hours. Days with clear, blue sky, sunshine, and a hint of a chill are a pure delight.

HIGH RAINFALL

Rainfall is on the increase and November can be a soggy month. The wettest parts of the country are the Highlands of Scotland and Ireland. Here, the rainfall can be as much as 267mm (10½in), compared to the eastern parts of England, where it can be as little as 47mm (1¾in). Get on with soil cultivation as soon as the weather permits and protect some ground from the worst of the wet with polythene sheeting.

SOME SNOW

Snow is on the agenda now in north-eastern parts. Braemar in Aberdeenshire can expect, on average, five days of snow on the ground. Rarely, other parts of the country may see snow, ranging from none at all in the south to 1.7 days in central Scotland.

AROUND THE GARDEN

ORDER SEED CATALOGUES

The sooner you do this and get your seed orders off, the more likely you are to get all the varieties you want before they are sold out. It's exciting to plan what you are going to grow in the coming season, and the catalogues are usually full of new varieties every year to tempt you.

KEEP RAKING UP FALLEN LEAVES

In dry weather, rake up fallen leaves on the lawn. Don't burn or bin these – they can be used to make leafmould, an excellent soil conditioner, mulch, and ingredient in potting composts. In wet weather, try to keep off the lawn altogether. If you have to go over the lawn when it is extremely wet to reach borders, then put down some planks to walk on, but ideally try to keep off it. Don't walk on the lawn when it is frosted, either.

CLEAN GARDENING EQUIPMENT

There will be few pests around now, but it is best to be on your guard as some will be hiding away in corners. The best way to avoid problems is to practise good hygiene, and this includes keeping sheds and equipment clean and tidy, as well as keeping borders in check. Any dirty pots and seed trays kicking about should be thrown out or recycled. Wash them in a weak solution of a garden disinfectant and store them away for the winter. Also clean the ends of stakes and canes before storing them for the winter as pests often lurk there.

TAKING CARE OF YOUR TOOLS

Clean metal tools – spades, forks, trowels, and rakes – after use. Brush off the soil, wash them thoroughly, and then dry.

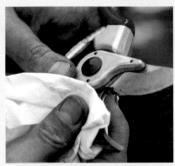

Remove dirt and sap from secateurs using some lubricant or ordinary household cleaner, and wipe off with a tissue.

To prevent carbon steel tools rusting, wipe them over with an oily rag. Blades can also be sharpened using a file.

To prevent secateurs rusting, smear lubricant onto the bevelled edge and rub gently with a nylon scourer.

CLEAN OUT BIRD BOXES

Old nesting material can harbour parasites; clearing them out will encourage birds to nest in them again next year. Do this job as soon as possible, as birds will soon be looking for winter roosts in which to keep warm. If they are already familiar with a box by spring, they are much more likely to select it as a nesting site.

CHECK BONFIRE PILE FOR WILDLIFE

If you are planning a bonfire, check the rubbish heap beforehand to see if any hedgehogs or toads are hibernating in it. If there are, leave them in peace, taking away some of the heap to burn elsewhere if you must, but leaving the creatures some debris. Do all you can to encourage these animals, as they are great allies in controlling pests.

INSULATE POTS

If pots are too large to bring inside, insulate them from the cold. The roots of plants in containers outside are more prone to frost damage than plants in the ground, and they need some protection from hard frosts. Insulate them by wrapping bubble polythene or hessian sacking around the pots. Tie up the leaves of plants like cordylines to protect the growing

Pots can be lagged with hessian to protect roots against the cold. Moving them closer to walls often offers some protection, too.

If you need to move heavy containers, use a plant mover: a stand on wheels that will help you to avoid straining your back.

REMOVE PUMPS AND LIGHTS FROM PONDS

If you didn't have time to do so last month, you should remove submersible pumps and lights now. Clean pump filters and dry them off before storing. If any problems have cropped up recently, send the equipment off to be repaired, or simply replace it. Check that the cabling is in good condition too. If you have any doubts whatsoever about the safety of outdoor cables or other electrical connections, call in an electrician. Water and electricity don't mix.

tip from excess winter wet which will rot it, and wrap in fleece. Containers can also be moved together for mutual protection.

Modern plastic or terracotta containers are usually frost-proof, but older terracotta pots may not be. Therefore, even if they are empty, wrap them or take indoors for the winter. Ensure containers are lifted off the ground slightly to improve drainage. There are decorative "feet" available from garden centres for this purpose.

KEEP TIDYING PONDS

Continue to cut down plants that are growing around the pond and in the shallows. Old growth and leaves falling in the pond will rot and give off gases that are toxic to fish, so get debris out of the water as soon as possible.

TREES, SHRUBS & CLIMBERS

CHECK TREE TIES AND STAKES

These should be checked on a regular basis to see that the stakes are sound and that ties are not cutting into the trunks of the plants; if they are, they will strangle the plant as the trunk expands outwards over the years.

PLANT BARE-ROOTED STOCK

At this time of year, bare-rooted stock of most deciduous trees and shrubs is available, and can be planted throughout the dormant season (from now until March), provided that soil conditions allow. They are cheaper than container-grown plants, but take a look at the root systems before you buy to ensure that they have been lifted with care and are not dried-up. Make sure they are well wrapped

Angled stakes give support to trees low down where it is needed, and can be inserted without damaging the plant's rootball.

before transporting, and plant as soon as possible. If the plants arrive by post and are not satisfactory, phone the supplier straight away to arrange an exchange.

To plant, prepare the ground well, incorporating plenty of organic matter. Dig a hole large enough to take the root system without cramping the roots. Put a stake in first for trees and tall shrubs on the windward side, so the plant is blown away from the stake to prevent rubbing. Then plant the tree or shrub to the same depth as it was planted before, easily seen by the darker part of the stem near the roots. Fill in the hole and firm in gently with your boot.

Make sure all newly planted trees and shrubs are well staked and tied. After spending a lot of money on them, it's a job worth doing well. The stake should come at most about a third of the way up the trunk. The only exception is when staking top-grafted standards such as dwarf weeping trees, when the stake should reach the graft point. For all other trees, a low stake allows the top of the tree to flex in the wind, strengthening the trunk. Secure the tree to the stake using a plastic tree tie; this can be loosened as the tree grows and the trunk expands.

Container-grown trees and shrubs can be planted all year. The soil requires the same preparation as for bare-root trees and shrubs. If container-grown plants have a solid mass of roots, it is a good idea to tease out some roots, otherwise they will continue to grow round in circles, forming a weak root system.

TIE IN CLIMBERS

Tie in long, whippy shoots of climbers and wall shrubs to prevent them being blown about and damaged in bad weather. If there isn't a gap in the framework where you can secure the shoot, prune it back to five or six buds.

Make sure all whippy shoots are well secured before winter winds pick up.

PLANT BARE-ROOTED ROSES

Bare-root roses should be available from this month through to March. They are slightly cheaper than container-grown plants, and they do establish better. For roses to give their best, thorough preparation of the soil is essential. Cultivate as large an area as you can or dig as large a hole as possible and work in plenty of organic matter.

Never allow the roots to dry out; if the roses have just arrived by mail order and the roots are dry, soak them in a bucket of water for a couple of hours. Plant the rose deep enough so that the point at which it was grafted (the

PLANTING BARE-ROOTED ROSES

1 Remove any damaged growth and spindly shoots, and any stems that cross the centre of the plant. Trim off any roots that are damaged.

2 Dig a generous hole so you don't cramp the root system. If the soil wasn't prepared beforehand, incorporate organic matter and add a little bonemeal.

joint between the stems and roots) is about 5cm (2in) below ground level. Work soil in amongst the roots well and firm with your boot as you go. To finish, mulch the surface with well-rotted garden compost or manure.

If you are considering planting new roses in the same patch where the old ones were, you might encounter problems. Roses planted in soil that has grown roses for a number of years are prone to a disease known as rose sickness. If you must plant new roses in this situation, then take out as much of the old soil as possible and replace it with fresh soil from another part of the garden which has not grown roses before.

3 Place the rose in the hole with the roots well spread out. Lay a cane across the hole to check that the point of grafting will be below soil level.

4 Fill in the hole by gradually working soil in around the roots with your hands, and pressing down firmly. Lightly tread the soil and water well.

FLOWERING PLANTS

PROTECT PLANTS FROM FROST

In colder parts, kniphofias (red-hot pokers) may not be reliably hardy, especially when young, but they can be protected. Tie the foliage together firmly; this protects the crown of the plant, so even if the foliage is damaged by hard frosts the crown should be unaffected.

Other slightly tender herbaceous plants like penstemons should also be protected. Bracken or straw placed over the plants and held there with netting, or a layer of a dry, loose mulch such as leafmould or bark chippings, will give a good degree of protection. Check the plants now and then through winter to ensure no diseases have set in.

Protect tender bulbs left in the ground, such as nerines and agapanthus, with a thick mulch of garden compost. Try to grow them in a sheltered area, at the base of a south-facing wall or fence.

CLEAR LEAVES FROM PLANTS

Remove any leaves that have accumulated on top of clumps of perennials. If the leaves are left there for an extended period of time, the plants will suffer due to lack of light, and the dark, moist conditions are likely to attract slugs and snails. Don't burn the leaves that you collect; you could either add them to the compost heap, or make a separate leaf heap to make leafmould.

CUT DOWN OLD PLANT GROWTH

The routine job of cutting down old growth can continue, but if you live in a colder part of the country it may be better to leave some of the old growths on now, as they will provide protection for

Cut down and clear growth of perennials once they lose their ornamental value.

the plants during severe weather. Some of the more attractive or architectural dead stems can look quite stunning when covered with frost or snow.

CUT DOWN GRASSES AND BAMBOOS

Those that are not ornamental in winter are best cut back now as they can look messy at this time of year. Some bamboos with thick canes can be cut, cleaned up, and stored, then used for supporting plants next season.

Use loppers to cut down bamboo canes; wear gloves as you do so, as some bamboos can give you a nasty cut.

KEEP EXAMINING FORCED BULBS

If you are forcing any bulbs for early flowering, remember to keep tabs on them. When they have made approximately 2.5cm (1in) of growth, they should be moved into a cool greenhouse or cold frame. If you don't have either of these, a cool windowsill is also ideal. When hyacinths and narcissi such as 'Paper White' and 'Soleil d'Or' begin to form flower buds, you can bring them into warmer conditions so that they flower just in time for Christmas.

KEEP CHECKING STORED BULBS

Continue to check stored bulbs, corms and tubers. Any that are showing signs of rotting should be thrown away. If only small parts of the bulb, corm or tuber are affected, you may get away with cutting out the infected part with a sharp knife and dusting the cut surface with flowers of sulphur – but keep them separate from the others in store to avoid spreading the infection.

POT UP HIPPEASTRUMS

If you want hippeastrums (amaryllis) in flower at Christmas, start them into growth at the beginning of this month. Pot up and water the bulbs, and put them in a warm place to get them going quickly. Some people start them off in an airing cupboard, but check them regularly if you do this as they grow so rapidly that they may be a couple of feet tall before you know it. Over a radiator (a place most houseplants hate) is also ideal.

PLANT TULIPS

By planting tulips once other spring-flowering bulbs are in, there is a better chance of preventing them being infected with the fungal disease tulip fire. Try to get them in before the end of the month. You can, of course, grow tulips in pots. One advantage of growing them in pots is that they can be planted, pot and all, in any part of the garden lacking colour in the spring, and then are easily lifted out again when the flowers are over. Plant tulips in borders and pots just as you would other bulbs.

Plant tulip bulbs on a layer of coarse grit to prevent them rotting off, especially if your soil is heavy clay.

TULIPS TO TRY

'Dreamboat'

'Keizerskroon'

'Fringed Beauty'

'Dreaming Maid'

KITCHEN GARDEN

PRESS ON WITH WINTER DIGGING

Do this as the weather allows – make sure the soil is not so wet that it sticks to your boots when you walk over it. You can cover the ground with polythene sheeting to keep off the worst of the rain. Pull it back on a fine day to dig, and cover the soil again when you are finished.

LIFT PARSNIPS

Parsnips taste much better when they have had a touch of frost on them, but if you wish, lift and store them now in the same way as carrots. Pack them in boxes of sand and they will keep well through the winter. If you haven't much room for storing crops, you could always heap them up outside the back door and cover them with a thick layer of straw. Hold this in place with some netting pegged into the ground.

KEEP HARVESTING BRUSSELS SPROUTS

Harvest these from the bottom of the plant upwards, as the largest sprouts form at the base of the plant first. Very tall plants which look as if they are in danger of blowing over in high winds can be staked and tied to a cane.

NET REMAINING BRASSICAS

If there are still brassicas you haven't yet netted, you should finish off the job this month. As the weather gets colder and there is less food around, pigeons will be increasingly attracted to the winter crops in your garden. There are many different types of bird scarer on the market, but by far the best way to protect the crops is by covering them.

Make sure traditional netting is properly secured at ground level so that small birds don't get caught

PROTECTING CAULIFLOWERS

This time of year, mature cauliflower curds can be damaged by severe frost.

Protect them by wrapping the leaves around the central curd, then secure with string.

up in it; a safer alternative for birds is the very fine mesh sheeting used as a barrier to pests like carrot fly, or even spare pieces of horticultural fleece. If you do use netting as a cover, hold it up off the plants with cane supports or the birds will peck through it. Remember to shake it after a heavy fall of snow, or the weight may bring supports down or rip the netting, making it useless.

SNAP LEAVES OVER CAULIFLOWERS

Protect the curds of cauliflowers to keep them white and delay the time when the flowers will open up. The inner leaves can be bent over the curd and tied in place. However, there are some modern cultivars with leaves that naturally bend over the curd, protecting it from the elements, so you might not have to do this yourself.

PLANT FRUIT TREES AND BUSHES

Bare-root trees and bushes can be planted from now until March, whenever the soil is not frozen or too wet. Prepare the ground by incorporating organic matter in the form of garden compost or well-rotted farmyard manure.

Dig a hole that will accommodate the roots, then loosen the subsoil at the bottom, without bringing it to the surface. Work some organic matter into the hole (ideally well-rotted farmyard manure). Fruit trees on dwarfing rootstocks will need staking for most of their lives, so hammer in a good stout stake before planting the tree, so as not to harm the root system.

As always, plant to the same depth as they were previously (with the exception of blackcurrants), indicated by the darker mark on the stem. With grafted fruit trees, the point of grafting – the swollen part low down on the main stem – should always be kept above ground level. Otherwise the variety part of the tree (the upper part which produces the fruit and was grafted onto the rootstock) will begin to root into the soil, and so any control over the vigour of the tree will be lost.

Gradually fill in, working the soil between the roots, and firm gently with your boot. Level off and water in thoroughly, then tie to the stake with an adjustable tree tie. Finish by mulching with a thick layer of organic matter. Garden compost or well-rotted manure is ideal; straw is also good in sheltered spots.

The kink in the stem indicates the graft union, where the variety part has been grafted onto the rootstock. With fruit trees, this must be above soil level when planting.

PLANT BLACKCURRANT BUSHES

Blackcurrants are a slight exception to the planting rules in that they should be set lower in the planting hole, with 8–10cm (3–4in) of stem below ground level. This encourages new growth from the base of the plant. The newly planted bushes should then be pruned to 10cm (4in) from the ground to produce strong growth for future fruiting.

START PRUNING APPLE AND PEAR TREES

Winter pruning of established trees can commence now – this consists mainly of pruning back the leaders of branches by about one-third. Any older branches which are crossing and rubbing against one another should be cut out completely to prevent damage and to keep the centre of the tree as open as possible. This allows air to circulate more freely between the branches, reducing the risk of diseases affecting the trees.

MULCH PRUNED FRUIT

After pruning, mulch fruit trees with a layer of organic matter to retain moisture and revitalize the soil. Mulching will also help prevent weed seeds germinating and competing for the nutrients in the soil. Any kind of organic matter is suitable as a mulch, as long as it is unlikely to hold any diseases that could infect the fruit plants.

Always remove one of two branches that rub together, or the chafing will create an entry point for disease.

NOVEMBER PROJECT

PLANT A COLOURFUL WINTER BORDER

Winter is not necessarily a dull time in the garden. There won't be an abundance of flowers at this time of year, but if you select a variety of herbaceous shrubs with colourful bark, stunning effects can be created. Also, if you leave the dry seed heads on your plants over winter they can look terrific, especially when covered with a sparkling of frost on a sunny day.

In addition to the plants featured in this border, try winter-flowering heathers and bulbs, such as snowdrops and winter aconites, as well as a few evergreen shrubs to add form and structure. Scent is also valuable in the winter garden and fragrant shrubs, such as *Viburnum × bodnantense* 'Dawn', will fill your garden with perfume – plant them near a path or close to the house for maximum effect.

Rubus thibetanus
The ghostly white arching stems of this shrub make it a beautiful plant for winter. In spring, cut back shoots to two or three buds for the best-coloured stems.

***Salix alba* var. *vitellina* 'Britzensis'**
This is a fast-growing willow that can be treated as a shrub. It has eye-catching, fiery orange-red stems in winter. Prune hard in spring for the brightest shoots.

Stipa tenuissima
This elegant, feathery grass, which billows in the slightest breeze, adds movement to the border. The flowerheads fade to buff and contrast well with other winter plants.

***Sedum* 'Herbstfreude'**
Known for its deep pink flat flowerheads in autumn, this sedum's tawny-red, long-lasting heads also look stunning covered with frost on a bright winter's day.

PYRACANTHA [1]

Pyracantha 'Golden Charmer' ♥
A robust, spiny evergreen shrub, which
has bright orange berries from autumn
through winter. In early summer, it bears
clusters of small white flowers, and glossy,
bright green leaves all year.
‡3m (10ft) ↔ 3m (10ft)

CULTIVATION Grow in any fertile,
well-drained soil. Trim hedging in
summer. On wall-trained plants, shorten
outward- and inward-growing shoots in
mid-spring. Trim sideshoots to two or
three leaves after flowering to expose
the berries.

STINKING IRIS [2]

Iris foetidissima ♥ A vigorous,
rhizomatous evergreen perennial. In early
summer, it bears subtly coloured dull
purple flowers suffused with yellow; in
autumn, the seed pods split to reveal
bead-like scarlet seeds. The strap-shaped
dark green leaves give off an unpleasant
scent if crushed.
‡30–90cm (12–36in) ↔ indefinite

CULTIVATION Grow in any well-drained
soil in sun or shade. Divide congested
clumps in autumn.

SMOKE BUSH 3

Cotinus **'Grace'** A fast-growing,
deciduous shrub. A haze of tiny purple-
pink flowers appear in summer giving the
plant the common name of smoke bush.
The oval purple leaves turn a brilliant
translucent red in late autumn.
‡6m (20ft) ↔ 5m (15ft)

CULTIVATION Grow in any moderately
fertile, moist but well-drained soil. To get
larger, brighter coloured foliage, prune all
shoots back hard in spring, but let plants
become well-established before doing so.

2

3

PAMPAS GRASS [1]

Cortaderia selloana **'Sunningdale Silver'** ♀ A vigorous perennial grass. In late summer and autumn, it sends up feathery, silvery white flower plumes that are very weather resistant. Clumps of arching bluish-green leaves all year round.
‡3m (10ft) or more ↔ 2.5m (8ft)

CULTIVATION It prefers an open, sunny site, but tolerates dappled shade. Grow in fertile, well-drained soil. In late winter or early spring, carefully cut or comb out old foliage; the leaves have viciously sharp edges.

WILD ROSE [2]

Rosa moyesii A robust, upright, open deciduous shrub with long, arching branches. In summer, it bears single, cupped, red or pink flowers that are very attractive to honey bees. It produces large, crimson, flask-shaped hips in autumn.
‡to 4m (12ft) ↔ 3m (10ft)

CULTIVATION Grow in any fertile, moist but well-drained soil in sun or light, dappled shade. Every three to four years, in winter, cut one or two old shoots to the ground. Overlong, wayward shoots can be shortened at any time.

HONEYSUCKLE 3

Lonicera fragrantissima A bushy, spreading, semi-evergreen winter-flowering honeysuckle. In winter and early spring, it bears richly scented flowers. It has dark green leaves that are blue-green beneath.

‡2m (6ft) ↔ 3m (10ft)

CULTIVATION Grow in any fertile, well-drained soil in sun or light shade. After flowering, prune back flowered shoots to strong buds or shoots lower down the stems.

2

3

WINGED SPINDLE 1

Euonymus alatus ♥ A dense, bushy, deciduous shrub. The leaves turn brilliant crimson in autumn, setting off the red-purple fruits that split to reveal orange seeds. The stems have corky "wings" and the dark green leaves are attractive throughout the summer.
‡ 2m (6ft) ↔ 3m (10ft)

CULTIVATION Autumn colour is best in full sun, but it will tolerate part-shade. Grow in any well-drained soil. Prune in winter, if necessary, to shape the shrub and to remove any wayward, dead, or damaged shoots.

CLEMATIS 2

Clematis 'Bill MacKenzie' ♥
A vigorous, late-flowering clematis. From late summer until autumn, it produces hanging, bell-shaped flowers in bright golden yellow, followed by fluffy silver seedheads that persist into early winter. Attractive foliage all through the summer.
‡ to 7m (22ft) ↔ 2–3m (6–10ft)

CULTIVATION Plant in fertile, humus-rich, well-drained soil, with the plant's base in the shade and the upper growth in sun or light shade. In spring, prune to a pair of strong buds about 20cm (8in) from the ground.

ORNAMENTAL VINE ③

Vitis coignetiae ♈ A clinging, spreading deciduous climber. Undoubtedly at its best in the autumn when the large, heart-shaped leaves turn gold then brilliant red and purple. The deep green spring and summer leaves are wrinkled and deeply veined with thick brown felt beneath.
↕15m (50ft) ↔ indefinite

CULTIVATION Grow in sun or part-shade in well-drained, neutral to slightly alkaline soil. Prune in winter and again in summer to confine to allotted space.

2

3

WHAT TO DO IN
DECEMBER

WEATHER WATCH

Any sunshine this month will be weak, but if you wrap up well you can still have some pleasant days in the garden. Catch up on maintenance jobs and make the most of any bright weather by pruning and protecting plants for the winter.

WINTER CHILL

Although there can be a few relatively mild December days, it's generally a cold month and there's no getting away from it. With sharp frosts and driving winds, some days the temperature will rarely climb above freezing. However, on the whole the weather is not usually too bad and the cold can be beneficial in the garden, killing off pests and diseases that would otherwise survive to cause trouble in spring.

WINDS AND GALES

Definitely a windy month, with bitingly cold winds at times. But it can be calm, especially in frosty weather. The most intense gales are likely in western coastal areas close to the Atlantic as weather depressions are driven across from America. Northern areas can expect from two to five days on average of gale-force winds. Southern areas experience up to two days of gales.

LIMITED SUN

The days are very short now and the north of the country comes off worst in the sunshine stakes in December. In the far north there are only 13 hours sunshine in the month, and up to about 50 hours in the north-east. Southern parts can expect up to 54 hours.

A WET MONTH

It can be quite wet this month too, with all areas seeing more rain. All coastal areas can be wet, as well as hilly areas like the Highlands of Scotland. Here you can expect around 275mm (11in) of rain, whereas in the south the average is 53mm (2in). Avoid walking on sodden soil or you will do more harm than good.

SOME SNOW

There is an increased chance of snow this month, but rarely does it last, or lie on the ground, for long. We may hope for a white Christmas, but although it happens more rarely in England these days we can still have a surprise when heavy snow falls before the end of the year. A good covering of snow can turn the garden into a winter wonderland, transforming bare stems and seed heads. But do be aware that it can also damage plants. Snow on trees and shrubs can break the branches, so shake it off before the damage occurs.

AROUND THE GARDEN

REMOVE GARDEN DEBRIS

Although there are few pests around in the garden now, it pays to be vigilant; milder winters, much more common of late, lead to many pests surviving the winter when they would normally be killed off. Practising good garden hygiene will go a long way to reducing problems in spring and summer. Clear away any debris or fallen leaves around plants, and burn or bin diseased material.

For those who want to garden in a more natural way, there is a paradox in advice about clearing the garden. To encourage wildlife into the garden to eat pests, we must provide places for them to hibernate.

For instance, hedgehogs hide in leaf litter, while ladybirds, which control aphids, hibernate in all sorts of little crevices. They have even been known to come out of the masonry of old stone-built houses where the stone is a bit flaky. So bear this in mind when you are clearing up, and leave a few safe havens for these creatures.

Hedgehogs like a heap of leaves to winter in, so leave the odd pile in an out-of-the-way corner of the garden.

FEED BIRDS IN COLD WEATHER

Birds are terrific allies in the garden, even though they try to eat the fruit grown for our consumption. It is very hard for them to find food when the ground is frozen or there is a thick layer of snow. So make sure you put something out for them regularly. Purchase bird food rather than leaving out your leftovers – cooked food can attract vermin. Do also leave a shallow dish of water out, and thaw it with warm water as necessary; dehydration can be as harmful for birds as hunger.

Buy special bird food rather than leaving out household scraps, as seed and nut mixtures provide a better diet for birds.

PROTECT PLANTS FROM FROST

It's important to protect plants vulnerable to frost as the year is now entering its coldest phase. Take in under cover any plants that have been overlooked. Plants *in situ* such as penstemons will benefit from a layer of protection, particularly in colder parts of the country. Herbaceous perennials are very easy to protect now that plants have died back – though it won't harm them even if they are in leaf. Just put a thick layer of straw or bracken over the crown of the plant, and hold it in position with some wire netting secured by pegs stuck into the ground. Taller shrubs can be "lagged" with straw held in place with hessian or sacking. Don't use plastic, as even when plants are dormant they still need to breathe.

WRAP INSULATION AROUND GARDEN TAPS

As water turns to ice, it expands and can burst pipes; this could affect the water supply to the house. You can insulate taps by binding them in several layers of hessian, or there are products on the market specifically designed to insulate outside taps. If possible, turn off the supply to outside taps during the winter; in this way you will avoid any possibility of burst pipes.

SHRED PRUNED MATERIAL

Winter is pruning time for ornamental and fruiting woody plants. If you haven't done so before, consider shredding prunings rather than burning them. Shreddings make a terrific mulch, or can be added to the compost heap to rot down with greener material. If your garden is mostly shrubs and lawn, leaving little bulky material for the compost heap in summer, keep a pile of shreddings to mix in with grass clippings in the summer months. These need plenty of air in them if they are to rot down properly and not form a slimy, stinking mess. Don't shred any diseased material as the disease will be spread around the garden.

ORDER OR BUY MANURE

If you didn't dig any manure into the soil in autumn, try to lay your hands on some now. You can usually get some from farms or riding stables. If you're digging manure in straight away, make sure you get well-rotted stuff, but you can stack fresher manure to rot down, or add it gradually to other composting material to make the most wonderful mix. Even in towns, manure is not as difficult to get as most people think. Just look for local riding stables in the business directory. Most cities and towns now have riding stables on their outskirts. Some may charge a nominal amount for the manure but most will be only too glad to see the back of the stuff.

TREAT TIMBER WITH PRESERVATIVES

Sheds and fences need to be protected from the winter weather. There are many different types of timber preservative on the market, in a range of colours, but make sure what you buy isn't harmful to plants. You might have to untie climbing plants on fences to apply the preservative.

Creosote used to be a regularly used preservative, but has now been withdrawn; if you want to achieve the same effect as creosote, there are substitutes available. However, there are a host of other alternatives to choose from, many of which are not harmful to plants.

CLEAN MOSS AND LICHEN FROM PATHS

Paths can become treacherous at this time of year when wet. There are many proprietary path and patio cleaners on the market today, and all are easy to use. Just mix according to the instructions and apply to the area to be cleaned.

The weather this month is often fairly dry, allowing painting jobs to be done; wood will then be protected throughout winter.

Using a solution of household bleach will get the job done just as well. Water on the solution, leave for a few minutes, then scrub the moss and lichen off. On large areas, a power washer will make light work of this necessary chore – these can be hired quite cheaply. You'll be amazed the difference being blasted clean makes to any stonework or woodwork.

TREES, SHRUBS & CLIMBERS

SHAKE SNOW OFF TREES AND SHRUBS

Although we rarely get lots of snow this month, beware of the odd snow flurry. Plants do look terrific with a layer of snow on them, but it can bring down branches. Conifers planted as specimen trees, where the shape is all-important, can be protected by tying thin wire or strong string around them, preventing branches opening up when snow falls on them. Brush snow off dense evergreen climbers and wall shrubs too; accumulating snow can break stems and put strain on ties and supports. Don't worry about snow on low plants: it actually protects them against cold, blanketing them from frost.

As long as the layer of snow hasn't frozen hard, brush it off branches as soon as possible to prevent damage.

KEEP AN EYE ON NEW TREES AND SHRUBS

Check newly planted trees and shrubs, including roses, to see if they have been loosened by winds or lifted by frost. When this happens, gaps form around the roots, causing them to dry out because they are not in close

contact with the soil. If you see cracks around the plant, gently firm in with your feet. If there is still planting to be done, then press on with it, as long as the soil is not frozen or waterlogged.

PRUNE TALL BUSH ROSES

Tall bush roses should be cut down by half to prevent wind rock – the stiff branches catch the wind like a sail, and can loosen the plant. Eventually, a hole will form at the base of the plant where water will collect and cause the roots to rot. In frosty weather the water may freeze, resulting in further damage to the root system. Note that cuts do not need to be precise as the rose will be pruned again in spring.

PRUNE ORNAMENTAL VINES

Vines can produce growths up to 3m (10ft) or more in one season, so over several years, if they are not pruned you will end up in a mess. Thin out overcrowded shoots, and then prune sideshoots to two buds from the main stems that are kept as a framework.

PRUNE OVERGROWN DECIDUOUS HEDGES

No matter how often we trim hedges such as beech and hornbeam through the summer, they imperceptibly creep outwards, taking up more space and becoming more difficult to cut. The plants are dormant this month, so this is a good time to reduce the hedge to a manageable size. On an old established hedge you may need loppers or a pruning saw to cut some of the larger branches.

Cut back the sides until the hedge is no more than 45–60cm (18–24in) wide at the top, tapering it so that the bottom is wider. This shaping will protect the hedge from damage by heavy snowfalls. The top can be trimmed to whatever height you want. To get the top level, you may need to put up a line at the height required.

PRUNE DECIDUOUS TREES AND SHRUBS

Don't prune for the sake of it: unnecessary pruning weakens growth, and the fewer wounds you can make on a plant the better, as each is a potential entry point for disease. Some trees, most particularly walnuts, "bleed" an enormous amount of sap when pruned, too, so unnecessary cuts are dangerous.

However, on most deciduous trees, dead, diseased and damaged wood should be removed, as although pruning creates wounds these are, on balance, less risky than leaving unhealthy wood on the plant. Any further cuts you make will probably be cosmetic, but consider the effect carefully before removing anything substantial – it's not only the effect of removing growth that you must envisage, but also the direction in which the new growth will come.

You will need a good pair of secateurs, a pair of loppers, and a

CUTTING OFF A LOW BRANCH

1 Reduce the weight of the branch so that the final cut can be made cleanly. To prevent downward tearing, make an undercut.

2 Supporting the weight of the branch, cut downwards straight through it about 5cm (2in) beyond the undercut.

pruning saw for cutting off larger branches. Chainsaws can be hired from local hire shops, but unless you are familiar with them, they are best left to the experts; they can be very dangerous in inexperienced hands. Likewise, very large or high branches should be left to a tree surgeon. Check with your local council before pruning old established trees as they might have a tree preservation order on them.

Firstly, remove any dead or diseased wood and any crossing

3 Now cut back the stub cleanly, cutting just beyond the swollen ring or "branch collar" where it meets the trunk.

branches that are rubbing together, cutting out whole shoots to a joint whenever possible rather than just tipping them back. If the plant is taking up too much room in a smaller garden, it can be trimmed. The harder you prune, the stronger will be the resulting growth, so when restricting size, light pruning will have a much more satisfactory effect than hacking away. Don't just give freestanding plants an all-over "haircut", as when trimming a hedge. Try to open up the centre of the plant to allow air to circulate and reduce the amount of shadow cast on lower-growing plants in the border.

Take your time when pruning. Stand back and look at the plant and consider what effect removing a branch will have on the plant's appearance before making the cut. You can't stick a branch back on once it's removed. Remember to feed after pruning, preferably with an organic fertiliser, and mulch with organic matter.

FLOWERING PLANTS

CONTINUE CUTTING DOWN DEAD GROWTH

Pay attention to dead foliage on herbaceous perennials, and generally weed and tidy borders. The sooner this is done, the less work there will be left in the busy spring period. But robust stems with seedheads, as on sedums, can be left uncut until the spring, as you will find they are beautiful when wrapped in a layer of frost: a lovely sight, especially on a clear, sunny morning.

KEEP AN EYE ON CONTAINER PLANTS

Permanent plants in containers should be checked over regularly and any debris that remains cleared out. Fallen leaves can get in around the base of plants in containers, encouraging disease and giving pests somewhere to hibernate, as well as making the plants look untidy.

WATCH FOR DISEASE ON STORED BULBS

Keep checking bulbs, corms, and tubers in store for signs of disease. Diseases such as botrytis and rotting can quickly spread through bulbs and tubers kept in store through the winter. If any diseases do start to show, remove the affected bulb or tuber – or if only part of it is affected, cut out the diseased portion and dust the cut surface with flowers of sulphur. This should prevent the disease spreading further.

KEEP POTTING UP LILIES

Continue to pot up lilies for a succession of blooms. Put four or five bulbs into an 18cm (7in) pot containing coir compost, and cover the bulbs with about 10cm (4in) of compost. Water them in and wait for the stunning flowers to appear in spring.

Set hippeastrum bulbs in a pot just large enough to hold them. By late winter, they will bear beautiful flowers like those of Hippeastrum 'Apple Blossom', right.

POT UP HIPPEASTRUM BULBS

Hippeastrum bulbs make popular Christmas gifts. If you want to pot one up as a present, or if you have been given one yourself, simply set them so that the nose of the bulb is just at the surface of the compost, within a pot that is large enough to take the bulb comfortably. Then place them somewhere cool and light to grow.

BRING FORCED BULBS INTO A WARM ROOM

Bulbs like prepared hyacinths and daffodils, which were plunged outside in the autumn and then brought into cool conditions a few weeks ago, can be brought into the warmth to encourage them into flower in time for the Christmas festivities. Hyacinths are a particular favourite as they fill the room with their scent.

KITCHEN GARDEN

TEND TO BRASSICAS

Earthing up spring cabbages and other winter brassicas will give them better anchorage in strong winds. Tall-growing Brussels sprouts are particularly prone

Brassicas need a good roothold to withstand windy weather, so earth them up by drawing up soil around the base of the plants.

to being blown over. It may also be necessary to put in canes and tie the plants to them. Remove yellowing leaves regularly, as these encourage fungal diseases. Harvest sprouts from the stem upwards once they have reached 2.5cm (1in) in diameter.

Spring cabbages are normally planted in the autumn at a distance of about 15cm (6in) apart. During the winter, cut every other one as winter greens, leaving the others to grow on and heart up in the spring. Earth up these remaining cabbages, and remove yellowing leaves whenever they appear.

BRING BAY TREES UNDER COVER

Bay trees grown in pots should be taken indoors if cold weather is forecast, or at least moved to the most sheltered part of the garden. The leaves are very susceptible to cold winds and need protection.

This is a good time to prune blackcurrants: the lack of foliage makes it easier to see old stems that need to be removed. A healthy bush will produce a profusion of berries come summer.

PRUNE BLACKCURRANTS

Blackcurrants fruit on both new and old wood and they are grown as a stool plant (that is, with the branches growing in a clump from, or just under, ground level). Pruning is all about maintaining a balance between the old and the new wood. Around one-third of the bush should be removed each year to maintain the vigour of the plant – this leaves a more open bush that will fruit more readily. Wherever possible cut older stems to the ground, leaving younger wood to fruit in summer, although you will probably cut out some young growth at the same time. When finished, you should have a balance between old and new branches on a fairly open bush. Mulch after pruning, ideally with well-rotted farmyard manure, but do not let it touch the stems.

DECEMBER PROJECT

WILDLIFE WALL

As many beneficial insects, such as ladybirds and ground beetles, struggle to find welcoming habitats in our neat, modern environment, we should do all that we can to encourage them to make our gardens their home.

One simple solution is to leave a quiet corner of your garden a little untidy, with perhaps a pile of logs left to rot down naturally. Alternatively, you could create a wildlife wall. Most insects love to live in cracks and crevices in wood or stone, and a wildlife wall imitates these ideal conditions.

The wall is easy to construct with alternate layers of wood, bricks, old canes, broken tiles and other building materials, and its textures and patterns make an attractive garden feature. If you haven't got suitable material at home, try your local refuse centre.

1 *Construct the wall* in a quiet area of the garden. Make an initial layer of bricks and tiles, leaving plenty of gaps. Place planks or plywood on top and then add another layer or bricks. Top off with roof tiles, to keep excess moisture out.

2 *Cut bamboo canes* to short lengths and pack them into any gaps to make homes for solitary bees. Corrugated cardboard rolled up tightly makes a perfect home for ladybirds. Use moss, straw and twigs to fill any other gaps.

3 *Once built*, your wildlife wall should be left alone. The more established (and dishevelled) it is, the better it will be for wildlife. Occasionally you may need to top up the lighter materials, such as straw, which may be removed by birds.

COTONEASTER

Cotoneaster frigidus **'Fructu Luteo'**
An erect then spreading deciduous tree
or large shrub. Large clusters of tiny
white flowers appear in summer followed
by creamy yellow fruits in autumn. The
flowers attract bees, and the fruits are
eaten by birds in hard winters.
‡ to 10m (30ft) ↔ to 10m (30ft)

CULTIVATION Tolerates almost any
soil including dry ones, but best in
moderately fertile, well-drained soil in
full sun. Prune lightly to shape in winter,
if necessary.

VIBURNUM

Viburnum × *bodnantense* **'Dawn'** ♀
A sturdy, upright, vigorous deciduous
shrub. From late autumn to early spring,
it bears small, rounded clusters of fragrant
pink flowers, on bare branches. It has
deeply pleated, bright green leaves that
are bronze when young.
‡ 3m (10ft) ↔ to 2m (6ft)

CULTIVATION Thrives in any reasonably
fertile, well-drained soil in sun or dappled
shade. It needs little pruning other than
to shorten any shoots that spoil the shape
and to thin out congested shoots on
mature plants. Prune after flowering.

WINTER JASMINE 3

Jasminum nudiflorum ♀ A very hardy, deciduous, scrambling shrub. In winter and early spring, it bears masses of bright yellow flowers on bare branches. The green shoots and dark green leaves persist for most of the year.

↕ to 3m (10ft) ↔ to 3m (10ft)

CULTIVATION Grow in any fertile garden soil. After flowering, cut back flowered shoots to strong buds. Every three or four years, take out some of the oldest growths at the base.

ENGLISH HOLLY [1]

Ilex aquifolium **'Handsworth New Silver'** ♀ A dense, evergreen shrub of columnar outline. All year, its dark purple stems bear glossy dark green leaves with spiny cream margins. Vivid, bright red berries in winter.

↕8m (25ft) ↔ 5m (15ft)

CULTIVATION Full sun produces the best variegation, but it tolerates dappled shade. Grow in any fertile, well-drained soil. Prune to shape, if necessary, in early spring.

SPOTTED LAUREL [2]

Aucuba japonica **'Variegata'** An evergreen shrub of dense, bushy growth with attractively variegated foliage all year round. Upright clusters of small red flowers appear in mid-spring; on female plants, like this cultivar, they are followed by bright red berries.

↕to 3m (10ft) ↔ to 3m (10ft)

CULTIVATION Exceptionally tolerant of a range of difficult sites, from deep, dry shade to coastal cliffs. It grows in any but waterlogged soil. Prune, or trim hedges, in spring. Very tolerant of hard pruning.

MAHONIA 3

Mahonia × *media* **'Charity'** An upright, bushy, evergreen shrub. From late autumn to early spring, it bears long spikes of fragrant, deep yellow flowers. During the rest of the year, it has attractive, glossy dark-green, sharply toothed leaves.
↕ to 5m (15ft) ↔ 4m (12ft)

CULTIVATION Grow in moist but well-drained, humus-rich soil, in part-shade or in sun if soils are reliably moist. It needs little pruning; if it becomes leggy, or outgrows its allotted space, prune after flowering.

WILLOW [1]

Salix alba var. *vitellina* **'Britzensis'** ♀
Large, upright, deciduous tree; pruned
regularly, it makes a twiggy shrub. It
has bright orange-red young shoots in
winter. In spring, it bears slender, yellow
catkins with the emerging, narrow mid-
green leaves.

‡ 25m (80ft) ↔ 10m (30ft)

CULTIVATION Grow in any moist but
well-drained soil. Each year – or for
catkins, every other year – cut all stems
back hard in early spring, either to the
ground or to a short trunk. Young shoots
have the best colour.

AMARYLLIS [2]

Hippeastrum **'Apple Blossom'** One
of the most spectacular bulbs to grow
as a houseplant. In winter, it bears large,
white, funnel-shaped flowers with pink-
flushed petal tips.

‡ 30–50cm (12–20in) ↔ 30cm (12in)

CULTIVATION Plant the bulbs in
autumn, with "neck and shoulders" above
soil level. Water little until growth is well
underway then water freely and feed
every two weeks with a balanced liquid
fertilizer. After flowering gradually reduce
watering as the leaves begin to die down.

2

ELAEAGNUS 3

Elaeagnus x *ebbingei* 'Gilt Edge' ♀
A moderately vigorous evergreen shrub.
All year round, it has lustrous dark leaves
with gleaming, creamy yellow margins.
The autumn flowers are fragrant but
visually insignificant.
↕ to 4m (12ft) ↔ to 4m (12ft)

CULTIVATION The leaves colour best in
sun, but it tolerates dappled shade. Grow
in any fertile, well-drained soil; it does
not thrive on shallow, chalky soils. Prune
lightly to shape in mid- to late spring;
cut out shoots with all-green leaves.

3

YEAR AT A GLANCE

January

Ensure that birds have food and water.

Continue with winter digging as soil conditions allow.

Cover ground to keep out the wet.

Order seeds and summer-flowering bulbs.

Protect plants vulnerable to wind and cold.

Aerate lawns to improve drainage.

Keep a small area of ponds free from ice.

Keep on top of winter-germinating weeds.

February

Top up the food and water supplies for garden birds.

Apply organic-based fertilisers.

March

Mulch bare soil in beds and borders.

Move evergreen shrubs.

Reseed bare patches on the lawn.

Mow lawns regularly.

Retrieve pumps from store and put them in the pond.

April

Continue watering new trees and shrubs when dry.

Feed established lawns.

Plant new aquatic plants.

May

Water plants that need it regularly.

Protect young plants from slugs.

Replenish water plants with aquatic fertiliser.

Feed fish regularly.

Feed, weed, and mow lawns to encourage good growth.

Cover plants with horticultural fleece whenever night frosts are forecast.

June

Weed and deadhead to maintain beds, borders, and container displays.

Introduce new fish into the pond.

Remove blanket weed and duckweed to prevent them clogging up water features.

Mow the lawn and trim edges regularly.

Energise tired lawns with a liquid feed.

Water new lawns made in the spring.

Water containers regularly as temperatures rise.

Water new and young plants as necessary.

July

Ensure birds have water in dry weather.

Water new and young plants during the summer, but use water wisely.

Watch out for pests and diseases.

Feed and water all plants in containers regularly.

August

Ensure birds and other wildlife have fresh water, and keep ponds topped up.

Feed and water plants in containers.

Mow less frequently if the weather is hot and dry.

September

Start clearing autumn debris to prevent pests and diseases overwintering.

Move evergreen shrubs.

Scarify and aerate established lawns.

Net ponds to keep out autumn leaves.

October

Rake up fallen leaves, and pile them up to make leafmould.

Continue clearing up the garden, and burn or bin debris that shows signs of fungal infection.

Dig over empty areas of soil.

Tidy ponds and remove pumps for the winter.

November

Tidy the garden for winter.

Clear out bird boxes, and put food out for birds.

Check the bonfire heap for hibernating creatures before lighting it.

Continue with winter digging.

Clean or throw out old pots and trays.

Keep off the lawn in frosty weather.

Install pond heaters.

December

Feed birds in cold weather, and do not allow ponds and bird baths to freeze over.

Continue winter digging, incorporating organic matter.

Clean paths, and repair sheds and fences.

Repair lawns if weather conditions allow.

Shred the prunings from ornamental plants and fruit trees and bushes.

January

Refirm newly planted trees and shrubs if lifted by frost.

Brush snow off trees and shrubs so branches don't break.

Check supports of trees and shrubs.

Plant deciduous hedging.

Prune trees and shrubs to shape.

Prune wisteria and other vigorous climbers.

February

Continue planting trees and shrubs as the weather allows.

Firm newly planted trees and shrubs if lifted by frost.

Prune winter-flowering shrubs that have finished flowering.

Prune summer-flowering shrubs that flower on new wood.

Prune hardy evergreen trees and shrubs.

Prune jasmines and late-summer-flowering clematis.

Repot or top-dress shrubs in containers.

March

Prune bush and shrub roses.
Prune shrubs with colourful winter stems.
Renovate climbers and plant new ones.

April

Plant evergreen trees and shrubs.
Erect windbreaks around new trees and shrubs if needed.
Trim grey-leaved shrubs to keep them bushy.
Tie in the new shoots of climbers.
Prune early-flowering shrubs.
Prune shrubs grown for large or colourful foliage.

May

Prune spring-flowering shrubs that have finished flowering.
Prune *Clematis montana* after flowering.
Trim box and other formal hedging lightly.
Move tender shrubs in pots outside for summer.

June

Prune spring-flowering shrubs.
Watch for pests and suckers on roses.

July

Prune shrubs that flowered in early summer.
Trim conifer hedges and take cuttings.
Summer-prune wisteria.

August

Trim hedges.
Prune rambling roses after flowering.

September

Start planting new trees, shrubs and climbers.

Stop feeding trees and shrubs in containers.

October

Finish planting evergreen shrubs.

Plant new climbers.

November

Plant bare-rooted trees and shrubs and new roses.

Plant fruit trees and bushes.

Protect tender and newly planted shrubs from frost and wind.

December

Prune woody ornamental plants and fruit trees and bushes.

Prune ornamental vines.

Shake snow off trees, shrubs, and hedges.

FLOWERING PLANTS

January

Clear the plant crowns of damp leaves.
Check forced bulbs for growth.
Sow sweet peas under cover.

February

Prune off old stems of herbaceous perennials.
Start dahlia tubers into growth.
Divide and plant snowdrops.
Bring the last of spring bulbs being forced inside.

March

Lift and divide overgrown clumps of perennials.

Split polyanthus after flowering.

Plant summer-flowering bulbs.

Sow hardy annuals where they are to flower.

Sow sweet peas outdoors or plant out young plants.

Pinch out tips of young sweet peas to encourage sideshoots.

Water indoor plants regularly now the weather is warmer.

Protect young, tender plants from slugs.

Cut down old growth left over winter.

April

Divide perennials.

Stake tall-growing perennials.

Protect young growth from slugs and snails.

Remove annual weeds with your hands.

Remove perennials weeds by digging them out.

Deadhead daffodils.

Sow annual climbers and grasses.

FLOWERING PLANTS

May

Divide and cut back spring-flowering perennials.
Plant out dahlias at the end of the month.
Clear out spring bedding.
Harden off summer bedding plants.
Thin out annuals sown earlier.

June

Tidy and cut back spring-flowering perennials.
Take cuttings from pinks.
Sow seed of perennials.
Cut down the faded foliage of bulbs.
Lift and divide overgrown clumps of bulbs.
Plant out summer bedding in borders and containers,
  including hanging baskets.

July

Deadhead flowers as they fade.

Divide bearded irises.

Layer and take cuttings of carnations and pinks.

Plant autumn-flowering bulbs.

Transplant seedlings of biennials sown earlier.

August

Collect ripening seed from plants you wish to propagate.

Trim lavender after the flowers have faded.

Water plants that need it regularly.

Take cuttings from tender perennials such as pelargoniums
and fuchsias.

September

Start planting new perennials.

Start dividing overgrown perennials.

Support tall, late-flowering perennials.

Plant spring-flowering bulbs.

Plant out spring-flowering biennials.

Plant up containers with spring bedding.

October

Plant new perennials.

Plant tulip and lily bulbs.

Divide overgrown perennials.

Lift and store dahlias, gladioli, and summer-flowering bulbs.

November

Plant tulip bulbs.
Insulate pots left out for the winter.

December

Water plants overwintering under cover sparingly, to avoid the risk of overwatering and rotting.
Tend to pot plants to get the best of their winter display.

January

Chit early potatoes.
Protect fruit trees from bird damage.
Continue planting and winter-pruning of fruit.
Force rhubarb.

February

Prepare seedbeds for vegetables.
Lime vegetable plots if necessary.
Continue planting fruit trees and bushes.
Mulch fruit trees after feeding.

March

Sow vegetables outside.
Plant early potatoes.

April

Continue sowing and planting vegetables outdoors.
Plant container-grown fruit trees.

May

Thin out vegetables sown earlier.

Sow and plant out tender vegetables later this month.

Protect crops from carrot fly.

Continue successional sowing of vegetables.

June

Harvest vegetables as they mature.

Plant winter brassicas, and protect them from pests.

Water fruit and vegetables thoroughly during dry spells.

July

Water vegetables regularly.

Lift new potatoes, onions, and garlic.

Pinch out runner beans when they reach the top of canes.

Pinch out outdoor tomatoes when four trusses have formed, and remove sideshoots.

Pick raspberries and currants.

Harvest herbs for drying.

August

Lift and dry onions.

Cut and dry herbs for winter use.

Water and feed tomatoes at regular intervals, and remove yellowing leaves.

Plant new strawberry plants, and keep them well watered.

Harvest the first apples and pears.

September

Harvest the last marrows and courgettes, and lift maincrop potatoes.

Plant out spring cabbages.

Sow winter lettuce.

Continue harvesting apples, pears, and autumn-fruiting raspberries.

October

Cut down the dying tops of perennial vegetables.

Lift and divide rhubarb.

November

Continue to lift and divide rhubarb crowns.

Winter-prune fruit trees and bushes.

December

Earth up tall Brussels sprout stems to support them.

Bring bay trees under cover to protect them from cold.